Baha'i and Globalisation

RENNER Studies on New Religions

RENNER Studies on New Religions is an initiative supported by the Danish Research Council for the Humanities. The series is established to publish books on new religions and alternative spiritual movements from a wide range of perspectives. It includes works of original theory, empirical research, and edited collections that address current topics, but will generally focus on the situation in Europe.

The books appeal to an international readership of scholars, students, and professionals in the study of religion, theology, the arts, and the social sciences. It is hoped that this series will provide a proper context for scientific exchange between these often competing disciplines.

BAHA'I AND GLOBALISATION

Edited by Margit Warburg,
Annika Hvithamar & Morten Warmind

Printed in Denmark by Narayana Press
ISBN 87 7934 109 8

AARHUS UNIVERSITY PRESS
Langelandsgade 177
8200 Aarhus N
Denmark
Fax (+ 45) 8942 5380

73 Lime Walk
Headington, Oxford OX3 7AD
United Kingdom
Fax (+ 44) 1865 750 079

Box 511
Oakville, Conn. 06779
USA
Fax (+ 1) 860 945 9468

www.unipress.dk

Published with the financial support of the Danish Research Council for the Humanities and the Humanistic Faculty of the University of Copenhagen.

Renner Studies on New Religions:

Vol. 1: Robert Towler (ed.), *New Religions and the New Europe*, 1995
Vol. 2: Michael Rothstein, *Belief Transformations*, 1996
Vol. 3: Helle Meldgaard and Johannes Aagaard (eds.), *New Religious Movements in Europe*, 1997
Vol. 4: Eileen Barker and Margit Warburg (eds.), *New Religions and New Religiosity*, 1998
Vol. 5: Mikael Rothstein (ed.) *New Age Religion and Globalization*, 2001
Vol. 6: Mikael Rothstein and Reender Kranenborg (eds.), *New Religions in a Postmodern World*, 2003
Vol. 7: Margit Warburg, Annika Hvithamar, and Morten Warmind (eds.), *Baha'i and Globalisation*, 2005

Contents

Introduction

The Danish RENNER project is a **RE**search **N**etwork on the study of **NE**w **R**eligions. This research network, which is supported by the Danish Research Council for the Humanities, has been active since 1992. In 1998, a new grant from the Research Council allowed us to conduct a specific study on new religions and globalisation, and we initiated the project with several separate studies of new age religion and globalisation. The present book, *Baha'i and Globalisation*, which is the seventh volume of the book series *Renner Studies on New Religion*, is the second of the case studies of the project. Another book, which emphasises the theoretical and methodological aspects of the study of new religions and globalisation, will be volume eight in the series, rounding off this special RENNER topic.

Globalisation is the conventional term used to describe the present, rapid integration of the world economy facilitated by the innovations and growth in international electronic communications particularly during the last two decades. Globalisation carries with it an increasing political and cultural awareness that all of humanity is globally interdependent. However, the awareness of this global interdependency has been aired by philosophers and politicians much before the term globalisation was introduced. Thus, the founder of the Baha'i religion, the Iranian prophet, Husayn-Ali Nuri (1817-1892) called Baha'u'llah, claimed in the late 19th century that the central doctrine of the Baha'i religion is the realisation that the human race is one and that the world should be unified: 'The utterance of God is a lamp, whose light is these words: Ye are the fruits of one tree, and the leaves of one branch'. This is a goal that 'excelleth every other goal'.[1]

Present-day globalisation is a continuation of a historical process over several hundred years. This process gained momentum in a crucial period from around 1870 and the subsequent fifty years. It is notable that this period coincides with the period when the central doctrines of the Baha'i religion were formulated by Baha'u'llah and his son and successor, Abdu'l-Baha (1844-1921). The sociologist of religion,

1 Both quotations are from Baha'u'llah (1988: 14).

James Beckford has noted that in some senses the faith of Baha'u'llah 'foreshadowed globalization, with its emphasis on the interdependence of all peoples and the need for international institutions of peace, justice and good governance' (Beckford 2000: 175).

The synchrony between the take-off of globalisation and the emergence of Baha'i on the world scene should not be dismissed as insignificant. Baha'u'llah's message that the world should be unified would probably not have fallen on fertile soil much before the 1870s, because the impact of globalisation was not yet begun to be felt among potential proselytes. In the late nineteenth century and in the beginning of the twentieth century, the climate for this idea was more receptive.

From the Baha'i point of view, the unification of the world is a consequence of the culmination of the spiritual development of humanity. This spiritual development has been achieved through the successive revelations of God's will in the prophecies of the different religions since the time of Abraham, with the Baha'i religion as the latest of the divine revelations. The Baha'is also perceive themselves as the vanguard of this historical process, which is destined to result in a new world civilisation, called the World Order of Baha'u'llah. This golden age for humanity, the 'Most Great Peace' is believed to be preceded by the 'Lesser Peace' in which the nations of the world reach an agreement to abolish war and establish the political instruments to secure world peace and prosperity, consonant with the Baha'i call for the unification of the world.

Thus, to study the Baha'is and their religion in the light of globalisation is to grasp an essential aspect of the Baha'i teachings, and it is with good reason that Baha'i and globalisation stands as a central case in the RENNER study of new religions and globalisation. Few other religions express so clearly in their doctrines the view that the world should be unified, politically and religiously. The Baha'is are also globalised in the sense that they live all over the world, and they deliberately aim at being present in as many locations as possible. In 2003, there were Baha'i communities in 190 countries and 46 territories of the world, and excerpts of Baha'u'llah's writings had been translated into 802 languages (*The Bahá'í World* 2003: 311).

The Baha'i Religion

The different chapters of this book assumes a basic knowledge of the Baha'i religion and its historical development. A brief review will therefore be given in the following.

The Baha'i religion has its origins in religious currents within Shi'i Islam in the first half of the nineteenth century. In 1844, a millenarian movement, called Babism, rose from these currents. The Babis provoked the Islamic establishment by insisting that their leader, Ali Muhammad Shirazi (1819-1850), called the Bab, was a new prophet and a source of divine revelations. This implied in principle that the age of Islam was over. The rapid growth of the Babi movement occurred in a general climate of public unrest, and from 1848 the Babis were engaged in a series of bloody fights with the Iranian government. By 1852, however, the movement seemed to have been crushed, and the surviving Babi leaders including Baha'u'llah were exiled to the neighbouring Ottoman Empire. After a break in 1866-67 with a minority of the Babis who acknowledged Baha'u'llah's half-brother Subh-i-Azal (ca. 1830-1912) as their leader, Baha'u'llah openly declared that he was a new source of divine revelation. The great majority of Babis soon recognised the theophanic claims of Baha'u'llah, and he gradually transformed Babism into the present Baha'i religion.

Although Baha'u'llah abolished many Babi doctrines and practices, in particular the militancy and the harsh treatment of unbelievers, there is also a strong element of continuity between Babism and Baha'i. The Bab occupies a central and visible position in the Baha'i religion, and his remains are buried in a splendid golden-domed shrine on the slope of Mount Carmel in Haifa, adjacent to the Baha'i administrative headquarter, the Baha'i World Centre. The year 1844, when the Bab made his declaration, is the year one in the Baha'i calendar, which was devised by the Bab.

Through systematic mission initiated by Baha'u'llah's son and successor, Abdu'l-Baha (1844-1921), Baha'i gradually expanded outside its Muslim environment. Baha'i missionaries came to the USA and Canada in the 1890s and to West Europe around 1900. Effective growth in Europe did not occur, however, until after World War II, when Abdu'l-Baha's grandson and successor, Shoghi Effendi (1897-1957) organised a Baha'i mission in Europe assisted by many American

Baha'is who came to Europe as Baha'i missionaries or 'pioneers' in the Baha'i terminology.

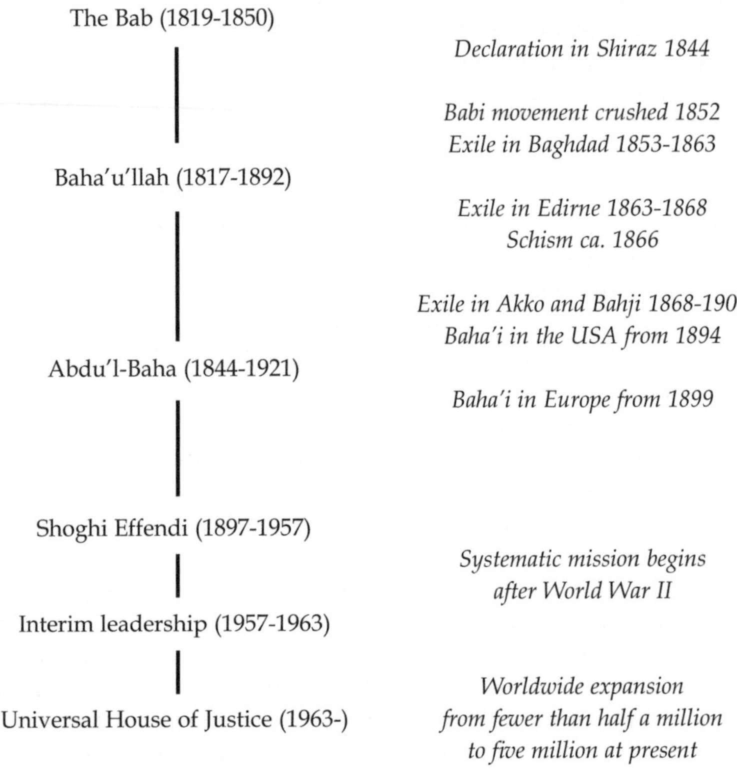

The above figure gives a brief chronology of Babism and Baha'i, showing the names of the leaders and some major historical internal events in the Baha'i religion. Shoghi Effendi was the last individual to lead Baha'i. Abdu'l-Baha had appointed him as leader of the Baha'is with the title of 'Guardian of the Cause of God', and he was meant to be the first in a line of 'Guardians'. However, when Shoghi Effendi died in 1957 without an appointed successor, an interim collective leadership established in 1963 the present supreme ruling body of the Baha'i religion, the Universal House of Justice.

The writings of the Bab, of Baha'u'llah, and of Abdu'l-Baha make up the canon of Baha'i sacred texts. The writings of Shoghi Effendi are not considered sacred but they are still binding in doctrinal and legislative matters. The Baha'i leaders were prolific writers and left both books and a massive corpus of letters of doctrinal significance, called tablets. Some of the central Babi and Baha'i texts are introduced and analysed in the different chapters with a view of elucidating the globalisation aspect of the religion.

Diachronic Perspectives

We have sought to study the relation between Baha'i and globalisation from its historical beginning in early Babism until today. To do so, RENNER and the University of Copenhagen invited an international group of scholars to participate in a three-day conference in August 2001. The scholars who represented different fields were asked to apply their specialisations in a study of Baha'i and globalisation. All contributions are original and are published here for the first time.

The chapters of the first part of *Baha'i and Globalisation* roughly follow a chronological scheme and together they make up a diachronic sweep of the rise of the global orientation of the Babi and Baha'i religions. The opening chapter by Stephen Lambden aims at showing that the Babi-Baha'is were not unprepared for Baha'u'llah globalist thoughts. In his paper, Lambden emphasises the continuity between the globalism in the Bab's early major work, the *Qayyum al-asma'*, and Baha'u'llah's globalism, but also the breaks, notably the abandoning of *jihad* as a means of promoting a globalisation process. Todd Lawson's chapter is a philological analysis of Baha'u'llah's important early work, the *Hidden Words* from the 1850s, and with this example Lawson elucidates the further development of the global orientation of the Babi-Baha'i religion in the cosmopolitan atmosphere of Baghdad. Juan R. I. Cole shows in his chapter on Abdu'l-Baha that the globalist thinking in Baha'i was now far-reaching and truly international in character. Abdu'l-Baha embraced many of the ideas of liberal modernity, and he clearly perceived that the world had become a single place even in the early twentieth century.

Abdu'l-Baha was a determined leader, and Moojan Momen's chapter gives much substance to the tight connection between Abdu'l-Baha's thinking and his practical directives in the exceptional global expansion of the Baha'i religion in the first two decades of the twentieth century. In connection with this expansion Robert Stockman argues how Abdu'l-Baha's thinking inspired much of the practice of the Baha'i proselytising, and he brings to attention the practical activism of the early American Baha'is and the mutual bonds of assistance between the Baha'i communities of North America and Iran. It was, however, precisely the international orientation of the Iranian Baha'is which gave rise to allegations of unpatriotism from nationalist circles in Iran. This is shown by Fereydun Vahman who analyses a broad selection of Iranian anti-Baha'i polemic literature before the Iranian revolution of 1979. The global ambitions of the Baha'is are furthermore illustrated in Zaid Lundberg's chapter on Shoghi Effendi's *World Order of Baha'u'llah*. Lundberg carefully describes Shoghi Effendi's understanding of the Baha'i religion as part of a global evolution aiming at a world commonwealth which were to be identical with a Baha'i commonwealth. Morten Warmind puts the Baha'i emphasis on globalisation and modernity into perspective by comparing and contrasting it with another break-off movement from Islam in the 19th century, Ahmadiyya. Margit Warburg concludes the chronological section with a chapter that integrates a view of the historical development of the Baha'i religion into a general understanding of globalisation, based on a model originally proposed by the sociologist Roland Robertson. This model is further developed in the chapter and is used in an analysis of the changing attitudes of the Baha'i leadership in relation to international politics.

Some Synchcronic Themes

The second part of the book gives a thematic, synchronic coverage of contemporary Baha'i and globalisation. Wendi Momen opens with a chapter on the globalisation thinking in Baha'i from a politologic exegesis of the Baha'i writings, in particular the writings of Abdu'l-Baha and Shoghi Effendi. With the Internet, the individual Baha'is' reflections on their religion can now be expressed in a truly global forum. David Piff treats the Baha'i discourse on the Internet and shows its potentials for creating a new transnational community feeling among the participants and for being a seedbed for diverging and sometimes controversial discourses on Baha'i doctrines.

The ideas conveyed in the sacred texts are reflected and reinterpreted in the minds of the followers, and this is treated in several of the following chapters. Two chapters are based on interviews of Baha'is with regard to their understanding and conceptualisation of the global ideas of Baha'i. Lynn Echevarria has conducted interviews among 21 of the oldest living Canadian Baha'is, showing how ideas of the 'oneness of mankind' and of 'world consciousness' were salient in the early Baha'i mission. Will van den Hoonaard has interviewed 18 Baha'is world-wide and has also made extensive use of Baha'i secondary and core literature to elucidate the discourse of the idea of 'unity in diversity' in different Baha'i communities. Sen McGlinn continues the thread of interpretation and re-interpretation of texts and he brings to the surface a number of divergent Baha'i stances on issues following in the wake of modernisation and globalisation, such as the relation between state and church or the equality of the sexes. Finally, Denis MacEoin points to the triumphalist aspect of the Baha'is' self-understanding as representing the religion to unite all religions in the culmination of globalisation. However, on the path ahead lie issues of secularism, and MacEoin discusses the challenges which secular values present to a religion that - rooted in Islamic thinking - aims to fuse the spheres of religion and society.

Issues of Terminology

Having completed the fifteen chapters of *Baha'i and Globalisation*, the observant reader may have noted certain inconsistencies with respect to spelling (British or American usage, as regards the central term globalisation/globalization!) and the use of diacriticals. There are (good?) reasons why inconstancies are hard to eradicate. Many Baha'i names and terms are of Persian or Arabic origin, and Baha'is usually transcribe these words with full diacritical marks in all official texts of the religion. However, their transcription does not always follow modern academic transcription systems; apart from some spelling particularities the most conspicuous difference is that the Baha'is have retained an earlier practice of using the acute accent instead of the horizontal stroke over the long vowels, a, i and u.

Fortunately, for the convenience of most of the readers who have no particular interest in the details of transcription, also many scholars who are themselves Baha'is have now chosen to reduce the use of diacriticals to a minimum. This trend set by leading specialists in the Baha'i religion is a refreshing liberation from the spelling orthodoxy of earlier Baha'i research, and we have not wished to interfere with this in the edition of the work. Nor have we wished to standardise the denotation of the Baha'i religion itself, whether it is called the Baha'i Faith (the official Baha'i term), Bahaism, or just Baha'i.

Among the new religions of the modern age, Baha'i has indeed been one of the most successful. Today, the Baha'is claim that there are more than five million registered Baha'is world-wide and the religion is represented in almost all countries in the world. Nevertheless, the Baha'i religion has attracted less interest among students of new religions than it deserves, and the number of scholars who have Baha'i as their main research topic is limited. Most of them are, in fact, represented in this book, which is the first anthology in Baha'i studies that deals with globalisation. On behalf of RENNER and the authors I hope that it will catch the interest of students of new religions and globalisation as well as promoting the academic study of the Baha'i religion and its followers.

Margit Warburg
Copenhagen, August 2005

References

The Baha'i World 2001-2002 (2003). Haifa: Baha'i World Centre, 2003.

Baha'u'llah (1988), *Epistle to the Son of the Wolf.* Wilmette: Baha'i Publishing Trust.

Beckford, James A. (2000), 'Religious Movements and Globalization'. In Robin Cohen and Shirin M. Rai (eds.), *Global Social Movements*, 165-219. London: The Athlone Press.

Part I

Diachronic Perspectives

CHAPTER 1

The Messianic Roots of Babi-Baha'i Globalism

Stephen N. Lambden

Ideas of the oneness of a globally united humanity has a rich and variegated history, reaching back to antiquity (Baldry 1965; Kitagawa 1990). A substantial part of this global thinking is represented by major world religions, which have been theologically globally-minded through most of their existence. This is especially the case as far as their eschatological hopes, messianisms and apocalyptic visions are concerned. Eschatological expectations within diverse apocalyptic traditions include religious messianisms which are associated with national, global and / or cosmic renewal. It was expected by many that God would one day through the instrumentality of one or more exalted messiah figures, set the whole world and its peoples in order. At least within the main Abrahamic religious traditions (Judaism, Christianity and Islam), messianic hopes have often presupposed that in the 'latter days' a messianic advent of global import would take place alongside a cosmic re-creation.

Scriptures and traditions held sacred within Judaism, Christianity and Islam all give value to predictions that their religion would ultimately be made truly global through acts of eschatological warfare and divine judgment (Klausner 1956; Levey 1974; Sachedina 1981; Neusner 1984). A final world-embracing battle, an Armageddon, a major *jihad* achieving the universal defeat of ungodliness, should take place throughout the earth and perhaps throughout the cosmos. It was anticipated that injustice, evil and ungodliness would be challenged and ultimately defeated, resulting in the universal establishment of world order and truth. One or more warrior-messiah figures along with an elect would induce many of the peoples of the whole world to turn towards God. Those that refuse meet an unpleasant end as spelled out in various apocalyptic texts. This final act of universal 'holy war' would be supplemented by acts of supernatural divine intervention such that the whole world would become an earthly expression of the heavenly 'kingdom of God'.

Globalism in eschatological thinking is thus pictured as being achieved by militaristic means through the defeat and complete annihilation of all forms of evil and ungodliness. Within streams of ancient Judaism, Christianity and Islam the waging of a universal holy war is fundamental to and preparatory of millennial peace.

A global religious perspective fuelled by world-wide eschatological hopes has always been and remains something absolutely central to Babi-Baha'i religiosity, despite the fact that narrow Shi'i exclusivisms were dominant within the mindset of the 19th century Persianate world into which both the Bab and Baha'u'llah were born. Cloaked for a while in the - at times - opaque garment of messianic secrecy, they, as will be seen, harboured universalist messianic sentiments. Almost from the outset they directly and indirectly addressed all humanity and its religious and ecclesiastical leaders. By the late 1860s a global soteriological call was clearly voiced to all humankind by the Persian born messianic claimant Mirza Husayn 'Ali Nuri entitled Baha'u'llah ('The Splendour of God', 1817-1892). By the 1880s in a large number of his writings he came to frequently voice as a divinely revealed, universalist dictum, 'The earth [world] is but one country and all humankind its citizens' (Baha'u'llah 1978: 167).

It will be argued in this paper that the world-embracing, globalistic nature of the Baha'i religious message has religious roots in Shi'i and Babi messianisms and related visions of universal, global, eschatological renewal. One of the aims of this paper will be to argue that Islamic, especially Shi'i messianic and associated apocalyptic traditions, underpin present day Baha'i globalism, internationalism and universalism, and that this underpinning was achieved through a reinterpretation of the *jihad* doctrine in early Babism.

Globalism after Eschatological Warfare in Shi'i Islam

Islamic messianisms and apocalyptic scenarios frequently echo, mirror or creatively refashion aspects of Zoroastrian, Jewish, Christian and, to a lesser extent, Manichaean materials pertaining to the wars and tribulations attendant upon the consummation of the ages (cf. Pedersen, 1996). This, along with the associated 'signs' of the 'Hour', the onset of the *yawm al-qiyama* (Day of Resurrection) and the *yawn al-din* (Day of Judgment). Predictions of a militaristic latter-day, global *jihad* are common in a very wide range of Islamic eschatological and related literatures. They predict that a universal holy war is to be waged by a messianic savior figure at the time of the end. This results in the internationalism and globalization of the religion of God established in the final age.

The Shi'i messianic Mahdi (Rightly Guided One) is essentially an eschatological warrior figure often referred to as the Qa'im (messianic 'Ariser'), or the *Qa'im bi'l-sayf* (the messianic 'Ariser' armed with the sword). He is a military figure who should establish global justice and true global religiosity. Through his actions, evil, anarchy and ungodliness will be defeated and justice, righteousness and peace be established throughout the world.

The first Imam by Shi'i reckoning 'Ali b. Abi Talib (d. 40/661) is one of the key prototypes of the Shi'i eschatological messiah. His militaristic prowess has long been celebrated as is reflected, for example, in such diverse sources as the *Tarikh al-rusul wa'l-muluk* (History of Prophets and Kings) of al-Tabari (d. 310/922) and the semi-*ghuluww* ('extremist') *Khutba al-tutunjiyya* ('Sermon of the Gulf') ascribed to Imam 'Ali himself (delivered between Medina and Kufa) and containing messianic and apocalyptic passages well-known to both the Bab and Baha'u'llah (al-Tabari 1997; 'Ali b. Abi Talib 1978). In eschatological times the militaristic genius of Imam 'Ali is echoed in that of the twelfth Imam and his Shi'i followers who are to redress injustices in these final decisive battles.

This militaristic vision of global justice informs and lies behind aspects of the Babi-Baha'i concepts of messianic universalism and its claimed fulfillment in the religions of the Bab and Baha'u'llah. The following few notes sum up select Islamic eschatological *jihad* traditions which directly or indirectly inspired the Bab and his first Shi'i-Shaykhi-rooted followers.

A number of Shi'i traditions state that the messianic Qa'im will be characterized by various qualities central to previous sent Messengers. One such tradition from the sixth Shi'i Imam, Ja'far al-Sadiq

(d. c.145/765) as cited by Ibn Babuya al-Qummi (d.280/991) in his *Kamal al-din...* (The Perfection of Religion), reads as follows:

In the [messianic] Qa'im ('Ariser') is a sign from Moses, a sign from Joseph, a sign from Jesus and a sign from Muhammad... As for the sign from Jesus, it is traveling *(al-siyaha)* and the sign from Muhammad is the sword *(al-sayf)*. (Ibn Babuya 1991: 39).

The location from which the messianic Qa'im will call for universal holy war is variously indicated in the Shi'i sources. They often give considerable importance in this respect to al-Kufa, the location of the shrine / mosque of 'Ali b. Abi Talib and to Karbila, the Iraqi site of the shrine of the martyred Imam Husayn (d. 61/680). Both these sacred places are intimately associated with the parousia of the Qa'im and his role in initiating and waging an ultimately global *jihad*.

Another very lengthy, composite Shi'i tradition on eschatological lines is that ascribed to Mufaddal b. 'Umar al-Ju'fi (d. c. 145/762-3) an associate of Imam Ja'far al-Sadiq and recorded in Majlisi's *Bihar al-anwar* ('Oceans of Lights') (Majlisi, *Bihar* 53:1-38, in al-Mufid 1979: 346ff). This tradition associates eschatological events with Syria, Iraq (Baghdad) Iran (Khurasan) and other places. A Hasanid Sayyid is mentioned who calls all people to the messianic Qa'im when pious souls from Taliqan (Khurasan, Iran) arm themselves for *jihad* and mount swift horses. It is predicted that at Kufa they will slay numerous enemies of God and come to settle in this sacred city. In time they are to further assist the Mahdi in *jihad* activity involving much slaughter and the globalization of religion.

Several further Islamic traditions presuppose that the messianic Qa'im, the *sahib al-amr* (bearer of a Cause /Command) will establish a new religious *amr* (religious 'Cause') which will be propagated throughout the globe. One *hadith* again originating with Ja'far al-Sadiq as cited by Shaykh al-Mufid is fairly explicit in this respect:

When the Qa'im... rises, he will come with a new *amr* (religious 'Cause'), just as the Messenger of God [Muhammad] *(rasul Allah)* ...at the genesis of Islam summoned unto a new *amr* (religious 'Cause'). (al-Mufid 1979: 364)

A number of Shi'i traditions registered in the final section of the *Kitab al-ghayba* (The Book of the Occultation) of Muhammad b. Ibrahim b.

Ja'far al-Nu'mani (d. Damascus 360/971), entitled 'What has been [authoritatively] relayed [from the Imams] about the duration of the [final] *mulk* ('rule', 'dominion') of the Qa'im... subsequent to his rising up' (al-Nu'mani 1973: 231-32). Ja'far al-Sadiq is recorded as having stated that the messianic Qa'im 'will rule' (*yamlaka al-qa'im*) for 'nineteen and some months' (al-Nu'mani 1973: 231ff). This and similar traditions mentioning 'seven', 'nine' and other periods of time, are sometimes understood messianically in Babi-Baha'i literatures. The allusions to a 19 or so year messianic period was understood as reflecting the period separating the advents of the Bab (1260/1844) and Baha'u'llah (1279-80/1863) viewed as the twin eschatological advents of the Qa'im and the Qayyum ('Divinity Self-Subsisting').

Any messianic claimant appearing in Qajar Iran claiming to be (or to represent) the eschatological Qa'im would of necessity have to clarify his position regarding holy war for his Shi'i contemporaries. Such traditions as are summarized above would need to be interpreted. The Bab did this in certain of his earliest writings - not that all of his listeners were satisfied with his statements.[1]

The Bab, the *Qayyum al-asma'* and Globalization through *Jihad*

It has not been my purpose here to examine all that the Bab has written about *jihad* or review the nature of the Babi upheavals in this light.[2] Rather, the focus of attention will be on the move towards universalism as a result of the messianic call for global, eschatological *jihad*.

The first major work of the Bab originating at the time of his Shiraz disclosure of his actual or imminent messiahship (*Qa'imiyya*) before

1 The earliest attack on emergent Babism was penned by the Kirmani Shaykhi leader Hajji Mirza Muhammad Karim Khan Kirmani (d. 1871). He questioned the legitimacy of the Bab's call for holy war in the *Qayyum al-asma'* and elsewhere since such a call can only legitimately be made by the Qa'im in person, not by one who commits *i'jaz,* the production of non-revealed qur'anic type verses as Kirmani meant the Bab had done (Kirmani 1972-3: 127ff).

2 See, for example, MacEoin (1982; 1988); Zabihi-Moghaddam (2002a; 2002b); Lambden (1999-2000; 2004). A survey of the writings of the Bab is given by MacEoin (1992), and the reader is referred to this work for a description of the Bab's major works discussed in the present paper.

Mulla Husayn Bushru'i on 22 May 1844, is his bulky, over four hundred pages long, neo-qur'anic *Qayyum al-asma'* (loosely, 'Self-Subsistent Reality of the Divine Names'; mid. 1844 CE). Its first chapter is entitled *surat al-mulk,* the Surah of the Dominion.[3] This title is highly eschatologically suggestive, being intended to remind humankind that the eschatological 'Hour' or 'Day' is shortly to be realized, the time when earthly dominions would return to God Himself through the imminent global sovereignty of His messianic representatives. Just as qur'anic *surah* ('chapter') titles derive from key words used in the surahs so named, so does the title of this *Surat al-mulk* derive from a seminal verse halfway through, where we read:

O concourse of kings and of the sons of kings! Lay aside, in truth, as befits the Truth, one and all your (Ar.) *mulk* (dominion) which belongs unto God (Bab 1976: 41 revised).

Global rulership is to be returned to God Himself through His messianic representatives the Mahdi-Qa'im, twelfth Imam, the *Dhikr* (Remembrance), or their servant the Bab himself. It is the Bab's *Surat al-mulk* which sets the theological-eschatological parameters whereby the words *al-mulk li-láhí* (the Kingdom belongs to God) can be realized. The mediator for this process is the Bab who communicates with the hidden Imam who directs the carrying out of God's will. This involves the relinquishment of worldly kingship by human kings and rulers. It is also related to the immanent advent of the messianic Qa'im (Ariser) who is the true ruler of the eschatological age on account of his imminent global victory.

For the Bab the *mulk Allah,* the rule of God should ideally be established by kings who become faithful servants of the promised messiah. If such kings take personal part in a global *jihad* with the messianic twelfth Imam they would be amply rewarded (*Qayyum al-asma'* 1: 29ff). About half-way through the *Surat al-mulk* the Bab addresses the 'King of the Muslims' most likely indicating the Persian Muhammad Shah

3 The Arabic word *mulk,* has a wide range of meanings including, `dominion', 'kingdom' or 'sovereignty', This word *mulk* (cf. *malik* = king) actually occurs 8-9 times within key verses of the first chapter of the *Qayyum al-asma'* (see esp. *Qayyum al-asma'* 1: 20ff). The *surat al-mulk* has been translated by Lambden and is electronically available, see references.

(reigned 1834-1848) calling him to aid the messianic Remembrance. The Shah should purify or purge the 'holy land' *(al-ard al-muqaddas),* most likely the *'atabat* or shrine cities of Iraq.[4] Then, as a devotee of the messianic *Dhikr* and his *amr* (religious 'Cause'), he should 'subdue' the various *al-bilad,* the regions or countries of the earth. If he accomplishes this task of holy war he is promised by the Bab a place in *al-akhira,* the post-resurrection 'Hereafter', among the *ahl al-jannat al-ridwan* the inhabitants of the paradise which is the 'Garden of Ridwan'.

In the *Qayyum al-asma'* the Bab further explicitly calls Muhammad Shah and other kings to render God victorious through their 'own selves' and 'by means of their swords' in the shadow of the messianic Remembrance. Eschatological victory through *jihad* is clearly referenced. In an address to Hajji Mirza Aqasi (d.1265 /1848), the *wazir al-mulk* (minister of the King, Muhammad Shah), the Bab bids him relinquish his *mulk* (dominion) in view of the fact that he, the Bab, has inherited the earth and all who are upon it. The *mulk* (dominion) of kings is now something 'vain', 'false' or 'ephemeral'.

The Bab also called upon the kings to hastily disseminate his revealed verses to the Turks and to the *ard al-hind,* the people of India as well to those beyond these lands in both the East and the West. Such statements most clearly illustrate the universalism or globalism of the Bab at the very onset of his mission.

In the course of the *Surat al-mulk* (the first *surah* in *Qayyum al-asma'*) the Bab not only raises the call for universal *jihad* and announces the imminent *mulk* (dominion, state, rule, etc) of God and /or the Qa'im, but utilizes the above-mentioned motif of a new *amr* (religious 'Cause'). About half-way through the forty-two or so verses in the *Surat al-mulk,* the Bab refers to his emergent messianic religion as *al-amr al-badi'* ('the new Cause', 'novel religion') (cf. Bab 1976: 41 which has 'wondrous revelation').

The question of latter-day *jihad* and its messianic centrality is evidenced in both the initial 3-4 pages of the *Surat al-mulk* and, most notably, in seven or more sometimes adjacent chapters within the complete 111 surahs of the *Qayyum al-asma'*. Most of the titles of these surahs were named by the Bab himself in his early *Kitab al-fihrist* (Book

4 The *'atabat* are the Iraqi cites of Najaf, Kufa, Karbila, Kazemayn and Samarra where the shrines of six of the twelver Imams and other places of Shi'i visitation are located.

of the Index written in Bushire in 1261/June, 1845) and his *Kitab al-Ruh* (Book of the Spirit). Several manuscripts of the former work identify these seven adjacent surahs, spanning from *surah* (95) 96 until *surah* 102, as all designated either *Surat al-qittal* (The Surah of the Slaughter) in four recensions or *Surat al-jihad* (The Surah of Holy War) in three recensions.

These seven surahs all contain rewritten qur'anic materials having to do with holy war and its eschatological application relative to the combative role of the messianic person of the *Dhikr-Allah.* They are not merely repetitions of qur'anic verses relating to *jihad* but are at times infused with a millennial excitement centering upon the realization of the long-awaited *nasr Allah,* the 'victory of God', pronounced near at hand. The following passage must suffice to give an idea of the Bab's innovative refashioning of qur'anic motifs as evidenced in *surah* 102, the last of the four *Surat al-qittal* (The Surah of the Slaughter):

O Qurrat al-'Ayn! [= the Bab] Should the following directive *(al-amr)* come from before Us [God], 'So summon ye the people for killing *(al-qittal)!'* then [know ye] that God has stored up for your [eschatological] Day men even as powerful mountains. For such were indeed [written] in the Archetypal Book *(umm al-kitab),* [as persons] manifest for the name of the Exalted Dhikr-Allah (messianic Remembrance of God) (*Qayyum al-asma'* 102:408).

For the Bab, God is capable of raising up very strong male warriors even as 'powerful mountains' for fighting in the messianic *jihad.* Qur'anic laws of holy war are repeated or modified in the *Qayyum al-asma'* without explicit abrogation (cf. Qur'an 74:31b).

Eschatological Warfare and the Religion of the Bab

From a study of the Bab's writings it will be evident that the Bab did not shrink away from the issue of the holy war expected to occur universally in the last days by all Shi'i and most other Muslims. In his many writings the Bab quite frequently made reference to *jihad* and to an anticipated eschatological *nasr* (victory). Yet, despite the later sporadic engagements between the Babis and the government troops, *jihad* never seems to have been straightforwardly or collectively called by the Bab during his lifetime (MacEoin 1982).

Though this matter cannot be discussed in detail here, it may be noted that an early Arabic prayer of the Bab was composed in response to questions associated with the above-mentioned eschatological events at Kufa. In this prayer the Bab appears to respond to questions raised by such messianic and militaristic traditions as are ascribed to the abovementioned Mufaddal b. 'Umar. In this early expository prayer the Bab states that he only knows what God has taught him regarding the [advent of the] *al-nafs al-zakiyya* (The Pure Soul) 'who will be slain in the land of Kufa', 'the one who will emerge from Khurasan and Taliqan' and regarding the [militaristic] 'decree of the Husaynid Sayyid'. He then states that he is nothing but 'the like of what God has stipulated' and continues to add that he would, if necessary and in accordance with the will of God, blot out such matters through *al-bada'* ('innovation'), the alternation of the divine plan. Then such eschatological affairs would through *al-bada'* 'be rescinded consonant which whatsoever hath been promised the trustees of the All-Merciful' (Bab, 'Prayer in reply to questions').

From this prayer it seems clear that the Bab was made aware – through his questioner – of certain traditions relating to figures who will proceed and assist the messianic Qa'im in his holy war activities. He apparently disclaimed personal knowledge of the meaning of these traditions and appears to indicate that such expectations may or may not be realized in the light of his possible implementation of *al-bada'*, (loosely) the emergence of a change in the divine plan.[5] Through the Bab, God can change his mind about the realization of such expectations. The militaristic messianism of the *hadith* of Mufaddal and others need not take place and could be 'demythologized' if God so willed. The early plans for a literalistic fulfillment of Shi'i expectations of global *jihad* centering on Kufa and Karbila, were thus cancelled, despite that from the outset of his messianic activities the Bab invited the kings of the world to a global *jihad* and taught that God would 'wreak his vengeance' upon such as had martyred Imam Husayn (d. 61/680) (*Qayyum al-asma'* 21: 69, cf. Bab 1976: 49).

5 The Arabic word *bada'*, literally means 'emergence', indicating the emergence of new circumstances which require a change to an earlier circumstance or ruling. It indicates the alteration of a previously divinely ordained plan. God may change his mind as it were.

The historical fact is that when the Bab returned to Shiraz in June 1845 from his pilgrimage to Mecca, he decided not to go to Karbila as planned, maybe because of the *fatwa* issued against him in connection with Ali Bastami's trial.[6] After his cancellation of the Karbila rally, a formal call for *jihad* seems never to have been categorically reissued by the Bab himself, although *jihad* by kings and others still remained a future possibility in the achievement of the global spread of his religion (Bab, *Dala'il-i Sab'ih*: 43; Bab, *Haykal al-din*: 15ff).

The Terrestrial and Cosmic Universalism of the Bab

In the *Qayyum al-asma'* and numerous other writings the call of the Bab is not restricted to Iran, Iraq and the Middle East, but is addressed to all humanity and even beings beyond this world. Within the over 100 surahs and more than 500 pericopae of the *Qayyum al-asma'* there are scores of universalistic and cosmic addresses.[7] While outside of the *Surat al-mulk* in the 63rd *Surat al-Rahman* (Surah of the All-Merciful) the Bab bids all worldly kings fear God respecting his position as messianic Gate, in the 9th *Surat al-tawhid* (Surah of the Divine Unity) he addresses all the 'people of the earth'. Influenced by qur'anic cosmology, the Bab called all within and betwixt the heavens and the earths to have faith in him / the messianic *Dhikr* and his divinely inspired message. He communicated a global and extra-global cosmic message. He called out to human and supernatural beings including the *jinn*, the celestial concourse *(mala' al-a'la)* and beings associated with the divine Throne *(al-'arsh)* in the 'sphere of lights'. This also sets the scene for Babi-Baha'i internationalism and globalism.

6 Mulla Ali Bastami was among the Bab's close disciples ('the Letters of the Living') who had gone to Karbila to spread the teachings of the Bab. Large crowds of expecting adherents gathered while arms were purchased for the preparation of *jihad*. Bastami was, however, arrested and imprisoned, and in 1845 he appeared before a joint Sunni-Shi'ite tribunal in Baghdad - an unusual reconciliation of Sunni and Shi'ite *ulama*. The tribunal issued a *fatwa* condemning the Bab as blasphemous and an outright unbeliever; however, because of internal disagreement between the Sunni and Shi'i parties Ali Bastami was spared a death sentence. See MacEoin 1982; Momen 1982.

7 They frequently commence with the Arabic vocative particle *ya* or its extended form *ya ayyuha al-*.

The final two paragraphs of the *Surat al-mulk* again underline the global scope of the Bab's 1844/1260 message. They are addressed to 'the servants of the All-Merciful' and to all the 'people of the earth'. In addressing the people of the earth later in another *surah* of the *Qayyum al-asma'* (No. 59), the Bab states that through the power of God his book and message has pervaded both earth and heaven. The 'Mighty Word of God', relating to the supreme messianic testimony, has been firmly established throughout the East and the West (*Qayyum al-asma'* 59: 234; cf. Bab 1976: 59-60).

Also worth noting at this point is the fact that in *Qayyum al-asma'* 53, God addresses the Bab with the following words:

> Be ye patient O Qurrat al-'Ayn (loosely, 'the Apple of his Eye'), for God hath indeed pledged [guaranteed], to [establish] Thy might [sovereignty] over [all] the countries (lit. *'izz 'ala al-bilad)* and over those that dwell therein' (*Qayyum al-asma'* 53: 208, cf. Bab 1976: 57).

In his early and partly lost, neo-qur'anic *Kitab al-ruh* (The Book of the Spirit, 1845, see MacEoin 1982: 61, 189), the Bab again has an address to all of 'the people of the earth'. Many later paragraphs of this work are also addressed to the worldly 'concourse' while within *surah* 21 there is an address to the assemblage of all of 'the *jinn* and men'.

In his *Persian Bayan* from 1848, *wahid* 5 (p. 158) the Bab stated that every past religion was fit to become universal and that it was the incompetence of the followers which prevented its universal adoption.[8] A thorough reading of the Bab's many writings makes it obvious that he anticipated his 'pure religion' (*al-din al-khalis*, see *Qayyum al-asma'* 1: 4) becoming universal as he did that of the many successive future Babi messiah figures known as *man yuzhiru-hu Allah* ('Him whom God shall make manifest') (*Persian Bayan*, *wahid* 5; *Kitab-i panj sha'an*, 314-15, cf. 397).

The anticipated Shi'i-Babi *jihad* predicted in numerous traditions of the Prophet Muhammad and the Imams, was never realized in worldly terms as discussed above. Neither 'kings' nor the 'sons of kings' rose up for any *jihad* episode called for in the Bab's first major

8 This has also been noted in a letter written on behalf of Shoghi Effendi dated Feb. 10th 1932 and cited in *Living the Life* (National Spiritual Assembly of the Baha'is of the UK 1972: 11).

book. Even the later Babi upheavals (1848-1852) appear never to have been actualized by a specific call of the Bab for *jihad.* While *jihad* activity remained a distinct, future theological possibility for the Bab, it never came to have any concrete, militaristic realization. As time went on the Bab tended more and more in the direction of a demythologized reading of Islamic apocalyptic (Lambden 1998).

From, at latest, the time of the Persian and Arabic Bayans and *Dal'il-i Sab'ih* (Seven Proofs, c. 1848), the Bab generally demythologized Islamic apocalyptic eschatology though he never abandoned the vision of the universal spread of his religion or that of the Babi messiah, the *man yuzhiru-hu Allah* (The One Whom God shall make manifest). However, he never totally ceased using *jihad* language until his execution in July 1850.

In what is probably the last substantial work of the Bab, the *Haykal al-din* (The Temple of Religion, 1850) the waging of a kind of holy war is spelled out when the Bab states that a future Babi king should, as a manifestation of the 'wrath of God' *(qahr Allah),* put all non-Babis to death. This drastic measure, which does not quite go along with the developed Baha'i image of the Bab, would in principle result in instant Babi globalization! It is, though, fully in line with the implications of one of the tablets of 'Abdu'l Baha.[9]

The Abandoning of *Jihad*

Twenty years after the Bab's 1260/1844 messianic disclosure in late April–early May 1863, Baha'u'llah continued transforming Babism into a movement for peace realized without concrete holy war. As a devout Babi he argued in his *Kitáb-i Íqán* (Book of Certitude, 1862), that the sovereignty of the Bab as the Qa'im was destined to be more like that of Jesus Christ than Muhammad. It was a 'spiritual', unworldly sovereignty not a concrete theocratic rule established by warmongering followers.

9 This tablet of 'Abdu'l-Baha can be found in the compilation *Makatib-i Hazrat-i* 'Abdu'l-Baha, vol. 2: 266, and reads in part, 'In the Day of the manifestation of His Holiness the Exalted One (= the Bab) the striking of necks [cf. Qur'an 8: 12], the burning of books and treatises (*kutub va avraq*), the demolition of buildings and the universal slaughter (*qitl-i-amm*) of all except such as believed and were steadfast was clearly enunciated.'

From the very outset of his post-Baghdad mission, Baha'u'llah abrogated outer *jihad* waged by means of the sword.

In a highly Arabized Persian letter of Baha'u'llah, dated 1293/1876, he speaks of three 'words' (principles) which he annunciated at the time of his 1863 Ridvan declaration on the outskirts of Baghdad. The very first word was the abrogation of Islamo-Babi *jihad*:

> On the first day that the Ancient Beauty [Baha'u'llah] occupied the Most Great Throne in a garden (orchard, *bustan*) which has been designated Ridvan, the Tongue of Grandeur uttered three blessed proclamations (1) The first of them was that in this [Baha'i] theophany [dispensation] *(zuhur)* the [use of the] sword *(sayf)* [in holy war] is put aside *(murtafi')*.[10]

These fundamental aspects of post-1863 Baha'i doctrine were categorically affirmed and repeated in the decade later *Kitáb-i-Aqdas*, the 'Most Holy Book' of Baha'u'llah (1992: 76) and in numerous supplementary tablets. In the *Tablet of Bisharat*, the very first Glad-Tiding, like the first 'Word' uttered at the time of the Ridvan declaration, is as follows:

> O people of the earth!
> The first Glad-Tidings which the Mother Book hath, in this Most Great Revelation, imparted unto all the peoples of the world is that the law of holy war (jihad) hath been blotted out from the Book...(Baha'u'llah 1978: 21).

Distinctly echoing the Isaiah 2: 4, Baha'u'llah also desires, according to the *Bisharat*, that 'weapons of war [Isaiah = 'swords'] throughout the world may be converted into instruments of reconstruction [Isaiah = 'ploughshares'] and that strife and conflict may be so removed from the midst of men and shall learn war no more' (Baha'u'llah 1978: 23, cf. Isaiah 2: 4 and Micah 4: 1-2).

10 Refer to the Persian text reproduced in Iran National Baha'i Manuscript Collection, 44: 225f. The other two 'words' were (2) that no new theophanological claimant would appear for a millennium (1,000 years) and (3) at that time [of this Ridvan announcement] there was a divine self-revelation *(tajalli)* upon all of the Divine Names. On a fourth supplementary 'word', see further Iran National Baha'i Manuscript Collections, [Tehran] 44: 226.

For the former Babi, Baha'u'llah, the Bab's promise of the theocratic sovereignty of God can only be befittingly realized when wholly detached from militaristic 'holy war' activity. For Baha'is non-violent religion should be propagated through the peaceful means of religious exposition (Ar. *bayan)* characterized by spiritual *hikma* ('wisdom') such as would maintain peace and unity in the diversity of humankind. Thus, in Baha'u'llah's understanding of *jihad*, the (Islamic) non-militaristic 'greater' *jihad*, the conquering of the lower self, becomes foundational for the greater *jihad* propagated with utterance of *hikma.* This, Baha'is believe, can peacefully transform the whole world and all humankind.

A well-known Persian Baha'i prayer of Baha'u'llah underlines the relationship between human unity and the 'kingdom' returning to God. It reads:

> God grant that the light of unity may envelop the whole earth and that the seal *al-mulk li-llahi* (the Kingdom is God's) may be stamped on the brow of all its peoples. (Baha'u'llah 1983: 11)[11]

In the *Kitáb-i-Aqdas* Baha'u'llah confidently announces that through his presence the kingdom of God is realized independently of any *jihad* activity:

> O kings of the earth! He Who is the sovereign Lord (*al-malik* lit. Ruling One, King) of all is come. The Kingdom is God's (*al-mulk li-lahi*), the omnipotent Protector, the Self-Subsisting. (Baha'u'llah 1992: 48; author's reference to the Arabic)

The above citation is centered upon words derived from the Arabic root M-L-K (indicative of possession, dominion and kingship, etc.) illustrates that the divine *mulk* (kingdom, rule), the sovereignty of God, had potentially or spiritually been realized in view of his messianic status as kingly Ruler and architect of a peace centered religion. The realized eschatology of Baha'u'llah presupposed that, independent of any militaristic *jihad* activity, the kingdom of God was universally realized through the establishment of his spiritual sovereignty.

11 Persian text in *Muntakhabati az Athar-i Hadrat-i Baha'u'llah,* Hofheim-Langenhaim: Baha'i Verlag, No. 7: 11.

The Closing of the Circle

Though there are important pacifist aspects to the Babi religion, the Bab never actually abandoned the *jihad* concept as associated with the globalization of Babism under the messianic Qa'im, a future Babi king or as achieved by *man yuzhiru-hu Allah* (Him Whom God shall make manifest). It is a significant doctrine having connotations of universalism and divine victory throughout his mission.

From the outset Baha'u'llah categorically abrogated *jihad*, advocating instead a pacifist attitude to the propagation of (middle) Babism or the nascent Baha'i religion. However, he made this transformation to be both a continuation and a break with the Babi doctrines of *jihad* and globalism. In an Arabic Tablet to a certain (unidentified) 'Ali, partially published in the compilation *Ma'idih-yi Asmani*, Baha'u'llah states,

> We indeed lifted up the *hukm al-sayf wa'l-sinan* (decree of the sword and spears) and We decreed that victory (*al-nasr*) be through exposition [of the sacred Word] (*al-bayan*) and that which comes out from the tongue. He indeed is the Sublime (*Ma'idih* 4:18) (Baha'u'llah 1972: 18).

Some 20 years after the Bab's communicating the *Surat al-mulk* (*Surah* of the Dominion), in the *Qayyum al-asma'*, Baha'u'llah penned his 70 page wholly Arabic *Surat al-muluk* (The Surah of the Kings). Its preamble begins on distinctly universal lines, with an address to 'the concourse of the kings of the earth', the *ma'shar al-muluk*, (Baha'u'llah 1968: 4). This probably alludes to the *Qayyum al-asma'* 1: 34, which also was addressed to 'the concourse of the kings', cf. above. Baha'u'llah further calls their attention to the 'story of 'Ali' (the Bab = 'Ali Muhammad Shirazi) who came with a 'glorious and weighty Book' (= the *Qayyum al-asma'*?). Baha'u'llah continues to admonish the kings as persons who failed to heed the Bab as the *Dhikr-Allah* (Remembrance of God), referring to the Bab after the terminology of the *Qayyum al-asma'*. The kings who rejected the Bab should not be heedless of the counsel of Baha'u'llah through whom true *mulk* 'sovereignty' has been established:

> Beware not to deal unjustly with anyone that appealeth to you and entereth beneath your shadow. Walk ye in the fear of God, and be ye of them that lead a godly life. Rest not on your power, your armies, and treasures. Put your

whole trust and confidence in God, Who hath created you, and seek ye His help in all your affairs (*Surat al-muluk,* verse 10).

Many other passages in the writings of Baha'u'llah in one way or another bear upon the undesirability of *jihad,* the folly of warfare and the necessity of peace, collective security, and the means for the globalization of his religion. Only a few examples have been cited here.

The *Surat al-muluk* (The *Surah* of the Kings) stands as the early central proclamation of globalism among the writings of Baha'u'llah. The similarity of its title with the first surah of the *Qayyum al-asma',* the *Surat al-mulk,* and the many references to the Bab's message in 1845, show that Baha'u'llah's globalism is deeply imbedded in Shi'i and Babi eschatology, while at the same time it radically transcends the idea of globalisation by the sword.

References

'Abdu'l Baha (1912). *Makatib-i Hazrat-i 'Abdu'l Baha,* vol. 2. Cairo: Matba'a Kurdistan al-'Ilmiyya.

'Ali b. Abi Talib (1978). 'Khutba Tutunjiyya' in Rajab al-Bursi, *Mashariq anwar al-yaqin fi asrar Amir al-muminin,* Beirut: Dar al-Andalus: 166-170.

Bab [n.d.]. 'Ali Muhammad Shirazi, the, *Dala'il-i Sab'ih* (The Seven Proofs), [n.p.] (Azali edition).

Bab [n.d.]. *Haykal al-Din,* [n.p.].

Bab [n.d.]. *Kitab al-Fihrist,* Iran National Baha'i Archives, Tehran ms. TBA 6006/7C: 339-348 and Iran National Baha'i Archives, Tehran ms. TBA 5014C: 285-93 esp.: 289-90.

Bab [n.d.]. *Kitab al-ruh* (The Book of the Spirit), (Incomplete) Mss: Iran National Baha'i Archives, Tehran 4011C63.

Bab [n.d.]. Persian Bayan: *Kitab-i panj sha'an* [n.p].

Bab [n.d.]. *Qayyum al-asma',* International Baha'i Archives, Haifa mss. 1261 in hand of Shah Karam.

Bab (1905) *Qayyum al-asma'* Afnan Library, U.K.

Bab [n.d.] 'Prayer in reply to questions' in Iran National Baha'i Archives, Tehran ms. 6006C: 173ff.

Bab (1976) *Selections from the Writings of the Bab,* Haifa: Baha'i World Centre.

Baha'u'llah (1968) *Surat al-muluk* (Tablets to the Kings and Rulers of the Earth), Alvah-i nazilih khitab bi muluk va ru'asa-yi ard, Tehran: Baha'i Publishing Trust.

Baha'u'llah (1972) *Maídih-yi Asmani,* vol. 4, Tehran: Baha'i Publishing Trust.

Baha'u'llah (1978) *Tablets of Bahá'u'lláh,* Haifa: Baha'i World Centre.

Baha'u'llah (1983) *The Kitáb-i Íqán. The Book of Certitude,* Wilmette, Ill.: Baha'i Publishing Trust.

Baha'ullah (1983) *Gleanings from the Writings of Baha'u'llah,* Wilmette, Ill.: Baha'i Publishing Trust.

Baha'u'llah (1992) *The Kitáb-i-Aqdas,* Haifa: Baha'i World Centre.

Baldry, H.C. (1965) *The Unity of Mankind in Greek Thought,* New York & Cambridge: Cambridge University Press.

Ibn Babuwayh [Babuya] al-Qummi (1991) *Kamal al-din wa tamam al-na'ima,* Beirut: Muassa'at al-Al-a'la.

Kirmani, Muhammad Karim Khan (1972-73), *Risala Izhaq al-batil fi radd al-babiyya,* Kirman: Matba'at al-Sa'ada.

Kitagawa, Joseph, M. (1990) *The Quest for Human Unity, A Religious History,* Minneapolis: Fortress Press.

Klausner, Jospeh (1956) *The Messianic Idea in Israel,* London: George Allen & Unwin.

Lambden, S. (1999-2000) 'Catastrophe, armageddon and millennium: Some aspects of the Babi-Baha'i exegesis of apocalyptic symbolism', *Baha'i Studies Review*: 81-99.

Lambden, S. 'The Bab, Qayyum al-asma', 'Surat al-mulk' (The Surah of the Dominion')' trans. Stephen Lambden, URL: http://www.hurqalya.pwp.blueyonder.co.uk/03-THE%20BAB/QAYYUM%20AL-ASMA'/Q-ASMA.001.htm.

Lambden, S. (1998) 'Eschatology, Part. IV' In E. Yarshater (ed), *Encyclopedia Iranica* (vol. 8: 581). New York: Bibliotheca Persica Press.

Lambden, S. (2004) 'The Bābī-Bahā'ī religions, warfare and peace' in Gabriel Palmer Fernandez (ed.) *Routledge Encyclopedia of Religion and War,* no. 5, London: Routledge: 33-36.

Levey, Samson, H. (1974) *The Messiah. An Aramaic Interpretation. The Messianic Exegesis of the Targum. Cincinatti,* New York: Hebrew Union College Press.

MacEoin, Denis (1982) 'The Babi concept of Holy War', *Religion,* vol. 1: 93-129.

MacEoin, Denis (1988) 'Babism', in Ehsan Yarshater (ed), *Encyclopædia Iranica*, vol. 3, London, Routledge & Kegan Paul: 309-317.

MacEoin, Denis (1992) *The Sources for Early Babi Doctrine and History*, Leiden: E. J. Brill.

Momen, Moojan (1982) 'The Trial of Mulla 'Ali Bastami: a Combined Sunni-Shi'i Fatwa against the Bab', *Iran: Journal of the British Institute of Persian Studies*, vol. 20: 113-43.

al-Mufid, Shaykh [Muhammad b. Muhammad al-Nu'man al-'Akbari al-Baghdadi] (1979) *Kitab al-Irshad*. Beirut: Mu'assat al-A'lami. Translated by Howard, I.K.A., *Kitab al-Irshad*. Horsham and London: Muhammadi Trust, Balagha Books.

National Spiritual Assembly of the Baha'is of the UK (1972) *Living the Life... two compilations*, Wilmette, Ill.: Baha'i Publishing Trust.

Neusner, Jacob (1984) *Messiah in Context, Israel's History and Destiny in Formative Judaism*, Philadelphia: Fortress Press.

al-Nu'mani, Muhammad b. Ibrahim b. Ja'far (1973) *Kitab al-Ghayba*. Beirut: Muassat al-A'lami.

Pedersen, Nils A. (1996) *Studies in the Sermon of the Great War. Investigations of a Manichaean-Coptic text from the fourth century*, Aarhus: Aarhus University Press.

Sachedina, A. (1981) *Islamic messianism*, NewYork: Suny Press.

al-Tabari, Muhammad b. Jarir (1997) (trans. M. Fishbane), *The History of al-Tabari*, VIII, 'The Victory of Islam', New York: Suny Press.

Zabihi-Moghaddam, Siyamak (2002a) *Vaqi'i-yi Qal'iy-I Shaykh Tabarsi*. Darmstadt: 'Asr-i Jadid Publisher.

Zabihi-Moghaddam, Siyamak (2002b) 'The Babi-State Conflict at Shaykh Tabarsi', *Iranian Studies*, vol. 35: 37-112.

CHAPTER 2

Globalization and the *Hidden Words*

Todd Lawson

From Tehran to Baghdad

Baghdad (traditionally known as 'the City of Peace') is, we have all recently come to learn, a very diverse place both ethnically and religiously.[1] As such, it may be thought a faithful emblem of islamicate culture and history.[2] There are Sunni Muslims, Shi'i Muslims, Sunni Kurds, Syriac Christians, and Jews, among others. Moreover, it has been this way for a very long time indeed. Seventeenth century travelers 'were impressed with the great admixture of race, the diversity of speech and the rare freedom enjoyed by non-Muslims and the great toleration among the masses' (Durri 1975: 934b). Contrasted with the capital of its Eastern neighbor Iran, Baghdad was infinitely more cosmopolitan than the mainly Shi'i population of Tehran. Tehran, monochrome by comparison, had been mainly Shi'i for several hundred years as well. The significance this fact might have for the growth and development of the Bahai Faith is the main question treated here. The proposition is that the relatively communalistic and parochial Shi'i Babi movement

1 Note the prolonged difficulty the recently American-appointed Iraqi ruling council had in choosing a leader from amongst twenty-five members, finally settling on the Shi'i Ja'fari as the first president. Note also that this office is meant to rotate on a monthly (!) basis in alphabetical order. http://www.salon.com/news/wire/2003/07/30/interim/

2 The term 'islamicate' may require some explanation. It was coined by the historian Marshal G.S. Hodgson (1974, I: 57-60) who thereby sought to avoid doctrinal and normative complications by the use of 'Islamic' in such contexts.

was transformed as changes in audience occurred. If the Bahai prophet-founder Baha'u'llah had not been exiled to Iraq, and then Turkey and finally Ottoman Palestine (modern day Israel), it is possible that his writings would have remained more identifiably Shi'i than they did. In Baghdad, faced with an audience of widely divergent background and composition, Baha'u'llah was also faced with the task of distilling the vast complex of arcana and esoterica that was the revelation of the Bab into an essence that could move a much broader spectrum of believer than the virtually all-Shi'i audience of the Bab. In the process, his message was being universalized for an even wider audience than 19th century Baghdad. In order to demonstrate this proposition, we will analyze the opening passages of Baha'u'llah's *Hidden Words* with this factor of audience in mind.

The Sacralization of Globalization

How does such a discussion find its way into a book of essays devoted to the problem of the Bahai Faith and Globalization? To begin with, the doctrinal content of the Bahai Faith is nothing if not universal. One assumes that there is some kind of important connection between the 'universal' and the 'global'. Traditionally, a 'universal' truth or feature is thought to be one that migrates across long-standing boundaries or barriers of ethnos, nationality, language, culture, and geography to speak of something inherently, irreducibly and 'universally' human. To speak of a universal idea is to speak of one that is eminently susceptible of globalization – of being relevant or pertinent or even merely registrable, to human beings wherever they might be on planet Earth.[3]

Here, a unique phenomenon that has occurred in the growth and development of the Bahai Faith will be examined, namely the process

3 I should like to thank Professor Margit Warburg for her very helpful suggestions and comments on an earlier draft of this paper. I would also like to thank the editorial team, Dr Morten Warmind and Dr Annika Hvithamar, for their guidance and patience. Professors Peter Beyer of the University of Ottawa and Barbara Lawson, Ethnology Curator, Redpath Museum, McGill University, also read earlier drafts and made several very helpful suggestions touching both content and style, for which I am most grateful. Obviously, none of these kind readers is responsible for the remaining flaws.

by which a relatively marginal Islamic sect became a global 'World Religion' and in the process lost much of its original Islamic identity. No other similar movement of the last two hundred years has so completely left the 'gravitational pull' of Islam, to forge such a singular identity. This growth and development is no better characterized anywhere than in the words of Shoghi Effendi Rabbani (d. 1957) when he spoke of this process as the transformation of a 'heterodox and seemingly negligible offshoot of the Shaykhi school of the Ithna-Ashariya sect of Shi'a Islam into a world religion' (Rabbani 1970: xii).

Briefly, this statement refers to an intellectual history little studied in connection with the history of the Bahai Faith, but nonetheless necessary to understand it in its time and place. This is a history in which the Shi'i mystico-philosophical movement begun by Shaykh Ahmad al-Ahsa'i (d. 1826) plays a crucial and essential role. It was the activities and beliefs of this movement that would lead ultimately to the dramatic events associated with the chiliastic-cum-revolutionary activities of Sayyid Ali Muhammad Shirazi (b. 1819). This young charismatic and messianic prophet, known to history as the Bab (Arabic for *Gate*), was executed by Iranian state and religious authorities in 1850. Afterwards, many of his followers one of whom was Mirza Husayn Ali Mazandarani, *Baha'u'llah* (Arabic for *Glory of God;* d. 1892) would be dispersed throughout the Middle East. What the above quotation refers to is the move away from the extremely arcane, esoteric and highly exclusivist worldview of that Shi'i movement (Amanat 1989: 188-207) into a world religion with universal and global appeal (Smith 1987: 31-45 & 136-156). Some have characterized this trajectory as a move from heterodoxy to orthodoxy (MacEoin 1990: 329). While it may be reasonably argued and debated amongst scholars whether the Bahai Faith actually qualifies as a World Religion (Fazel 1994) rather than, say, a New Religious Movement or, 'NRM' (Internet discussion 1997), it is not debatable that there are now Bahai communities all over the world in regions and localities as culturally different as they could possibly be. So, whether as a *bona fide* World Religion or 'merely' an NRM (it may be more accurate in this instance to speak of New Religious Identities), the Bahai Faith is a global phenomenon in the process of constructing a global identity with the aid of universal teachings that apply to the human condition (Beyer 1998: Ch. 6; McMullen 2000: *passim*, esp. 109-125).

Of interest here is the stark contrast that its early, extremely parochial and exclusivist origins in the Shaykhi movement and the Babi faith provide to its current profile as promoter of the oneness of mankind, unity in diversity, tolerance, the abolition of prejudices and the honoring and valuing of the differences amongst the human family. A more compelling interest is precisely the manner in which this transformation occurred, what were its stages and how do we measure the process? (Smith 1987: 2-3).

Baha'u'llah, — who may be seen as a 19th century Persian theorist of modernism and globalization (Cole 1998: 14-15 & 32-47) - formulated his teachings in the mid to later 19th century, a crucial period in the rise of globalization. So, 'Bahai' has grown concomitantly with globalization, and there is reason to believe that there exists a close connection between the Bahai Faith and globalization from a historical as well as a sociological perspective. This connection can be elucidated by using material that comes from members of the Bahai community today (e.g., van den Hoonaard 1996, McMullen 2000). But it may be that the relationship between Bahai and globalization can also be studied and appreciated by working with religious texts. Here, another perspective may be illuminating, namely, the influence that the philosophical mysticism of Islam has had on the 'globalistic' doctrinal content of the Bahai Faith.

It is assumed that one of the chief factors facilitating the globalization of the Bahai Faith has been the relatively high degree to which people around the world have recognized themselves - their questions, problems, hopes, fears, sufferings and joys - as being addressed directly and in compelling ways by the Bahai teachings. This coupled with a dissatisfaction with their 'native' religions, has caused many to see in Bahai a fresh statement of what is most essential to religion as such. One of the best loved and most widely distributed and translated small compendia of Bahai teachings is a collection of Arabic and Persian apothegms known as *The Hidden Words of Baha'u'llah.* Quite apart from their literary beauty, a look at the circumstances of composition and the doctrinal contents of Baha'u'llah's *Hidden Words* will, it is hoped, offer us an insight into the transformation we are concerned with here. But before turning directly to this text, a bit of background is required.

Enchanted Ontology

One of the more prominent features of later islamicate spirituality and mysticism is the degree to which it is concerned with ontology, the nature of Being and/or Existence. Taking as a starting point traditional hylomorphism, Muslim sages and mystics would evolve a theory known as the Unity of Being, a kind of pantheism or panentheism which resulted in the divine unity of God being reflected and refracted, if not consubstantiated, in the resplendent multiplicity of creation. This basic apperception or spiritual axiom would be configured and articulated in a variety of ways. But the main idea, that creation was a mysterious expression of divine unity - that between and amongst all created things (including human beings) there was a living and sacred connection - would never be challenged. This basic and profoundly mystical or Sufi orientation represents the manner in which the world of Islamic mystical philosophy remains, to borrow a current term, enchanted. It is also the source and background of the teachings of Baha'u'llah (Cf. Rabbani 1973: 226).

Of course, the mystics and philosophers, being also rationalists, sought authoritative, logical explanations for this enchanted ontology, what they called 'unity in diversity' (*vahdat dar kasrat/wahdat fí 'l-kathrat*), a frequent Bahai watchword (Baha'i International Community 1997: 9; cf. Amuli 1989: 310) According to Islamic tradition, the Prophet himself was given the answer to this abstruse question by God himself. The answer has become one of the most important foci of meditation for Islamic spirituality and is preserved in the literary form known as *Hadith Qudsi*, extra-Quranic 'Sacred Saying of God', Who informed the Prophet:

I was a Hidden Treasure and yearned to be known
So, I created mankind (lit. 'creation').[4]

Thus the answer to the metaphysical question 'Why is there something

4 Arabic: *kuntu khanzan makhfiyan 'ahbabtu 'an 'urafu fakhalaqtu al-khalqa* (Amuli 1989: 102, 159, 162, 164, 601, 639, 662, 665, 682). Note: in this and the other transliterations to follow, 'ayn is represented by a simple apostrophe, nor is it possible to show velars and other similar sounds with the use of under dots.

rather than nothing - why are we here?' is linked to God's desire (lit. 'love') to be known. As a result, knowledge and love are indissolubly bound in a syzygical noetic and experiential dynamic that points to Being or Beyond.[5] It should also be mentioned that a standard hadith is composed of two equally important parts, its 'text' (*matn*, i.e. the part quoted above) and its credential or pedigree, known in Arabic by the word *isnad*, literally 'chain [of authority]', a long list of the names of teachers - 'spiritual ancestors' - who passed the knowledge from one to another. In Islamic learned discourse, one reveals (or conceals) one's deepest religious allegiances according to the composition of *isnad*s one uses for textual support. In the case of the kind of hadith represented here, namely *hadith qudsi*, there is an *isnad*, but these are frequently left out in published collections perhaps indicating that the important aspect is God's speaking directly to Muhammad, presumably through Gabriel, the angel of revelation, or in a dream (Robson 1971: 28-29). Thus, such statements are frequently unencumbered by the kind of sectarian sub-text afflicting other hadith. This type of hadith found favour amongst an earlier group of Islamic 'universalists', namely the Sufis. This particular hadith happens to be a favorite and may be seen as providing the foundational scriptural basis for the doctrine of the Unity of Being (*wahdat al-wujud*) associated with the greatest mystic of them all, Ibn Arabi (d.1240) and embraced by the many generations of his followers (and critics) who populate the world of Islam. Amongst such followers there are both Sunnis and Shi'is; in time, these followers would be criticized harshly for their 'pantheistic' beliefs. One of these opposing tendencies is referred to as Unity of Seeing (*wahdat al-shuhud*). Apparently at stake in the controversy is the transcendence of God.[6] The '*wujudi*s' were seen by some of their critics to violate this in their teachings. At times the debate would become quite intense. One example of such a heated controversy may be found

5 Note the Baha'i noonday prayer, 'I testify O my God, that Thou hast created me to know Thee and to worship Thee.' (*ashhadu yá iláhi bi-'annaka khalaqtaní li-'irfánika wa-'ibádatika*). Here 'worship' may be considered a near synonym for love. (Baha'u'llah 1982: 21; English translation by Shoghi Effendi in *Bahá'í Prayers* 1982: 4).

6 For a deeper reading of the terms of the debate, see Landolt 1971. Here, incidentally, it is pointed out that the term *wahdat al-wujud*, does not appear in any of Ibn Arabi's known writings.

in a work by the above-mentioned Shaykh Ahmad al-Ahsa'i himself. Here, Shaykh Ahmad takes to task, in virulent terms, one of the pillars of later Twelver Shi'ism, Mulla Muhsin Fayz Kashani (d. 1680) and virtually accuses him of unbelief (the most serious of crimes) for the doctrines he propagates. As a spokesman against the Unity of Being 'school', Shaykh Ahmad sought to elevate the Godhead beyond such terrestrial notions as 'being' and 'existence'.[7] This theological position was a key feature in the mysticism of the Bab and continues to be a part of basic Bahai belief (Lawson 2001). However, attachment and assent to the actual *hadith qudsi* was not restricted to so-called *wujudis*, for the *shuhudis* could easily find in it support for their opposing doctrine. Shaykh Ahmad himself comments on it and 'Abdu'l-Baha wrote an important, extensive commentary on it (Momen 1985). And, indeed, one of the Bahai obligatory prayers may be seen to reflect it almost verbatim (see above, note 5).

The *Hidden Words* were composed in Baghdad during the year 1857 (Taherzadeh 1980: 71-83). At that time, what we now call Iraq was governed by the Sunni Ottomans, although there was a very large, if not majoritarian, Shi'i element there. Not quite 25 years had passed since the violent communal riots in the Shi'i shrine city of Karbala (during which the second leader of the Shaykhi community, Sayyid Kazem Rashti, d.1844, had played an instrumental peacekeeping role). The Ottoman government eventually intervened. Thousands were killed and Iran was nearly forced to declare war against the Turkish authority (Cole and Momen 1986). The proposition put forth here is that 'Bahai universalism' would get its earliest impetus in works like the *Hidden Words* inasmuch as they were addressed to a previously unknown - i.e., in the case of Babism - heterogeneous (and potentially explosive) audience composed of Sunnis and Shi'is.[8] At the time of the revelation of the *Hidden Words*, Baha'u'llah's audience would have been divided into at least four major more or less mutually exclusive

7 There is no space here to discuss this in detail. The interested reader is referred to Lawson, 2005.

8 This is not to suggest that religious and confessional tensions did not exist in Iran. Note above the reference to the controversy surrounding *wahdat al-wujud*. This is only one example; see below the reference to Akhbaris and Usulis. And there are many other lines of fracture. It is true, however, that the Baghdad context was exponentially more 'multicultural'.

groups: the Sunnis, the Shi'is, the Wujudis and the Shuhudis. In turn, each of these groups, like the Shi'is, would be further divided into opposing factions, such as Akhbaris, the Usulis and the Shaykhis. This does not begin to take into account the stratified social variegation of 19th century Baghdad (Batatu 1978). Addressing such an audience, Baha'u'llah reduced the spiritual teachings of his religion to their most essential elements and thereby avoided placing unnecessary obstacles in the path of seekers of truth in the form of communalistic cues and insignia so common to much of Islamic religious literature of the time.[9] Indeed, he himself says so in the opening brief prologue to the *Hidden Words* (to which we will return).

What follows, is simply a demonstration of some of the ways in which the *Hidden Words* recasts traditional and contemporary Islamic teachings in a form innocent of any discernable communalistic provenance or allegiance, whether Shi'i, Sunni or organized Sufism. What emerges is a kind of catholic islamicate breviary, destined to appeal to a literary taste that had been cultivated in an islamicate milieu over the centuries and whose key reference points and inspirations, from the perspective of literary history, are the Qur'an, the Hadith and distinctive Sufi religio-literary presuppositions. But it is also a taste that is certainly not exclusively Muslim, let alone Shi'i. Obviously, it will not be possible to analyze the entire contents of this work. Only a few key examples have been chosen.

The Hidden Words

In the *Hidden Words*, no group or faction is preferred over another. Certainly, Baha'u'llah would have been known as a 'Babi'; but the vast majority of Baghdadis (along with a vast majority of Babis themselves) did not necessarily know what this meant as far as doctrinal detail might be concerned, apart from the general messianic mood of the movement. One indication of this mood is in the original title of the work at hand: *The Hidden Book of Fatima*. This explicitly points

9 As just one example from among literally thousands, the work mentioned above by the great scholar Mulla Muhsin Fayz Kashani, may be distinguished from Baha'u'llah's composition of the same name, in part, by the constant references to the authority of 'Ali and the Imams. See Lawson 2002.

to the fulfillment of the Shi'i Islamic eschaton which was to see, among other things, a number of books that had heretofore been hidden with the occulted and awaited Imam, and were expected to be published with his emergence from hiding (*zuhur*) (Lawson 2002, Amir-Moezzi 1992). The title was changed to its current status at some point, but we do not know exactly when (Taherzadeh 1980: 71). The change of title really underlines the overall achievement of the *Hidden Words.*

In the text at hand, brief quotations functioning almost like musical notes and phrases, are taken from the Qur'an, and Hadith, and heard throughout in an improvised form (Lawson 1997: 197-98; cf. also Lewis 1998). While the composition may be full of traditional Sufi terminology, there is no assumed allegiance to any of the many existing Sufi organizations. There can be no question of plagiarism here. The reader or hearer would instantly recognize these various cues and would deem it jarring if not insulting for the author to have disrupted the flow of the 'heavenly' discourse/performance to cite a 'source'. And, what is absent is just as important as what is there: nowhere in the book is there any mention of a proper name (not even Muhammad's) that could signal an allegiance to either Sunni, Shi'i or Sufi Islam. There are no *isnads*.[10] There are no legalistic doctrines or cultic pronouncements that could also be communalistically identified. What remains then is something that could easily appear to the mid-19th century Baghdadi, whether Sunni, Shi'i or Sufi, Christian or Jew as 'pure Religion'. A religion apparently unencumbered by the tragedy of history, appearing as a restatement of basic truths through the medium of a compelling religious literary art in both languages of the city: Arabic (71 'verses' and Persian (82 'verses').

Let us now turn to the text itself in order to illustrate this complex and seamless process. We will begin with the above-mentioned prologue to the *Hidden Words:*

He is the Glory of Glories
This is that which hath descended from the realm of glory, uttered by the tongue of power and might, and revealed unto the Prophets of old. We have

10 See the similar phenomenon in the writings of the Bab, specifically his first explicitly proclamatory book, the *Qayyum al-asma* (Lawson 1988b/1990).

taken the inner essence thereof and clothed it in the garment of brevity, as a token of grace unto the righteous, that they may stand faithful unto the Covenant of God, may fulfil in their lives His trust, and in the realm of spirit obtain the gem of Divine virtue.[11]

With this statement, which is completely free of Shi'i-specific references or cues, the message of oneness, unity, social harmony, social justice and peace may be seen as not merely emerging directly but literally escaping from the caldron of religious animosity exacerbated by the Safavid moment in history and continued to some degree by the 19th century socio-political reality of the Middle East. What is more, Baha'u'llah addresses his audience with a somewhat unusual but quite telling designation. In the English text, the word 'righteous' translates the Arabic word *ahbár*, a Quranic term meaning 'priests' but which likely means here in the first instance 'learned ones'. Such 'learned ones' are not identifiable as Muslims of *any* particular stripe. Indeed, the dictionary definition of the word is explicit: 'non-Muslim religious leaders'. If Baha'u'llah had wanted to designate Muslims specifically here, he could have chosen from a whole lexicon of alternate terms: 'learned Muslim religious scholars' (*ulema*), 'gnostic Muslims' (*urafa*), 'mystic philosophers' (*hukama*), not to mention the standard 'Muslims' (*muslimun*) or 'Believers [in Islam]' (*mu'minun*). Any of these other terms, including perhaps the most inclusive (but simultaneously exclusive) Quranic designation, 'people of the Book' (*ahl al-kitab*), used here would have lent an entirely different elan to this prologue.[12] With such a form of address, Baha'u'llah seeks to circumvent the exceedingly vexed problem of a 'correct' Islam as such, and attempts to create a new audience.[13] The mood is the time-

11 *Hidden Words*-English: 4-5; Arabic: *huwa 'l-bahá'u l-abhá hádhá má nuzzila min jabarúti 'l-'izzati bilisáni 'l-qudrati wa'l-quwwati 'alá al-nabyyín min qablu wa'inná 'akhadhná jawáhirahu wa'qmasnáhu qamísa 'l-ikhtisár fadlan 'alá 'l-ahbár liyúfú bi'ahdi 'lláhi wa yu'addú 'amánátihi fí 'anfusihim waliyakúnunna bijawhari 'l-tuqá fi 'ardi 'rrúh mina 'l-fá'izína* (*Hidden Words*-Arabic: 3)

12 Note 'Abdu'l-Baha's remark that long-standing Qur'anic notion of 'people of the Book' has been expunged from Bahá'í teachings (*Bahá'í World Faith* 1956: 246).

13 There are Shi'i hadiths identifying the Imams as *ahbár* (Isfahání 1954: 125). It is unlikely, but of course possible, that the word carries this meaning here.

less, perennial truth of prophecy. But no prophets are named, only God, as in 'covenant of God' (*'ahd allah*). *Allah* is the word for God in Arabic and is used by Arabs, whether Jewish, Christian, Muslim or members of any other group, to indicate the highest cosmic power. Although the word is habitually associated with Islam, there is nothing inherently Islamic about it (Gardet 1975). The *Hidden Words* have 'descended'. This translates the standard Arabic word for 'having been revealed', *nuzzila*. The descent, or revelation is from 'the realm of glory' (*jabarut al-'izza*) an appropriately abstract religio-philosophical technical term. 'Uttered by the tongue of power and might' (*bi-lisan al-qudra wa'l-quwwa*) namely, an anonymous angel of revelation (perhaps the tenth intellect of Muslim neo-platonists, or the faculty of the 'heart' of the Sufis, or any number of other 'islamicate' possibilities). Finally, it is the same message that was revealed unto the 'Prophets of old' (*al-nabiyyin min qablu*). Now, Islamic prophetology recognizes 124,000 prophets prior to Muhammad, so we are not even restricted here to thinking of Moses, Jesus and Muhammad. The sweep is magisterial. The audience could not be more vast.

The next two passages are equally 'anonymous' moral and ethical exhortations. The vocabulary is evocative of Sufism and its moral ethical and spiritual culture (Schimmel 1975: 228-241):

O Son of Spirit
My first counsel is this: Possess a pure kindly and radiant heart, that thine may be a sovereignty ancient, imperishable and everlasting.[14]

O Son of Spirit
The best beloved of all things in My sight is Justice; turn not away therefrom if thou desirest Me, and neglect it not that I may confide in thee. By its aid thou shalt see with thine own eyes and not through the eyes of others, and shalt know of thine own knowledge and not through the knowledge of thy neighbour. Ponder this in thy heart; how it behoveth thee to be. Verily justice

---

For a recent study of the relationship among scripture, reader/audience, and exegesis, based on recent insights of literary criticism, see McAuliffe 2000.

14 *Hidden Words*-English: 1:5. Arabic: *yá 'bna r-rúhi fí 'awwali 'l-qawli 'mlik qalbá jayyidan hasanan muníran litamlika mulká dá'iman báqiyan 'azalan qadíman* (*Hidden Words*-Arabic: 1: 4).

is My gift to thee and the sign of My loving-kindness. Set it then before thine eyes.[15]

Apart from the standard themes of ethical monotheism so beautifully expressed here, there are one or two clues to the mystic-philosophical tradition discussed above and out of which the Bahai Faith was born. But these are not explicitly identified with Shi'ism, or mysticism or philosophy. The reference to 'Justice' comes close to alluding to Shi'ism, and no doubt did so for a Shi'i audience. It is one of the prime religious preoccupations of that tradition, a tradition molded in marginalization and persecution. One of the hallmarks of the return of the Hidden Imam would be that he 'fill the earth with Justice as it is now filled with injustice.' (Amuli 1989: 102. Note that here the 15th century author connects this with the hadith 'I was a hidden treasure' discussed above.) But even here, Baha'u'llah makes a very deft adjustment. In Arabic, there are two closely related words to express the idea of justice. The one found most frequently in messianic texts of Shi'ism is *'adl*. The word used here is *insaf* and denotes fairness or equity more than justice. Thus, with a single word Baha'u'llah not only orients the discourse away from explicit and exclusive messianic Shi'ism, but also beyond the realm of Islamic law, whether Sunni or Shi'i. *Insaf* as equity implies a kind of Golden Rule in which it is necessary first to be equitable to oneself and then to others (Arkoun 1971: 1237). Certainly, the word can mean 'justice' but this concept, in an Islamic milieu is more accurately represented by the word *'adl*.

The topic of knowledge is also broached in this passage. The Arabic word *ma'rifa* refers to a specific kind of knowledge, namely spiritual or mystical, as distinct from the word *'ilm* which by comparison means religious, sacerdotal or legalistic knowledge. The exhortation is to 'know of thine own knowledge' (*ta'rif bima'rifatika*). This is quite a remarkable statement in the context of 19th century Shi'ism when the powerful office of the Marja' Taqlid – the so-called 'Shi'i pope' – was in the process of

15 Hidden Words-English 2: 6; Arabic: *yá 'bna 'r-rúh 'ahabbu al-ashyá 'indí al-insáfu. lá targhab 'anhu in takun ilaya rághibá wa lá taghfal minhu litakuna lí 'amínan wa 'anta tuwaffaqu bidhálika 'an tusháhida al-'ashyá bi'aynika lá bi'ayni 'l-'ibádi wata'rifahá bima'rifatika lá bima'rifati 'ahad fí 'l-bilád. fakkir fí dhálika kayfa yanbaghá 'an takúna. dhálika min 'atiyyatí 'alayka wa 'ináyatí laka fáj'alhu 'imáma 'aynayka.*(*Hidden Words*-Arabic: 2: 4).

being consolidated and institutionalized (Kazemi-Moussavi 1996). But, it is a direct continuation of the kind of anti-clericalism taught by Shaykh Ahmad (Cole 2001: 88ff) that would characterize much of the Bahai message and, no doubt, redound to its appeal. As such it may be seen as something of an improvisation on an equally iconic *hadith qudsi*:

He who has known himself has known his Lord.[16]

This is another one of a number of core 'verbal icons' whose contemplation enlivens and gives shape to Islamic mysticism. Note that the same words in 'improvised' form appear here: 'knowledge' (*ma'rifa*) a common derivation of the verb 'to know' (*'arafa*) and 'self' by means of the pronominal suffix *ka*. As mentioned above, it refers in this context to a mystical gnosis rather than a discursive knowledge (*'ilm*) (Landolt 2000: 31-32). It is a notion much loved and oft-repeated and commented upon because it ultimately points to the spiritual autonomy of the individual, rather than to a sacerdotal order of religious authorities. Baha'u'llah quotes it verbatim in numerous places (e.g. Bahá'u'lláh 1970: 102) to support his spiritual argument.

The next three brief passages (*Hidden Words*-English: 3-5, 7-8)[17] are analyzed here for the way they represent a restatement and artistic improvisation on the *hadith qudsi* discussed earlier:

I was a Hidden Treasure and yearned to be known.

So, I created mankind (lit. 'creation').[18]

The following verses from Baha'u'llah's *Hidden Words* read like a variation on this theme. For the convenience of the reader, the key correspondences are in bold:

16 See above note 5; Arabic: *man 'arafa nafsahu faqad 'arafa rabbahu* (Ámúlí 1989: 270, 307, 308, 315, 464, 675).

17 *al-Kalimát al-Maknúna / The Hidden Words of Bahá'u'lláh* was published as a trilingual Arabic, Persian and English edition. Here it is refered to as *Hidden Words*- Arabic, *Hidden Words*-Persian, or *Hidden Words*-English as appropriate. The English is the translation of Shoghi Effendi 'with the assistance of some English friends'(*Hidden Words*-English: 1).

18 *kuntu khanzan makhfiyan wa ahbabtu u'rifa fa khalaqtu al-khalqa.*

O Son of Man
Veiled in **My** immemorial **being** and in the ancient eternity of **My** essence, **I knew My love for thee**: **therefore I created thee**, have engraved on thee Mine image and revealed to thee My beauty.

O Son of Man
I loved thy creation, hence I created thee. Wherefore, do thou **love** Me, that I may name thy name and fill thy soul with the spirit of life.

O Son of Being
Love Me, that I may **love** thee. If thou **lovest Me** not, **My love** can in no wise reach thee. **Know this**, O servant.[19]

It should be borne in mind that the literary culture of the audience was a 'traditional' one; that is, as far as literary productions were concerned, a good commentary might stand for what our contemporary tastes would consider an original composition. Indeed, it could be argued that the literary tradition (and culture) with which we are concerned is in some ways, in its entirety, a commentary on the Qur'an (Lecomte 1965: 2). In the above three excerpts from the *Hidden Words* there is embedded in Baha'u'llah's text enough 'explicit allusions' to the original *hadith qudsi* to blur the line between original composition and commentary. The same literary method is at work in the Báb's *Qayyum al-asma* (Lawson 1988a&b/1990) and in numerous other works of Baha'u'llah (Lewis 1999/2000 & 1994).

The differences between Baha'u'llah's treatment of the themes of love, knowledge and creation here, and that found in other works by Shi'i religious thinkers and writers, are characteristic and quite illustrative of the point being made here. Ultimately, these differences are very revealing about the basic relationship between the Baha'i Faith and Islam. In Baha'u'llah's *Hidden Words* there is no partisan polemic on the scholastic problems of the primacy of being over quiddity or

19 (*Hidden Words*-English: 3-5: 7-8); Arabic: *yá 'bna 'l-'insáni* ***kuntu*** *fí qidam dhátí wa'zaliyyati kaynúnatí* ***'araftu hubbí fika khalaqtuka*** *wa'lqaytu 'alayka mithálí w'zhartu laka jamálí; yá 'bna 'l-'insáni* ***'ahbabtu khalqaka fakhalqtuka fa'ahbibní*** *kay 'adhkaraka wa fí rúhi 'l-hayát 'uthabbituka; yá 'bna 'l-wujúdi* ***'ahbibní li'uhibbaka*** *'in lam* ***tuhibbaní lan 'uhibbaka*** *'abadan* ***fa'rif*** *yá 'abdu* (*Hidden Words*-Arabic: 5: 5).

vice versa, there is no petitioning of the Qur'an or statements of the Imams to support the 'argument'.[20] Rather, Baha'u'llah's *Hidden Words* are presented by Him as being completely their own authority. And of course, Baha'u'llah's *Hidden Words* manage to state what might be considered the essence of the matter in a brief - and therefore, according to certain prevailing literary standards - more eloquent and masterful way than lengthier scholastic discussions - through the irresistible power of the aphorism. The *Hidden Words*, though not rhymed, lend themselves to memorization and as such can cross another barrier, that between the literate and the non-literate.

Standard Shi'i works seek to demonstrate the truth of a specific and controversial philosophical or religious position and of necessity must rely very heavily on discursive argumentation. As such they frequently entail the use of aphorism or brief quotation of some pithy saying from the Qur'an, the statements of the Imams, or poetry, in supporting his argument. While Baha'u'llah's work also reflects the words of the Qur'an and the Imams, it does so in a much less explicit way. There are no direct quotations, beyond the 'musical notes' mentioned above, from the Qur'an or any other source in the *Hidden Words*. However, much of this Book may be considered a reiteration and confirmation of the sacred teachings of Islam. A symbol of the inner workings of the transformation under discussion here may be found in the case of the Bab's disciple Mulla Ali Bastami whose conviction by a court composed of both Shi'i and Sunni judges represents an unusual example of agreement between the two communities (Momen 1982). It may be that the new movement's ability to attract such united negative attention was paralleled by an ability to attract a similar positive attention from the religiously diverse Baghdadi audience.

Thus, Baha'u'llah's composition is both timeless and 'wondrously new' (*badi'*). And in its newness it has managed to divest itself of communalistic baggage to become a neutral and transparent revelation in the social context of the mid-nineteenth century Ottoman 'province of Baghdad'. Of course such would eventually entail another allegiance. But that is a subject for another time. Today, this literary accomplishment, transposed onto a global scale with its attendant and exponentially more variegated audience, serves the idea of the greater unity

20 Note, however, Amuli's reading of this hadith as a clue to the understanding of the return of the hidden Imam (Amuli 1989: 102).

of the human race taught by the Bahai community.[21] It was an accomplishment in part inspired by and fashioned in response to the various dislocations attendant upon an earlier islamicate globalization.

References

Amanat, Abbas (1989). *Resurrection and Renewal: The Making of the Babi Movement in Iran, 1844-1850*, Ithaca, N.Y.: Cornell University Press.

Amir-Moezzi, Muhammad Ali (1992). 'FÁTEMA, i. In history and Shi'ite hagiography.', *Encyclopaedia Iranica*, online at: http://iranica.com/articlenavigation/index.html (August 19, 2003).

Amuli, Sayyid Haydar (1989, 1st ed. 1968). Jámi' al-asrár wa manba' al-anwár in H Corbin and O. Yahya (eds.) *La Philosophie Shi'ite*, Tehran: 1-617.

Arkoun, Mohammed (1971). 'INSÁF', in *Encyclopaedia of Islam, new edition*, Leiden: E.J. Brill, vol. III: 1236-1237.

Baha'i International Community (1997). *The Bahais*, http://www.bahai.com/thebahais/pg9.htm (August 19, 2003).

Baha'i Prayers (1982). *Baha'i Prayers: A Section of prayers Revealed by Bahá'u'lláh, the Báb and 'Abdu'l-Bahá*, Wilmette, Ill.: Baha'i Publishing Trust.

Baha'i World Faith (1956) *Baha'i World Faith: Selected Writings of Bahá'u'lláh and 'Abdu'l-Bahá*, Wilmette, Ill.: Baha'i Publishing Trust, 1971 (reprint of 1956 ed.).

Baha'u'llah, Mirza Husayn Ali-yi Mazandarani (1995). *al-Kalimát al-Maknúna / The Hidden Words of Bahá'u'lláh*, Rio de Janeiro: Editora Bahai - Brasil.

Baha'u'llah, Mirza Husayn Ali-yi Mazandarani (1970). *The Kitáb-i-Íqán: The Book of Certitude Revealed by Bahá'u'lláh, translated by Shoghi Effendi*, Wilmette, Ill.: Baha'i Publishing Trust.

Baha'u'llah, Mirza Husayn Ali-yi Mazandarani (1982). *Risálah-yi Tashbíh wa Tahlíl, compiled by 'Abd al-Hamíd Ishráq Khávarí*, New Delhi: Baha'i Publishing Trust.

21 Naturally, the *Hidden Words* had to be translated out of the original Arabic and Persian for this to happen. In the process of translation, much — but not all — of the 'confessional' Islam of the original has disappeared from view (Malouf 1997 and Lewis 1998).

Batatu, Hanna (1978). *The Old Social Classes and the Revolutionary Movements of Iraq: A Study of Iraq's old Landed and Commercial Classes and of its Communists, Bathists, and Free Officers*, Princeton: Princeton University Press.

Beyer, Peter (1998). *The Religious System of Global Society*. A Sociological Look at Contemporary Religion and Religions. *Numen* 45, vol. 1: 1-29

Beyer, Peter (1994). *Religion and Globalization*, London: Sage.

Cole, Juan R. I. (1998). *Modernity and the Millenium: The Genesis of the Baha'i Faith in the Nineteenth-Century Middle East*, New York: Columbia University Press.

Cole, Juan R. I. (2001). 'Shaykh Ahmad al-Ahsa'i on the Sources of Religious Authority', in L. Walbridge (ed.) *The Most learned of the Shi'a: The Institution of the Marja' Taqlid*, New York: Oxford University Press: 82-93.

Cole, Juan R. I. and Moojan Momen (1986). 'Mafia, Mob and Shiism in Iraq: The Rebellion of Ottoman Karbala', *Past and Present*: *A Journal of Historical Studies*, vol. 112: 112-43.

Durri, 'Abd al-'Azíz (1975). 'BAGHDÁD', in *Encyclopaedia of Islam, new edition*, Leiden: E.J. Brill, vol. II: 921-36.

Fazel, Seena (1994). 'Is the Baha'i Faith a World Religion', *Journal of Baha'i Studies* 6. An earlier draft is online: http://bahai-library.org/articles/jbs.6-1.fazel.html (August 19, 2003).

Gardet, Louis (1975). 'ALLÁH', in *Encyclopaedia of Islam, new edition*, Leiden: E.J. Brill, vol. I: 418-429.

Hodgson, Marshal G. S. (1974). *The Venture of Islam: Conscience and History in a World Civilization*, 3 vols., Chicago: University of Chicago Press.

Internet Discussion (1997). Juan Cole, Seena Fazel, Stephen Friberg, Denis MacEoin, Robert Stockman, Will C. Van den Hoonaard, and Ismael Velasco discuss the problems inherent in classifying the Bahai Faith as an New Religious Movement, online: http://bahai-library.org/essays/nrm.html (August 19, 2003).

Isfahaní, Abu al-Hasan al- (1954). *Tafsír mir'át al-anwár wa mishkát al-asrár*. Tehran: Matba' al-Aftab.

Kazemi-Moussavi, Ahmad (1996). *Religious Authority in Shi'ite Islam: From the Office of Mufti to the Institution of Marja'*, Kuala Lumpur: International Institute of Islamic Thought and Civilization.

Landolt, Hermann A. (1971). 'Simnání on Wahdat al-Wujûd', in M. Mohaghegh and H. Landolt (eds.) *Collected Papers on Islamic Philosophy and Mysticism,* Wisdom of Persia Series, vol. iv. Tehran: Institute of Islamic Studies: 91-112.

Landolt, Hermann A. (2000). 'Stages of God-cognition and the Praise of Folly according to Najm-i Rází (d. 1256)', *Sufi* 47: 31-43.

Lawson, Todd (1988b/1990). 'Interpretation as Revelation: The Qur'án Commentary of the Báb, (1819-1850) in A. Rippin (ed.) *Approaches to the History of the Interpretation of the Qur'án,* Oxford: Clarendon Press: 223-53; reprinted in *Journal of Baha'i Studies* 2:17-44.

Lawson, Todd (1988a). 'The Terms 'Remembrance' (dhikr) and 'Gate' (báb) in the Báb's Commentray on the Sura of Joseph', in M. Momen (ed.) *Studies in Honor of the Late Hasan M. Balyuzi,* Studies in the Bábí & Bahá'í Religions 5, Los Angeles: Kalimat Press: 1-63.

Lawson, Todd (1997). 'The Dangers of Reading: In libration, Communion and Transference in the Qur'án Commentary of the Báb', in M. Momen (ed.) *Scripture and Revelation.* Oxford, U.K.: George Ronald: 171-215, online: http://bahai-library.org/articles/reading.lawson.html

Lawson, Todd (2001). 'Coincidentia Oppositorum in the Qayyum al-Asma: the terms 'Point' (nuqta), 'Pole' (qutb), 'Center' (markaz) and the Khutbat al-tatanjiya', *Occasional Papers in Shaykhi, Babi and Baha'i Studies,* 5:10,000 words; online at: http://www.h-net.org/~bahai/bhpapers/vol5/tatanj/tatanj.htm (August 19, 2003).

Lawson, Todd (2002). 'The Hidden Words of Fayd Kashani', *Iran, Questions et Connaissances: Actes du Ive Congrès Européen des Études Iraniennes Organisé par la Societas Iranologica Europaea, Paris, 6-10 Septembre 1999, Vol. II: Périodes Médiévale et Moderne,* Studia Iranica. Cahier 26. Texts réunis par Maria Szuppe, Paris: Association pour l'Avancement des Études Iraniennes, Leuven: Peeters: 427-47.

Lawson, Todd (2005). 'Orthodoxy and Heterodoxy in Twelver Shi'ism: Ahmad al-Ahsá'i on Fayd Káshání (the *Risálat al- 'Ilmiyya*)', in R. Gleave (ed.) *Religion and Society in Qajar Iran,* London: Routledge Curzon: 127-154.

Lecomte, Gerard (1965). Ibn Qutayba (mort en 276/889): *L'Homme, Son Oeuvre, Ses Idées*. Damascus: Institute Français de Damas.

Lewis, Franklin (1994). 'Scripture as Literature: Sifting throught the Layers of the Text', *Baha'i Studies Review* 4; online at: http://bahai-library.org/articles/lewis.scripture.html (August 19, 2003)

Lewis, Franklin (1998). 'Translating the Hidden Words: An Extended Review of Diana Malouf's Unveiling the Hidden Words', *Baha'i Studies Review* 8; online at: http://bahai-library.org/articles/lewis.maloufhw.html (August 19, 2003)

Lewis, Franklin (1999/2000). 'Poetry as Revelation, Bahá'u'lláh's Mathnavíy-i Mubárak: Introduction and Provisional Verse Translation', *Baha'i Studies Review* 9: 101-157.

MacEoin, Denis (1990). 'Orthodoxy and Heterodoxy in Nineteenth-Century Shi'ism', *Journal of the American Oriental Society* 110: 323-29.

Malouf, Diana L. (1997). *Unveiling the Hidden Words: The Norms Used by Shoghi Effendi in his Translation of the Hidden Words.* Oxford: George Ronald.

McAuliffe, Jane Dammen (2000). 'Text and Textuality: Q. 3:7 as a Point of Intersection', in I. J. Boullata (ed.) *Literary Structures of Religious Meanin in the Qur'án,* Richmond, Surrey (U.K.): Curzon, 2000,

McMullen, Michael (2000). *The Baha'i: The Religious Construction of a Global Identity.* New Brunswick: Rutgers University Press.

Momen, Moojan (1982). 'The Trial of Mullá 'Alí Bastamí: A Combine Sunní/Shí'i fatwá against the Báb', *Iran* 20: 113-43.

Momen, Moojan (1985). ''Abdu'l-Baha's Commentary on the Islamic Tradition: 'I was a Hidden Treasure...' (a provisional translation)', *Bulletin of Baha'i Studies,* 3: 4-64; online, slightly modified, at: http://www.northill.demon.co.uk/relstud/kkm.htm (August 19, 2003).

Rabbani, Shoghi Effendi (1970, 1st ed. 1944). *God Passes By,* 'Introduction' by George Townshend. Wilmette, Ill.: Baha'i Publishing Trust.

Rabbani, Shoghi Effendi (1973). *Guidance for Today and Tomorrow.* London: Baha'i Publishing Trust.

Robson, James (1971). 'Hadith Kudsi' in *Encyclopaedia of Islam.* Leiden & London: E.J. Brill, vol. III: 28-29.

Schimmel, Annemarie (1975). *Mystical Dimensions of Islam.* Chapel Hill: University of North Carolina Press.

Smith, Peter (1987). *The Babi and Baha'i Religions: From Messianic Shi'ism to a World Religion.* Cambridge: Cambridge University Press.

Taherzadeh, Adib (1980). *The Revelation of Bahá'u'lláh: Baghdád 1853-63.* Oxford: George Ronald.

van den Hoonaard, Will C. (1996). *The Origins of the Baha'i Community of Canada.* Waterloo, Ontario: Wilfrid Laurier University Press.

CHAPTER 3

Globalization and Religion in the Thought of 'Abdu'l-Baha

Juan R. I. Cole

'Abdu'l-Baha (1844-1921) was among the Middle Eastern thinkers of the late nineteenth and early twentieth centuries who thought most deeply about the meaning of globalization, and his vast travels made him among the more cosmopolitan religious leaders of the day in that region. Although the leader of a distinctive, small religion with its origins in 19th-century Iranian Shi'ism, much of 'Abdu'l-Baha's intellectual production concerned issues in what we would now call globalization. Sociologist Roland Robertson has proposed a definition of globalization as the 'crystallization of the entire world as a single place'. He sees this process as occurring along four basic dimensions: societies, individuals, the international system, and the emergent category of the human. In each case, he posits that local actors construct new identities and social forms in interaction with the global. Thus, societalization is the 'globe-wide making of modern national society'. Individuation is the construction of the individual as a person. Internationalization has to do with the expansion of the state system, originating in Europe, to the rest of the world. By humanization, he says, he means the 'thematization of man- and womankind'. Here he seems to refer to a conception of the self as self-in-the-globe as opposed to earlier, tribal or national identities.

Robertson is careful to say that the construction of each of these four areas of human experience, while it takes place in dialogue with the rest of the world, is attended by significant controversy. That is, the making of the world into a single socio-cultural space does not only imply convergence among the various civilizations, though there is a great deal of that, but also conflict over strongly held values that do not change so easily. Globalization is not for Robertson a form of homogenization, as it is for other sociologists such as Anthony Giddens. In particular, Robertson instances the issue of the relationship of religion to politics, about which peoples in the various regions of the world feel quite differently. This is a matter on which there has been, he suggests, less global convergence and more local resistance. On the other hand, the very politicization of religion has global dimensions. Robertson also wishes to differentiate his project from the old 'modernization' or 'Westernization' master narrative, where other societies are only playing catch-up to a triumphant West. He wishes to de-centre globalization, to view it as lacking a predetermined script or a 'core' that defines all other societies as 'periphery'. He admits that there have been instances of 'de-globalization'. He also wishes to avoid the economic determinism that has characterized the thought of some other thinkers concerned with globalization. He locates the economic in only one of the four dimensions he addresses, i.e. societalization. His focus on religion signals the degree to which he feels that his four dimensions of globalization are closely intertwined with the question of values (Robertson 1987, 1989, 1992, 1995).

Oddly enough, given his engagement with religion, Robertson largely consigns it to a role in resisting the standardization of culture attendant upon globalization. Peter Beyer has pointed out this gap in Robertson's program (Beyer 1994). Some of the religious status groups have a generally positive outlook on globalization, whereas others reject it or contend with it. The post-Vatican II Roman Catholic church largely falls in the former category, whereas Khomeinism in Iran falls in the latter (*ibid.* 1994). Likewise, the international system is a system not only of states but also of global NGOs, including the World Council of Churches and Amnesty International (localistic bodies like the Druze of Lebanon would not fit in this category).

Beyer has argued that religious movements concerned with globalization have tended to be either liberal or conservative. Liberal religious groups often attempt to accommodate the social changes provoked by globalization as far as possible in the framework of their traditions, concentrating on charitable work and social justice. Fundamentalists resist globalization. By arguing in modernist style for these binary opposites, Beyer in my view elides the degree to which all religious movements contain both liberal and conservative emphases. The difference among them is a matter of the proportion of the mix. Conservative Roman Catholicism is as hostile to globalization as the largely Protestant New Religious Right, whereas liberal Shi'ite Islam, as with 'Abdu'l-Karim Surush, embraces globalization with open arms (Jahanbaksh 2001). With these clarifications, mostly inspired by Beyer, I believe Robertson's framework will serve well to explore the thought of 'Abdu'l-Baha on religion and globalization. My thesis is that 'Abdu'l-Baha addressed each of the four areas identified as important to globalization by Robertson, that with regard to each he put forth a vision of civil society and of religion, which he saw as distinct but overlapping, and that his vision was predominantly liberal but contained some conservative elements, as well.

'Abdu'l-Baha elaborated on the religious and social reformist thought of his father, Baha'u'llah (1817-1892). Baha'u'llah had engaged in a very Robertsonian dialogue with nineteenth-century global realities and thought, which I have described elsewhere (Cole 1998a). Born in Tehran, brought up and educated by tutors in Baghdad, 'Abdu'l-Baha went on to spend nearly 5 years in Edirne, in Turkish-speaking Eastern Europe, 1863-1868, where through the press or personal contacts he encountered the Ottoman political culture of the modernizing Tanzimat reforms and the dissident Young Ottoman group. He was exiled along with his father and dozens of other Baha'is to Ottoman Syria, where he continued his dialogue with the Young Ottomans in Akka. In the 1880s, he travelled to Beirut to attend the study sessions of famed Islamic modernist, Muhammad 'Abduh. After the Young Turk revolution in 1908 freed him from restrictions on his movements, he travelled to Egypt, Europe and the United States in the period 1910-1914. His last four years of life were spent under British colonial rule in the Mandate of Palestine. This confluence of cultures - Qajar Iran; Ottoman Iraq; Turkish-speaking Eastern Europe; the Syria of the Arab Renascence with its lively press; British Egypt; and Europe and the United States just before World War I was among the more remarkable to be encountered by any single Middle Eastern thinker in that era (Cole 1998a; Faydi 1971; Balyuzi 1971). It was nearly matched only by a few of his contemporaries from the region, such as veteran Iranian diplomat Mirza Husayn Khan Mushiru'd-Dawlih, the Pan-Islamic reformer Sayyid Jamal al-Din 'al-Afghani', also an Iranian, and Mirza Malkum Khan, the Iranian diplomatic and social thinker (Keddie 1972; Bayat 1982; Bakhash 1978).

Let me attempt to outline what I see as 'Abdu'l-Baha's conception of the four dimensions of globalization described by Robertson. In a talk at a church in Jersey City, New Jersey on 19 May 1912, 'Abdu'l-Baha spoke in terms similar to the ones used by Robertson, of levels of global unity. In Aristotelian style, he distinguished between the actual and potential brotherhood of humankind. Actual brotherhood derives from their being servants of a single God, members of a single family, and sentient ('intelligent') beings. That is, the actual brotherhood derives from the conceptual categories they fill. Their potential brotherhood, in contrast, comes about because they all inhabit 'this earthly globe' under a single sky. They are all 'elements of one human society subject to the necessity of agreement and cooperation'. ('Abdu'l-Baha 1982: 129). That is, their brotherhood in the material realm, what Robertson calls, societalization, was in 1912 still largely a potential development rather than an actual one. Labor historian E. P. Thompson made a famous distinction with regard to social class, of the class in itself and the class for itself. That is, workers on the shop floor can be categorized as a proletariat with interests that often diverge from that of their employers. Thompson pointed out, however, that the workers themselves do not begin by knowing they form part of a class. It is only through conflict and organizing that they come to do so. They begin as a class in themselves, but can end as a class for themselves (Thompson 1963; Sewell 1986). In the same way, it seems to me that 'Abdu'l-Baha is here making a distinction between humanity in itself and humanity for itself. Humankind was already actually global in 1912, but 'Abdu'l-Baha foresaw a slow and gradual realization of this globality in the succeeding decades and centuries. The global would have to be forged, as an identity for itself, in real-world struggle, compromise and realization.

Making the World One Place

'Abdu'l-Baha sees the emergence of the world as a single place as a quintessentially modern development, made possible by profound technological and social changes. In the past, he says, 'the unity of all mankind could not have been achieved'. Not only were the continents divided from one another, but even on the same continent 'association and interchange of thought were well-nigh impossible'. What changed was that the 'means of coming into contact' (*vasa'il-i ittisal*, presumably both communication and transportation) had multiplied ('Abdu'l-Baha 1978: 31, 'Abdu'l-Baha 1979: 29) He points out that it was, in the early twentieth century, easy for everyone 'to travel to every land, to associate and exchange views with its peoples, and to become familiar, through publications, with the conditions, religious beliefs and the thoughts of all nations [*milal*]' (My trans. of 'Abdu'l-Baha 1979: 29).

'Abdu'l-Baha had seen vast changes in the communications and transportation technology in his own lifetime. There were few newspapers in the Middle East when he was a youth, and those tended to be government-owned. By the 1870s in the Arab provinces of the Ottoman Empire, and after 1896 in Iran, private newspapers had proliferated. The first telegraph wires were laid in Egypt and Iran on a large scale in the 1860s and 1870s, but by the early twentieth century the Middle East was a key transit point for cables and wires carrying hundreds of thousands of telegrams annually between Europe and Asia. The dispatches of the international wire services, such as Reuters, were translated into Middle Eastern languages, and began to affect the style of local journalism. Middle Eastern elites, including many among the Baha'i community of Akka, began learning European languages. The first rail link between Alexandria and Cairo was finished in 1858, and in the early twentieth century the Ottomans connected their Arab provinces to Istanbul by rail. Passenger steamships proliferated. In the early twentieth century, they gradually began being powered by petroleum rather than coal (Cole 2002a; Fawaz and Bayly 2002). 'Abdu'l-Baha had thus seen with his own eyes the infrastructure of globalization being built up.

Simply being in much closer contact was not the only change he saw among the world's empires and nations. He continued, 'In like manner all the members of the human family, whether peoples or governments, cities or villages, have become increasingly interdependent. For none is self-sufficiency any longer possible, inasmuch as political ties unite all peoples and nations, and the bonds of trade and industry, of agriculture and education, are being strengthened every day'. ('Abdu'l-Baha 1978: 31-32, 'Abdu'l-Baha 1979: 30). This growing interdependence, and the inability of local communities to dispense with (*istighna'*) the rest of the world is what makes global unity now possible, he said. Not only can local units now articulate their identities, cultures, economies and politics with regard to the rest of the world, but they *must* do so. The way in which technological change actively deprives the local of independence seems to me an insight derived from 'Abdu'l-Baha's experiences in Western Asia and Eastern Europe. Palestine in the late nineteenth and early twentieth centuries would have been a particularly striking vantage point for the observation of globalizing movements. Zionist settler agriculture, the impact of the world market on Palestinian crops like oranges, and the Great Famine during World War I (as well as that war itself) all pointed to the globalization of markets and politics.

'Abdu'l-Baha not only recognized the reality of increasing global interdependence, but saw its achievement as a positive ethical ideal ('Abdu'l-Baha 1982: 287). Indeed, that the world is perceived in any other way is a mystery that needs to be explained. 'Racial prejudice or separation into nations such as French, German, American and so on is unnatural.' Why then does it happen? It 'proceeds from human motive and ignorance'. Elsewhere, he wrote,

> Then the establishment of various nations and the consequent shedding of blood and destruction of the edifice of humanity result from human ignorance and selfish motives. As to the patriotic prejudice, this is also due to absolute ignorance, for the surface of the earth is one native land. Every one can live in any spot on the terrestrial globe. Therefore all the world is man's birthplace. These boundaries and outlets have been devised by man. ('Abdu'l-Baha 1978: 299-300)

'Abdu'l-Baha was here putting forward what we would now call an instrumentalist theory of ethnicity and nationalism. It is for the advantage of politicians or other community leaders that they separate out some members of the human community as distinctive and promote a sense of division among them. The other possibility he admits is ignorance, that is, that some may not see that the world is a single place because they are poorly informed. He rejects what anthropologists now call the primordialist thesis that significant ethnic difference is natural or inherited. (For instrumentalism and primordialism see Bentley 1987. This debate has been superseded by the approach of Benedict Anderson to 'imagined' nations (Anderson 1991)).

Not only racial but also religious prejudices may interfere with the ability to perceive that 'this earth is one home and native land'. Religious prejudice derives from the overwhelming of science and reason by 'human misunderstanding' and 'ignorance' ('Abdu'l-Baha 1982: 287). Otherwise, he said, religion is mere 'superstition', and 'it would be better to do without it'. He believed, however, that it is possible to hold religion in such a way that it does not overwhelm reason, does not devolve into superstition, and does not produce religious hatred and fanaticism.

If we are to analyze 'Abdu'l-Baha's thought carefully, we must attend to a potential problem in his conception of religion as an element in making the world a single place. He himself argued that only a rationalized form of religion, which abandoned superstition and accepted the authority of science with regard to the physical world, could play a positive role in this effort. Yet at the same time that he advocated this religious liberalism and universalism, he himself was the leader of a particularistic religious tradition with its origins in popular Iranian Shi'ism. As a result, despite his own insistence on the rejection as 'superstition' of religious dogmas that contradicted science he himself had, at least before 1912, resisted scientific findings. He dismissed Darwinian conceptions of evolution, saying that the 'missing link' would never be found and that the similarities between humans and the primates were accidental, i.e. were like the resemblance of porpoises to sharks, based on function rather than heredity (Brown 2001). He also upheld the Virgin Birth of Jesus and ridiculed Western scientists who questioned it. 'Abdu'l-Baha therefore engages in both the possible religious responses to globalization. One, Beyer says, is 'to reorient a religious tradition towards the global whole and away from the particular culture with which that tradition identified itself in the past' (Beyer 1994: 10). In many ways 'Abdu'l-Baha's more liberal principles were aimed at universalizing and globalizing a Baha'i tradition still somewhat rooted in esoteric Iranian thought. His rejection of Darwin, and his acceptance of a 'magic garden' of correspondences between spiritual character and external events would be coded as conservative, fundamentalist motifs according to Beyer's schema. As

Beyer points out, the 'fundamentalist' approach is devoted to a 'particularistic revitalization of a tradition in the face of relativization' (Beyer 1994:10; cf. 115-17). 'Abdu'l-Baha wanted to affirm both science and religion, both the universal and the particular, leading him into paradox when they in fact disagreed. As Beyer implies, both strategies involve a grappling with issues in pluralization on a global scale.

Society

As noted, Robertson defines 'societalization' as the 'globe-wide making of modern national society'. He does not mean by 'national society' nation-states, but rather societies within national perimeters that nevertheless now have a global context. As noted, 'societies' is a vague term, and I would like to underline that in my understanding they would encompass all status and ethnic groups, including religious ones. 'Abdu'l-Baha was very much concerned with the need to transform the Qajar Empire into a modern Iranian national society. He admitted that in the late nineteenth century Europe and the Americas were renowned for the 'law and order, government and commerce, art and industry, science, philosophy and education' ('Abdu'l-Baha 1970: 9-10) to which he believed Iran must now aspire. He denied that Iranians were inherently inferior to others, pointing to their frequent past ability to excel other peoples and their country's vast natural resources ('Abdu'l-Baha 1970: 9-10). In addition, he argued, it needed practical steps such as the implementation of the rule of law, parliamentary democracy, amelioration of the condition of the poor, the adoption of Western technology, industrialization, a separation of religion and state, and religious toleration. He rejected the arguments of anti-liberal Shi'ite conservatives that such 'Western' reforms were inappropriate to Iran, asking ironically in what way it would be contrary to the interests of Iranians to benefit from good and responsive government or from technological progress ('Abdu'l-Baha 1970: 115). He also urged that Iran become deeply involved in international diplomacy and cultural and economic exchange. In a talk given decades later in America, he pointed out, 'In this life and being cooperation and association are essential. Through association and meeting we find happiness and development, individual and collective'. He argued that in an interchange between Iran and the U.S. both would have much to gain. ('Abdu'l-Baha 1982: 35-36). The formation of Iran as a modern, democratic national society within the matrix of an emerging global system formed only one of 'Abdu'l-Baha's aspirations in this sphere.

'Abdu'l-Baha argued that the Baha'i faith allowed individual freedom of conscience and that the global network of 'houses of justice' was not to punish believers for mere unorthodox belief, only for sinful behaviour. But in his era 'shunning', a highly conservative and anti-globalist practice, was introduced. Most of those declared shunned were Baha'is who felt uncomfortable with the magnitude of the claims made for 'Abdu'l-Baha by his partisans or who ultimately supported his brother Mirza Muhammad 'Ali in an attempt at rebellion and schism. The episode of the schism left a deep and enduring mark on the young religion, pushing many in it toward an often cult-like insistence on dogmatic correctness or 'firmness in the covenant' and a de facto attempt to demarcate doctrinal lines, the crossing of which would incur ostracization. This tendency was famously displayed in the U.S. during World War I, when a group of 'orthodox' Baha'is challenged other believers in Chicago for having set up a reading room with a Metaphysical (we would say 'New Age') orientation, with books on reincarnation (Baha'i Committee of Investigation 1917-1918; Smith 1987).

Whereas 'Abdu'l-Baha's thoughts on the reform of Iran as a national society were lucid, consistent, and clearly placed him on the side of liberalism and modernism, his writings on Baha'i administration demonstrate a bewildering mixture of liberalism and conservatism. His emphasis on tolerance, good social works, peace activism, theological inclusivism, welcoming of minorities, and support for world government are liberal in Beyer's terms. Yet, his emphasis on obedience to himself and the local assemblies, and his resort to systematic shunning, fall on the conservative side and in some ways seem innovations. Although his support for women's rights was unusual for a Middle Eastern religious leader of his generation, and although it, too, must be seen as a sign of liberalism, strong conservative and patriarchal values co-existed with it in his thought. He resisted women serving on houses of justice or spiritual assemblies until his 1912 visit to Chicago, when he changed his mind and allowed it. It is unclear whether he also changed his mind about women's service on the international house of justice, and subsequent Baha'i tradition has insisted that it must be all-male (Cole 1998a: 182-185).

The Individual

The construction of the individual as a person in the context of globalism is a central concern of 'Abdu'l-Baha. From the Judeo-Christian and Islamic traditions, as well as from Muslim Neoplatonism, he inherited a conception of the individual as theomorphic, as in the image of God. 'By man is meant the perfect individual, who is like unto a mirror in which the divine perfections are manifested and reflected' ('Abdu'l-Baha 1978: 61-62). He advocates that all be educated for ethical and intellectual progress, but admits the stubborn idiosyncrasy of the individual. 'That is to say, education cannot alter the inner essence of a man, but it does exert tremendous influence, and with this power it can bring forth from the individual whatever perfections and capacities are deposited within him'. ('Abdu'l-Baha 1978: 131-132).

Selflessness and working together with others is key to the development of the individual ('Abdu'l-Baha 1982: 337-338). Souls, he insists, must be educated so that the divine attributes or bestowals become apparent in them. This theomorphic education 'is possible through the power of the oneness of humanity'. That is, human beings' ability to manifest the divine attributes present within them is amplified by global unity and harmony: 'The more love is expressed among mankind and the stronger the power of unity, the greater will be this reflection and revelation, for the greatest bestowal of God is love'. All the prophets, he says, have endeavoured to cause love to be manifest in the hearts, because 'Until love takes possession of the heart, no other divine bounty [or emanation, *fayd*] can be revealed in it'. ('Abdu'l-Baha 1982: 14-15; 'Abdu'l-Baha 1984: 2,22). Although the conviction that human beings should strive to manifest the divine attributes is common in Muslim Sufism and wisdom-philosophy, I believe 'Abdu'l-Baha is being completely original and innovatory in making social harmony and human unity – that is to say peaceful globalization – a prerequisite for it. He gives us here a globalist anthropology, in which the unity of humankind is the matrix and sine qua non for mature individuation.

Ethical education must be accompanied by a firm grounding in reasoning. He insisted that, in accordance with Baha'u'llah's teachings, 'No individual should be denied or deprived of intellectual training, although each should receive according to capacity'. By the use of reason, 'He studies the human body politic, understands social problems and weaves the web and texture of civilization'. He sees 'science' (or perhaps we should say 'rational learning') as 'the very foundation of all individual and national development' ('Abdu'l-Baha 1982: 50). He endorsed for Iran the technology and knowledge characterizing modern civilization while insisting also on preservation of the particularities of Iranian culture.

He also upheld the right of the individual conscience. He said, 'Each human creature has individual endowment, power and responsibility in the creative plan of God. Therefore, depend upon your own reason and judgment and adhere to the outcome of your own investigation; otherwise, you will be utterly submerged in the sea of ignorance and deprived of all the bounties of God' ('Abdu'l-Baha 1982: 293). Muslim culture granted individuals more autonomy than is usually recognized, but it seems clear that 'Abdu'l-Baha's stance here was radically liberal. The exercise of the individual's own 'reason and judgment' is made the prerequisite for avoiding ignorance and receiving the divine bestowals. Addressing a Congregational church in Brooklyn in 1912, he said, 'Just as in the world of politics there is need for free thought, likewise in the world of religion there should be the right of unrestricted individual belief. Consider what a vast difference exists between modern democracy and the old forms of despotism. Under an autocratic government the opinions of men are not free, and development is stifled, whereas in democracy, because thought and speech are not restricted, the greatest progress is witnessed. It is likewise true in the world of religion. When freedom of conscience, liberty of thought and right of speech prevail—that is to say, when every man according to his own idealization may give expression to his beliefs—development and growth are inevitable' ('Abdu'l-Baha 1982: 197). This passage makes it clear that 'Abdu'l-Baha's vision of a social harmony and the education of the individual for cooperation and altruism must be seen as presupposing a democratic society, with individual rights and freedom of thought and expression and autonomy of conscience.

The International System

Building on the principles enunciated by Baha'u'llah, 'Abdu'l-Baha spoke a great deal about the sort of international system he wished to see in an era of globalization. He began discoursing on these matters in his 1875 *The Secret of Divine Civilization*, where he argued that Europe's material civilization of the nineteenth century had become unbalanced and had come to pose a danger to the world because it had not been accompanied by similar advances in spiritual civilization ('Abdu'l-Baha 1970: 59-64; 'Abdu'l-Baha 1911: 69-75).

In addressing the chaotic new world of aggressive, technologically advanced nation-states that ensued especially after the Italian and German unifications, he drew on his father's principles to argue for the need for a global civilizational framework to contain them:

> True civilization will unfurl its banner in the midmost heart of the world whenever a certain number of its distinguished and high-minded sovereigns – the shining exemplars of devotion and determination – shall, for the good and happiness of all mankind, arise, with firm resolve and clear vision, to establish the Cause of Universal Peace (*mas'alih-i sulh-i 'umumi*). They must make the Cause of Peace the object of general consultation, and seek by every means in their power to establish a Union [or association: *anjuman*] of the nations of the world. They must conclude a binding treaty and establish a covenant, the provisions of which shall be sound, inviolable and definite. ('Abdu'l-Baha 1970: 64)

In this passage 'Abdu'l-Baha actually went beyond the sort of measures advocated by his father, Baha'u'llah, who had called for similar peace consultations, international conventions attended by heads of state, and pacts of collective security.

The way in which 'Abdu'l-Baha continued to articulate these Baha'i ideals with global developments is demonstrated by his endorsement, after World War I, of President Woodrow Wilson's Fourteen Points (enunciated January 8, 1918) ('Abdu'l-Baha 1978: 109). Wilson had argued for open covenants of peace among nations (rather than secret treaties), reduction of armaments, the establishment of a general association of nations aimed at guaranteeing the territorial integrity of all, self-determination for the small nations that formerly lived under empires like Austria-Hungary and the Ottomans, and an adjudication of colonial territories that took into account the desires and welfare of the colonized (Walworth 1986). In addition to the international *'anjuman'* or association of his 1875 treatise, in his later works 'Abdu'l-Baha began calling for a world court (*mahkamih-'i kubra*). He added, 'questions both national and international must be referred thereto, and all must carry out the decrees of this Tribunal. Should any government or people disobey, let the whole world arise against that government or people' ('Abdu'l-Baha 1978: 249, 306-07, 'Abdu'l-Baha 1979: 241, 296-97). Despite his endorsement of the use of force by the international community against rogue states, 'Abdu'l-Baha did not wish to see the global institutions become oppressive. He put forward the federal system of the U.S. as a model, both for each country internally, and for the global association of nations as a whole. ('Abdu'l-Baha 1982: 167).

Along with international covenants and a permanent organization representing the nations of the world, 'Abdu'l-Baha foresaw the need for other infrastructural and cultural initiatives if modern, highly destructive warfare were not to reduce humankind to barbarity. In accordance with the teaching of Baha'u'llah, 'Abdu'l-Baha advocated in response an international language aimed at reducing misunderstanding and fostering a sense of unity among the peoples of the world ('Abdu'l-Baha 1982: 60-61, 182). Likewise, a global school system with ethics classes was required ('Abdu'l-Baha 1982: 182). Further, the global social economy had to be adjusted to ensure a basic standard of living for the poor. ('Abdu'l-Baha 1982: 181-82). Global movements of civil society, such as that of the more pacifist suffragists, he felt, also had an important part to play in promoting peace ('Abdu'l-Baha 1982: 167).

Nevertheless, 'Abdu'l-Baha remained deeply suspicious of politics and diplomacy as means to peace. He dismissed the 1907 Hague Peace conference this way: 'The wine sellers call a meeting so that they may discuss the evils of wine and remove from the world the drinking of wine; yet their own vocation is wine selling. Nations who are constantly thinking wither of worldly conquest, the expansion of their own dominion or waging war upon their contemporaries, send ministers and representatives to the congress of The Hague to discuss the problem of universal peace and legislative registrations for the prevention of war!' ('Abdu'l-Baha 1909-1916: 595-96). He therefore codes politics as inevitably the realm of unyielding, rapacious self-interest. Politics does not instill values in the populace, and is wholly instrumental and self-serving.

This impotence of politics and diplomacy to ensure peace demonstrates the necessity of yet another sphere of life, which specializes not in instrumental rationality but in ethics and values, i.e. religion: 'Universal peace is an impossibility through human and material agencies; it must be through spiritual power'. ('Abdu'l-Baha 1982: 108-09). Because true religion's specialty is just values and the production of harmonious feelings among adherents, it is the most suitable and most promising advocate of peace. He admitted that religion itself had occasionally been made a pretext for war, but insisted that this was only a misuse of an essentially good phenomenon, or the outcome of the people substituting conventionality and tradition (*taqalid*) for spirituality ('Abdu'l-Baha 1969: 135-36). For this reason, he was equally dismissive of an International Congress of Religions organized in Japan in 1906. He wrote, 'This congress had under discussion the politics of the religions. In truth, it is a political affair and not the attraction of the heart, faith, advancement toward God nor enkindlement with the fire of the love of God. This congress will not produce a lasting effect, for it is essentially politico-religious. What is effective and conducive to the penetration of the Word of God.' ('Abdu'l-Baha 1909-1916: 495-96). For him, feelings of spiritual harmony and high-minded, selfless ethics are the only basis for peace. Religion that contributes to such affect and such attitudes is laying the foundation for international peace. Religion that simply acts like another instrumental bureaucracy is not.

'Abdu'l-Baha uses various similes for the 'becoming' state of humanity. It is ill and needs to be cured. It is an infant and needs to mature. Its maturity is synonymous with globalization ('Abdu'l-Baha 1982: 37-38). The new humanity is not only potentially more spiritual, virtuous and advanced than ever before, but its intellect is more developed, as well. This rationalism is another sign of the liberal orientation of 'Abdu'l-Baha's religious vision. The globe's ultimate destiny, should it grasp it, is the 'Most Great Peace', a fresh stage of history in which war is rare and quickly ended by collective security arrangements. ('Abdu'l-Baha 1982: 38-39).

Conclusion

'Abdu'l-Baha was an original theorist of globalization who addressed issues at some length in all four of the areas which Robertson identified as characteristic of the phenomenon. He clearly perceived that the world had become a single place even in the early twentieth century, and foresaw the intensification of globalization. Analytically, he distinguished between actual and potential globalization. He saw as the reason for this transformation the extensive innovations in communications and transportation technology achieved in the nineteenth and early twentieth centuries. These changes not only enabled connectivity among the world's peoples but actually forced them into interdependence whether they liked it or not. In 'Abdu'l-Baha's era, globalization was often linked to Western (and, increasingly, Japanese) imperialism, but he rejected the idea that the two were synonymous. He fulsomely praised Wilson's 14 points, with their stress on self-determination and insistence on allowing the voice of the colonized to be heard regarding their future. He advocated a third way, between virulent nationalism and capitulation to the Western colonialists, which involved an emphasis on the ethical autonomy of spiritual individuals and their religious communities as a civil-society foundation for truly global values.

'Abdu'l-Baha grouped technological links and political interdependence under the rubric of 'physical' increased global unity. He was equally concerned with the necessity for a set of global values, a global subjectivity, which he felt was the work of religion. This he called 'spiritual' global unity. Global values would reject virulent nationalism, ethnic and racial hatred and separation, gender discrimination, and religious exclusivism, and would work for world peace. He further distinguished between spiritual religion and conventional or traditional religion. The former promulgated these universalist values, in part because it had accommodated itself to modern science and rationalism. The latter, in contrast, had become mired in superstition and had surrendered to particularistic prejudices. Although he saw the Baha'i faith as the most consistent exemplar of this spiritual religion, he frequently praised his Unitarian, Theosophical, and liberal Protestant hosts for participating in this globalizing, spiritual sort of religion.

Unlike conservatives in the Middle East, 'Abdu'l-Baha embraced much of liberal modernity, arguing for parliamentary democracy, the rule of law, human rights, mass education, modern science and technology, a separation of religion and state, and free commerce. He critiqued laissez-faire liberalism on several fronts, however. He insisted that the state and the wealthy must intervene to ensure a basic standard of living for the poor, and although he opposed Communism, he believed that the Left as a whole had an important future in the new world. 'Abdu'l-Baha's anthropology was similarly innovative. He spoke of a global community fostering peace and love as the matrix for the emergence of a new sort of spiritual individual. He argued for an ethical and rational education of all, with at least basic exposure to science, philosophy, civics and history. He upheld the rule of law and liberal juridical rights for the individual, as well as freedom of conscience and expression, both civil and religious.

He asserted the need for global political institutions, including an association of the nations and a world court. He urged the application of the federalist ideals of the U.S. both in individual states and on a global level, to avoid despotism. He nevertheless supported the development of a global school curriculum to be taught in a single world language. He was convinced that global women's organizations would play a central role in fostering peace among nations. He maintained that the prime role in promoting global values of tolerance and good will would fall to spiritual, non-instrumental and non-fundamentalist religion.

I find this positioning of religious liberalism as the pivot of what might be called subjective globalization an important proposal. I have at some points in this chapter suggested what I see as flaws or contradictions in 'Abdu'l-Baha's project, however, and these must be kept in mind. He himself appeared to premise its success on the accommodation of religion to science, rationalism and tolerance for diverse views. It is not clear, however, that organized religion as a phenomenon is capable of this accommodation. It was not always achieved by 'Abdu'l-Baha himself, as his many dismissive remarks in Persian about Western scientists and their findings demonstrate. Nor is it probably characteristic of the mainstream of the subsequent Baha'i community. Most religious belief is based on the authority of charismatic prophets, religious officials, and other institutions, on scripture and transcendence, on miracles and infallibility, and on the acknowledgment of prescribed dogmas and social conventions. The simple fact is that dogmatic ways of knowing are largely in conflict with scientific ways of knowing, and simply urging the 'unity of science and religion' cannot change that. It might be possible for liberal Baha'is to develop a process theology wherein 'Abdu'l-Baha's championing of the primacy of scientific discoveries about the material world would trump his rejection of ideas such as evolution, but only a few baby steps have been taken in this direction and they are certainly not being taken by the religion's leadership. It seems to me possible that the contradictions between the liberal and conservative elements in 'Abdu'l-Baha's thought and in the community as a whole have impeded, if not defeated, his hopes for a new sort of global spirituality.

Second, the idea that the religions foster, and might cooperate in fostering toleration was no doubt seen as preposterous by many of 'Abdu'l-Baha's secular critics in 1912, and it unfortunately has not gained in plausibility since then. The excesses of conventional religion, which 'Abdu'l-Baha knew very well and denounced in his own time, have not been attenuated, as September 11th and its aftermath demonstrated. Spiritual religion in the sense of congregations devoted to racial, gender and religious toleration and global unity was rare in 'Abdu'l-Baha's time and still today does not seem a widespread phenomenon. The Baha'i faith itself is much smaller than its officials claim, and a strong fundamentalist movement within it anyway raises questions about how tolerant it really is. The practice of shunning, which 'Abdu'l-Baha introduced in order to fight schism and such crimes as embezzlement, was expanded to other, instrumental, uses and has become a key source of intolerance and authoritarianism in the subsequent community (Cole 1998d; Cole 2002c). Many fundamentalist Baha'is have argued to me during the past thirty years for a future Baha'i theocracy in which non-Baha'is will be deprived of the vote. That such a vision seems bizarre in the light of 'Abdu'l-Baha's statements on the separation of religion and state and on equal civil rights for all do not appear to impede its increasing ascendancy in the community. The contradictions between 'Abdu'l-Baha's liberal commitments to freedom of conscience and expression and his conservative fears of social disorder, dissent and personal freedom have never been resolved in the community and if anything the latter has begun to predominate in the religion's power centres. Robertson might argue that even Baha'i fundamentalism can contribute to globalization by setting up a world-wide field of contention with more liberal values.

But Beyer is surely correct in seeing such a fundamentalism as conservative and localistic rather than truly global.

'Abdu'l-Baha's thinking about religion and globalization remains powerful and suggestive, nevertheless. Beyer made the point that the differentiation of life-spheres that has accompanied modernity has often disadvantaged religion. Law, politics, education, economics and other distinct spheres of life have their specialists, whose professionalization is made possible in part by the delimitation of the sector of society to which they attend. Religion, Beyer argues, began by encompassing all these spheres but has successively been pushed out of most of them. It has moreover had difficulty defining a new sphere that individuals would acknowledge as necessary to them. I would argue that 'Abdu'l-Baha attempted to address this matter by positioning religion as the source of global ethics and spirituality. He withdrew it from the sphere of politics and from interference in such realms as science precisely so that it could concentrate on non-instrumental values. Rather than being a third wheel, as it is often considered in rationalist, liberal nation-states, religion then becomes the essential bulwark against the pathologies of globalization. It ideally guards against the development of ethnic and nationalist hatreds, which are created and fostered by ambitious political entrepreneurs, rather as medical science fights disease. It provides a framework for individual and communal self-realization and development of the personality that is superior, he thought, to that provided by mere consumerism and materialism. Spirituality is, in his view, the sine qua non for global development and harmony. It is not clear, however, that an organized religion can manage to avoid falling into the instrumental rationality of the bureaucracy, and into sacrificing altruism and tolerance for narrow institutional and personal gain – thus coming to foster exclusion and intolerance. That is, the depoliticization of organized religion urged by 'Abdu'l-Baha may be a sociological impossibility. Still, spirituality and an ethics of toleration of the sort he advocated have played, and seem certain to continue to play, a key role in globalization.

References

'Abdu'l-Baha (1909-1916). *Tablets of 'Abdu'l-Baha 'Abbas,* 3 vols. Chicago: Baha'i Publication Committee.

'Abdu'l-Baha (1911). *Ar-Risalah al-Madaniyyah as-Sadirah fi sanat 1292.* Cairo: Matba'ah Kurdistan al- 'Ilmiyyah.

'Abdu'l-Baha (1969). *Paris Talks.* London: Baha'i Publishing Trust.

'Abdu'l-Baha (1970). *The Secret of Divine Civilization* (2nd edn.), trans. Marzieh Gail, Wilmette Ill.: Baha'i Publishing Trust.

'Abdu'l-Baha (1978). *Selections from the Writings of 'Abdu'l-Baha,* trans. Marzieh Gail, Haifa: Baha'i World Center.

'Abdu'l-Baha (1979). *Muntakhabati az Makatib-i Hadrat-i 'Abdu'l-Baha,* vol 1. Wilmette Ill. and Haifa: Baha'i World Centre and Baha'i Publishing Trust.

'Abdu'l-Baha (1982). *Promulgation of Universal Peace.* Wilmette, Ill.: Baha'i Publishing Trust.

'Abdu'l-Baha (1984). *Majmu'ih-'i Khitabat-i Hadrat-i 'Abdu'l-Baha fi Urubba wa Amrika,* 3 vols. in 1. Hofheim-Langenhain: Baha'i-Verlag.

Anderson, Benedict (1991). *Imagined Communities* (2nd rev. edn.). London: Verso.

Baha'i Committee of Investigation (1917-1918). *Report.* Http://www.2.h-net.msu.edu/~bahai/docs/vol5/RCI/RCI.html.

Bakhash, Shaul (1978). *Iran: Monarchy, Bureaucracy and Reform under the Qajars 1858-1896.* London: Ithaca Press.

Balyuzi, Hasan M. (1971). *'Abdu'l-Baha: Centre of the Covenant.* Oxford: George Ronald.

Bayat, Mangol (1982) *Mysticism and Dissent: Socioreligious Thought in Qajar Iran,* Syracuse: Syracuse University Press.

Bentley, G. Carter (1987). Ethnicity and Practice (in the Thin Line of Culture), in *Comparative Studies in Society and History,* vol. 29, No. 1. (Jan.): 24-55.

Beyer, Peter (1994). *Religion and Globalization.* London: Sage.

Brown, Keven (2001). *Evolution and Baha'i Belief: 'Abdu'l-Baha's Response to Nineteenth-Century Darwinism.* Los Angeles: Kalimat Press.

Cole, Juan R.I. (1998a). *Modernity and the Millennium: The Genesis of the Baha'i Faith in the 19th Century Middle East.* New York: Columbia University Press.

Cole, Juan R.I. (1998b). 'Abdu'l-Baha's 'Treatise on Leadership': Text, Translation, Commentary, in *Translations in Shaykhi, Babi and Baha'i Texts,* vol. 2, No. 2 (May), at: http://www2.h-net.msu.edu/~bahai/trans/vol2/absiyasi.htm.

Cole, Juan R.I. (1998c). Two Letters of 'Abdu'l-Baha to Mirza Haydar

'Ali Usku'i of Tabriz, in *Translations of Shaykhi, Babi and Baha'i Texts,* vol. 2, No. 5 (August), at http://www2.h-net.msu.edu/~bahai/trans/vol2/abevol.htm

Cole, Juan R.I. (1998d). The Baha'i Faith in America as Panopticon, 1963-1997, *The Journal for the Scientific Study of Religion,* vol. 37, No. 2 (June): 234-48.

Cole, Juan R.I. (2002a). 'Printing and Urban Islam in the Mediterannean World, 1890-1920,' in Leila Tarazi Fawaz and C.A. Bayly (eds), *Modernity and Culture from the Mediterranean to the Indian Ocean.* New York: Columbia University Press: 344-64.

Cole, Juan R. I. (2002c). 'Fundamentalism in the Contemporary U.S. Baha'i Community', in *Religious Studies Review,* vol. 43, no. 3 (March): 195-217 at: http://www-personal.umich.edu/~jrcole/bahai/2002/fundbhfn.htm

Fawaz, Leila Tarazi and C.A. Bayly (eds.) (2002). *Modernity and Culture from the Mediterranean to the Indian Ocean.* New York: Columbia University Press.

Faydi, Muhammad 'Ali (1971). *Hayat-i Hadrat-i 'Abdu'l-Baha,* Tehran: MMMA.

Jahanbakhsh, Forough (2001). *Islam, democracy and religious modernism in Iran (1953-2000): from Bazargan to Soroush.* Leiden and Boston: Brill.

Keddie, Nikki R (1972). *Sayyid Jamalu'd-Din 'al-Afghani': A Political Biography.* Berkeley and Los Angeles: University of California Press.

Robertson, Roland (1987). Globalization and Societal Modernization: A Note on Japan and Japanese Religion, *Sociological Analysis,* No. 47 (Mar.): 35-42.

Robertson, Roland (1989). Globalization, Politics, and Religion, in James A. Beckford and Thomas Luckmann (eds.), *The Changing Face of Religion.* London: Sage: 10-23.

Robertson, Roland (1992). *Globalization: social theory and global culture.* London and Newbury Park, Calif.: Sage.

Robertson, Roland (1995) Globalization: Time-Space and Homogeneity-Heterogeneity, in Featherstone, Mike, Scott Lash & Roland Robertson (eds.) *Global Modernities,* London: Sage.

Sewell, William (1986). *How classes are made: critical reflections on E.P. Thompson's theory of working-class formation.* Ann Arbor, Mich.: Centre for Research on Social Organization.

Smith, Peter (1987). *The Babi and Baha'i Religions: From Messianic Shi'ism to a World Religion.* Cambridge: Cambridge University Press.

Thompson, E.P. (1963). *The Making of the English Working Class.* New York: Pantheon Books.

Walworth, Arthur (1986). *Woodrow Wilson and His Peacemakers.* New York: Norton.

CHAPTER 4

The Globalization of the Baha'i Community: 1892-1921

Moojan Momen

The concept of globalization is one that has become very fashionable in social and political discourse in recent decades.[1] Mainly, it has come to be associated with its negative aspects related to the unbridled freedom of international companies to move capital around the world with minimal regard of the social consequences of their decision and the prospects of the increasing domination of the world by the one remaining super-power and the organs that it controls such as the International Monetary Fund and the World Bank. The positive aspects of globalization, such as the generation of financial and logistical support for areas of the world stricken by calamities or the mobilization of mass support for issues such as environmental causes, are not so frequently mentioned. What can scarcely be doubted is that both aspects are developing rapidly and with few signs of being reined in by government or any other forces of social control.

The term 'globalization', however, appears to point to something more than such facts as the international nature of business and trade, the increasing knowledge that we have of other human cultures, and the ease with which people can now travel to and communicate with all parts of the world. All of these phenomena can perhaps be encompassed by such words as 'international' and 'inter-cultural'.

1 This paper benefited from the valuable discussion of it on the Bridges e-mail list. Among those contributing to the discussion were: Dr Franklin Lewis, Ismael Velasco, Dr Robert Stockman, Dr Susan Maneck, and Dr Mark Foster.

The replacement of the use of the term 'international' with the word 'global' denotes the dawning of a consciousness that we are proceeding beyond a phase of relationships between peoples and states and on to a phase which can be summed up in the Marshall McLuhan terms 'global village' (1960) and 'all-at-once-ness' (McLuhan and Fiore 1967: 63) and Roland Robertson's concept of the 'world as a single place' (1992: esp. 182-84).

The phenomenon of globalization encompasses two seemingly-opposed trends. The first is the impulse of modernity towards unity around a common heritage of science and technology, along with the negative aspect of that: the trend towards uniformity under the cultural dominance of the West. The second is the post-modern impulse that emphasizes the diversity of human expression in its various cultural and textual manifestations (Cousins 1999: 210). Robertson discusses this same tension between these two trends using the words 'universalism and particularism' (Robertson 1992: 25, 141, 177-81).

In the field of religion, the fact of increased migration has led to an unprecedented mixing of different religions in the same locality. Religions that once claimed the sole authority to make metaphysical and ethical pronouncements are finding competitors in an increasingly crowded market-place. This reality resulting from the process of globalization of the world has led to the strengthening of two opposing tendencies. On the one hand, it has led to a conservative, xenophobic, ultra-nationalist response which is often linked to a religious fundamentalism; on the other hand, it has led some to reflect on the fact that goodness and piety can be found in all religions and has thus strengthened the liberal trend in religions (Momen 1999: 476-89).

The Baha'i Faith arose in Iran which was, and to some extent still is, deeply conservative, isolationist and xenophobic. This aspect of Iranian society has not always been to Iran's disadvantage. It should be remembered, for example, that, while the Arab Muslim conquests of the seventh century resulted in the obliteration of the languages and much of the ancient cultures of Mesopotamia, Syria and Egypt, they did not have the same effect in Iran, where the language and culture survived among the people and re-emerged centuries later. Not only did the Iranians cut themselves off from the rest of the Islamic Middle East by virtue of the re-emergence of the Iranian language and culture, but, they also isolated themselves from the rest of the Islamic world by their adoption of Shi'i form of Islam in the sixteenth century – a form of Islam that not only inculcated a deep hatred of the Sunni majority of Muslims, but also emphasises the idea that non-Muslims are impure and hence polluting. From all of this it can be seen that to bring to such a people a concept of globalization was indeed a formidable challenge.

The Baha'i Faith has throughout its 150-year history had globalization as a central theme. Despite this long connection, there has been little mention of the Baha'i Faith in reviews of religion and globalization.[2] The project of globalizing the Baha'i community began with Baha'u'llah (1817-92), who made it clear in his writings that he was directing his teachings to the whole world - all nations, all religions, all social strata. In his writings, he addressed Jews, Christians, Zoroastrians, as well as the kings and religious leaders of both Christian Europe and Muslim Asia. He also encouraged a widening of the boundaries of the Baha'i community by encouraging the conversion of Jews, Zoroastrians, Christians and Sunni Muslims. Although he did not announce specific expansion plans to the Baha'is in the way that later Baha'i leaders did, he appears to have initiated projects to attract to the Baha'i Faith specific groups of individuals. Thus for example, he directed certain individuals to take on the life-style of wandering Sufi dervishes and to see if they could attract Sunni Sufis in Egypt and the Ottoman Empire;[3] he directed Jamal Effendi to a specific project aimed at spreading the Baha'i Faith to India (Momen 1999-2000); and he encouraged a number of individuals to take the Baha'i Faith into Central Asia.[4]

There is some evidence that, as a result of Baha'u'llah's initiatives, the Iranian Baha'is had a somewhat broader perspective than most

2 See for example Beyer (1994) and Dawson (1998). Only Warburg (1999) has made the connection between Bahá'í and globalization.

3 Jamal Effendi appears to have been one person sent on such a mission in 1871-5, see Samandar 1973: 213 and Momen 1999-2000: 50; see also account of Haji Eliyahu, Mázandarání [n.d.], 6: 674; another was Sayyid Háshim of Kashan who spent seven years, on Baha'u'llah's instructions, wandering through Iraq, Syria and the Arabian peninsula dressed as a darvish (Vahid-Tehrani's, [n.d]: 1-2; see also Momen 2002).

4 Among these were Nabil-i Akbar and Mirza Abu'l-Fadl Gulpaygani (Mázandarání [n.d.], 6: 107, 371-73, Momen 1991).

Iranians.[5] It may, nevertheless, be stated that, when 'Abdu'l-Baha assumed the leadership of the Baha'i Faith in 1892, the Baha'i community was still overwhelmingly very narrowly Iranian in its ethnicity and Shi'i in its outlook. The drive to expand the religious base of new converts had resulted in a number of Jews from Kashan and Hamadan, some Zoroastrians in Yazd, a scattering of Sunni Muslims in the Ottoman domains and a very few Syrian Christians. All of these groups numbered probably no more than 2000 individuals (in the region of 1-2% of the total world Baha'i population).[6] The drive to expand the Baha'i faith among Sunnis in Central Asia had only resulted in the settlement of a number of Iranian Baha'is there. The project to recruit Sufis in the Sunni Ottoman domains had failed. The efforts of Jamal Effendi in India had only succeeded in recruiting Iranians or Persianate Indians (Indians who spoke Persian and were thoroughly immersed in Persian culture). The world Baha'i community consisted mainly of Iranians from a Shi'i background in Iran, with some scattered groups in India, Central Asia, the Caucasus, the Ottoman domains and Egypt, consisting mainly of ex-patriot Iranians.

The period of Baha'i history with which we are concerned in this paper, 1892-1921, covers the ministry of 'Abdu'l-Baha (1844-1921), the son and successor of Baha'u'llah. 'Abdu'l-Baha's globalization of the Baha'i community can usefully be considered in terms of the categories delineated by Jan Aart Scholte. Of the five modalities of globalization that he mentions, four are useful in considering the result of 'Abdu'l-Baha's work: normative, psychological, economic and institutional (the exception being the ecological modality, Scholte 1996: 46). Of course in using Scholte's modalities, we are not drawing comparisons between the present day which Scholte is describing and the time of 'Abdu'l-

5 See for example the words spoken to Browne by Iranian Baha'is in *A Year Among the Persians*, (see especially 1926: 235-36). There is also the evidence of a petition sent by the Bahá'ís of Baghdad to the U.S. Consul in Beirut in 1867 (Stauffer 1997).

6 All such numbers can of course only be estimates but the numbers of converts from minorities did not exceed 100 in each of a handful of Iran cities and similarly most Baha'is in cities outside Iran were ex-patriot Iranians, there were very few native converts (less than 20) in those few cities in Egypt, Syria, Anatolia, Iraq and India where there were Baha'i communities (see descriptions of these areas in Mazandarani [n.d.]).

Baha a century ago. What 'Abdu'l-Baha was striving to achieve would, in terms of today's situation, be considered as a merely embryonic movement towards globalization.

Normative Globalization

Normative globalization involves prescribing and establishing that the globalized world, 'the global village', is indeed the norm, the reality of the human world in the present age. The foundation of 'Abdu'l-Baha's many initiatives to promote globalization was his deeply-rooted belief in the unity and equality of the human race. Baha'u'llah had laid down the necessary groundwork for the globalization of the Baha'i community by removing it from the Islamic framework – a framework that divided the world into believers and unbelievers and reinforced that division by imposing upon unbelievers the condition of ritual impurity. Baha'u'llah had emphasized in his writings the equality of all believers, of whatever level of education or social rank. He had spoken of all as being 'created from the same dust' so that 'no one should exalt himself over the other' and hence that all should 'be even as one soul, to walk with the same feet, eat with the same mouth and dwell in the same land, that from your inmost being, by your deeds and actions, the signs of oneness... may be made manifest' (1990, Arabic, no. 68).

Baha'u'llah had also developed this theme into a statement of the need for each human being to have a global perspective:

> Let your vision be world-embracing, rather than confined to your own self... It is incumbent upon every man, in this Day, to hold fast unto whatsoever will promote the interests, and exalt the station, of all nations and just governments... Of old it hath been revealed: 'Love of one's country is an element of the Faith of God.' The Tongue of Grandeur hath, however, in the day of His manifestation proclaimed: 'It is not his to boast who loveth his country, but it is his who loveth the world.' (1983: 94-95, no. 43).

'Abdu'l-Baha, however, was to make this globalization a central feature of his rhetoric, thus bringing it to the forefront of the attention of the Baha'is. His talks in Europe and North America and well as his letters are full of statements asserting the normative nature of globalization ('we are all inhabiting one globe of earth. In reality we are one family and each one of us is a member of this family', 1945: 42) and unravelling the implications of this for the Baha'is. He asserted, for example, that globalization was the inevitable result of technological advances in travel and communication of the present age (1982: 101).

'Abdu'l-Baha insisted, however, that there were certain social prerequisites if globalization was not to be a negative and destructive moment in humanity's history. During his Western journeys, for example, he explored the implications of the unity and equality of all human beings in terms of raising the educational and social status of women and giving them a greater role in social affairs; in terms of the need to eliminate all forms of racial prejudice and inequality on the basis of race; and in terms of the need to avoid the discord, conflict and assumptions of superiority that go with political, national, religious and ethnic differences (1967: 160-63,148-50).

'Abdu'l-Baha also foresaw and responded to the other trend that we noted above, the post-modern concern with diversity. His vision of unity was not one of uniformity around a single expression of human culture, but rather a unity that encompassed and indeed gloried in diversity. He expressed this in numerous, often metaphorical, ways; for example:

> Consider the flowers of a garden: though differing in kind, colour, form and shape, yet, inasmuch as they are refreshed by the waters of one spring, revived by the breath of one wind, invigorated by the rays of one sun, this diversity increaseth their charm, and addeth unto their beauty. Thus when that unifying force, the penetrating influence of the Word of God, taketh effect, the difference of customs, manners, habits, ideas, opinions and dispositions embellisheth the world of humanity. This diversity, this difference is like the naturally created dissimilarity and variety of the limbs and organs of the human body, for each one contributeth to the beauty, efficiency and perfection of the whole. (1978: 291, cf. 1967: 51-53)

Psychological Globalization

Scholte describes psychological globalization as 'the growing consciousness of the world as a single place, an awareness reinforced by everyday experiences of diet, music and dress (1996: 46).' Of course in the time of 'Abdu'l-Baha, and especially in Iran, global experiences were by no means an everyday experience. We will look later in this paper at the manner in which 'Abdu'l-Baha spread the Baha'i Faith throughout the world. In parallel with this, however, 'Abdu'l-Baha promoted links between the various Baha'i communities in order to move the global nature of the Baha'i Faith from rhetoric to reality.

The links between the Baha'i communities and 'Abdu'l-Baha were natural and strong. But 'Abdu'l-Baha also encouraged links between Baha'i communities and between individual Baha'is in different parts of the world. Among the activities that emerged were the writing of letters between the various Baha'i communities and the spreading of news globally. Individual Baha'is wrote to Baha'is in other parts of the world and Baha'i communities wrote to each other and shared their newsletters. The Baha'i community became perhaps the first religious community to have a truly international news service accessible to the whole community, especially with the development of the *Star of the West* magazine, which, although published in the United States in English, had a Persian language section and had many subscribers throughout the Middle East, India, and Central Asia. Communities of interest were set up globally through letters. Iranian Baha'i women wrote to American Baha'i women, while European Baha'i Esperantists wrote to their fellow-believers in the Middle East and China. This international communication was facilitated by a growing number of Iranians who learned English and acted as translators both in Iran and after migrating to Europe and North America. While most educated Iranians of this period learned French as their second language, Baha'i students chose English, largely as a result of 'Abdu'l-Baha's guidance.[7]

As well as this interchange of correspondence, 'Abdu'l-Baha encouraged and instructed the Baha'is to travel and meet Baha'is in other parts of the world. 'Teachers must continually travel to all parts of the continent, nay, rather, to all parts of the world' (1993: 53-54). Of course 'Abdu'l-Baha's own journeys to Europe and North America were of great importance in bringing the Baha'is of the West firmly

7 There are numerous examples in the writings of 'Abdu'l-Baha of occasions when he specifically advises young Iranian Baha'is to learn English, and in some places he states that this is so that they can assist the Baha'i community by communicating with and translating for the American Baha'is (see Iranian National Baha'i Archives photocopied series of Baha'i scriptures, Afnan Library, Tonbridge, vol. 16: 181; vol. 52: 242; vol. 85: 190, 526; vol. 87: 237).

into the world-wide Baha'i community. But 'Abdu'l-Baha also directed the Baha'is to travel from their home countries and to meet Baha'is in other parts of the world. He made it clear that he saw this travelling and the subsequent cultural interchange as an important component of the globalization process:

> Let not conventionality cause you to seem cold and unsympathetic when you meet strange people from other countries. Do not look at them as though you suspected them of being evil-doers, thieves and boors. You think it necessary to be very careful, not to expose yourselves to the risk of making acquaintance with such, possibly, undesirable people.
>
> I ask you not to think only of yourselves. Be kind to the strangers, whether come they from Turkey, Japan, Persia, Russia, China or any other country in the world... Help to make them feel at home; find out where they are staying, ask if you may render them any service; try to make their lives a little happier... In this way, even if, sometimes, what you at first suspected should be true, still go out of your way to be kind to them – this kindness will help them to become better... After all, why should any foreign people be treated as strangers? ...
>
> What profit is there in agreeing that universal friendship is good, and talking of the solidarity of the human race as a grand ideal? Unless these thoughts are translated into the world of action, they are useless. (1967: 15-16)

'Abdu'l-Baha encouraged American Baha'is to travel to the Middle East and India and Middle Eastern Baha'is to travel to Europe and North America. Several Americans went on extensive journeys around the world visiting many Baha'i communities. Other Baha'is went on less extensive but more intensive journeys: American, British and French Baha'is to India, Egypt, and Iran and Iranian Baha'is to India, Europe and North America. The effect of these travels had an important impact not only on the travellers and their destinations but also on their home communities. Robert Stockman describes the effect of the American travelling teachers of the Baha'i Faith on the North American Baha'i community thus:

> The traveling teachers also had a major impact on the thinking of the Bahá'ís who stayed at home. Through books and circulated letters their experiences spread to Bahá'ís even in remote parts of North America. Burma, India and Persia entered in the consciousness of Western Bahá'ís and with them the awareness that one was a member of an international religious community... Exposure to the Asian Bahá'ís and their perspective on the Bahá'í religion also served to diminish the explicitly Christian understanding of the Faith that dominated American Bahá'í thinking at the turn of the century. (Stockman 1995: 353-54)

A similar process occurred in Iran, where the Baha'is increasingly began to feel part of a global community of Europeans and Americans. By the end of 'Abdu'l-Baha's ministry, this impression was so prevalent that it even spread to Iranian Muslims. Morgan Schuster, the American financier employed by the Iranian government, reported that the members of his mission were generally believed to be Baha'is simply because they were Americans. The American consular official Robert Imbrie was even murdered because of the same belief (Momen 1981: 462-65).

Another initiative of 'Abdu'l-Baha was to encourage inter-ethnic marriages. He greatly praised such marriages as that between Ali Kuli Khan and Florence Breed (Gail 1987: 215-16). In these ways, the global nature of the Baha'i community which was at first just rhetoric, gradually became a reality for many Baha'is.

Although 'Abdu'l-Baha's main efforts were towards bringing the Baha'i communities of East and West together and helping them through the inevitable cultural clashes that occurred, 'Abdu'l-Baha also directed his attention to the problem of racial prejudice towards the black races in his talks as well as by direct action. While he was in America, for example, he made a point of by inviting a black Baha'i to the position of honour at a dinner given by a high society Washington family (Morrison 1982: 52-54). He got the American Baha'is involved in improving race relations, instructing them to integrate Baha'i meetings and to start Race Amity Conferences (*ibid.*: 129-43). He also encouraged the inter-racial marriage of Louis Gregory, a black American Baha'i to Louise Mathew, a white British Baha'i (*ibid.* 1982: 63-72).

Financial Globalization

When Scholte speaks of financial globalization, he is referring to twenty-four-hour, round-the-world markets. In the time of 'Abdu'l-Baha, the move from local markets to national markets had only been achieved in a few spheres in a limited number of countries. It was still rare to find financial projects on a national basis, let alone a global initiative. 'Abdu'l-Baha, however, initiated a financial globalization of the Baha'i community by setting up the project of building a House of Worship in Wilmette, near Chicago. He then urged Baha'is from all around the world to contribute to what thus became a global financial project. Contributions for this project came from Baha'is in Europe, the Middle East, India and even from Mauritius (c. 1910, *Star of the West*, 28 April 1910, vol. 1, no. 3: 15).

Stories circulated among the Baha'is of the sacrifices being made worldwide for this House of Worship project. Examples include some which had resonances of the Gospel story of the widow's mite: the Iranian widow who sold her only possession, an earring, to make a contribution; the American widow, who could afford only to drag a stone to the site as her contribution (Whitmore 1984: 68, 46-8); and the British lady whose husband was unemployed and who, having nothing else to give, cut her long hair and offered it to be sold for the benefit of the temple ('Abdu'l-Baha 1978: 96-98; Momen 1974: 22).

'Abdu'l-Baha also encouraged the Baha'is of the East and West to make a positive contribution to the social and economic development of each other's communities. Thus for example, he directed a number of American Baha'is to move to Iran, where they helped set up schools and medical facilities. The American Baha'i women, in particular, became role models for the Iranian Baha'i women (Momen 2005). The American Baha'is also set up the Persian-American Educational Society in 1909 to help the Baha'i schools in Iran financially. Iranian Baha'is such as Mirza Abu'l-Fadl Gulpaygani were sent to Europe and North America in order to increase the knowledge of those communities about the Baha'i Faith. Other Iranian Baha'is went to Beirut, Europe and North America as students. Very often these students were helped by the communities that they went to.

Institutional Globalization

'Abdu'l-Baha commended to the Baha'is all moves towards globalization that occurred in the world (except communism). He attended the meetings of various peace societies and movements for international justice in America (Balyuzi 1971: 192-93), encouraged the Baha'is to learn Esperanto ('Abdu'l-Baha 1978: 308, No. 228), addressed the Central Organization for a Durable Peace at the Hague (Balyuzi 1971: 438-40), praised the Fourteen Points of President Woodrow Wilson ('Abdu'l-Baha 1978: 311-312, No. 232) and lauded the ideals behind the League of Nations (even as he warned of its problems; 'Abdu'l-Baha 1978: 306, No. 227).

'Abdu'l-Baha expended much more energy, however, on the spread and institutional globalization of the Baha'i community. The spread of the Baha'i Faith to North America and Europe occurred early in the ministry of 'Abdu'l-Baha and was largely unplanned. But later, 'Abdu'l-Baha directed and promoted further spread in the Far East, Australia, the Pacific, Central Asia, South America and Africa. By the end of his ministry, the Baha'i Faith could be said to have encircled the globe. There was also a spread of the Baha'i Faith among various religious groups. Jews and Zoroastrians had already begun to become Baha'is in the time of Baha'u'llah. Now this was extended to Christians in North America, Europe and the Middle East. In India, the first Hindus and Sikhs became Baha'is, while in China and Japan, followers of Buddhism and native religions were converted.

As well as the geographical spread of the Baha'i Faith, 'Abdu'l-Baha promoted its institutionalization. In Iran, he gave instructions for the Hands of the Cause to set up a Central Spiritual Assembly (1899) that would act as the organizer of Baha'i activities in Iran. In North America, he encouraged the Baha'i Temple Unity (elected in 1909) to move from its original purpose which was to supervise the building of the North American House of Worship to a much wider role as the coordinator of Baha'i activities in the continent. He instructed Dr Esslemont in 1920 to revive the National Baha'i Council in England that had originally been formed in 1914 but which had lapsed during the First World War. In addition to these national bodies, he also instructed the Baha'is in each place where a community had formed to elect local Baha'i councils and assemblies.

From about 1902, 'Abdu'l-Baha began to impose some sort of order on the array of local institutional arrangements that had evolved in different parts of the world. He instructed that all other usages such as 'House of Justice' and 'Board of Counsel' be dropped in favour of 'Spiritual Assembly' as the designation of these institutions. He then began to give instructions on how they were to be elected and what functions they should perform. He emphasized the importance of these Assemblies in a number of symbolic ways such as the following episode related by Shoghi Effendi:

> So great is the importance and so supreme is the authority of these assemblies that once 'Abdu'l-Bahá after having himself and in his own handwriting corrected the translation made into Arabic of the Ishráqát (the Effulgences) by Sheikh Faraj, a Kurdish friend from Cairo, directed him in a Tablet to submit the above-named translation to the Spiritual Assembly of Cairo, that he may seek from them before publication their approval and consent. (Shoghi Effendi 1968: 23)

The full development of these institutions was not to occur until after the passing of 'Abdu'l-Baha, but even from their earliest days they played an important role in the globalization of the Baha'i community by acting as foci of communications in the increasingly widespread network of the world Baha'i community. Travelling Baha'is, for example, would communicate with Baha'is in the country of destination through these assemblies and these assemblies would then in turn set up itineraries and hospitality for the travellers.

'Abdu'l-Baha provided plans for the continued globalization of the Baha'i community through his Tablets of the Divine Plan (written in 1916-17 and 'unveiled' at a convention in America in 1919). These writings gave instructions for how and to where the Baha'i Faith was to be spread. Though there was only a limited response to it in 'Abdu'l-Baha's own life-time, it became the basis for the global expansion of the Baha'i Faith under Shoghi Effendi.

Thus 'Abdu'l-Baha simultaneously promoted a) the normative globalization of the Baha'i community, by asserting in his writings that globalization was a reality towards which the world was inevitably and inexorably moving, and b) its psychological globalization, by creating and promoting numerous types of globalized interactions among the Bahá'ís of the world. In this way, he brought into the minds of the Baha'is the idea that they were part of a united worldwide community, a predecessor and exemplar of future world unity. These two goals were assisted and backed up by c) a financial globalization of the Baha'i community - through worldwide financial contributions to the project of building the American temple, and d) institutional globalization - through the creation of a worldwide framework of administrative institutions which acted as focal points for the global interactions of the Baha'is.

Universalism and Particularism

In his discussion of universalism and particularism, modernity and post-modernity, Robertson states that 'one of the main features of globalization is the *compression* of the world' resulting in 'an exacerbation of collisions between civilizational, societal and communal narratives' (1992: 141). 'Abdu'l-Baha in his programme of globalizing the Baha'i community may be said to have deliberately created a clash of narratives, in order to guide the Baha'i community in traversing the path to globalization and to demonstrate that unity is possible despite the clash of cultural and civilizational narratives.

'Abdu'l-Baha's main problem in his moves towards globalization was how to orchestrate these 'collisions between civilizational, societal and communal narratives' without the attendant danger of fracturing the Baha'i community into sects and factions. 'Abdu'l-Baha's solution to this was to advance the concept of the Covenant. This was 'Abdu'l-Baha's main theoretical framework for his project of globalizing the Baha'i community. He considered the Covenant to be the main element that would enable the Baha'i community to maintain its unity while at the same time exposing itself to the 'collisions between civilizational, societal and communal narratives'. In this context, the concept of the Covenant could be summarized thus: it maintains that it is possible and even desirable for different narratives, different viewpoints, different interpretations to evolve within the Baha'i community as long as the individual Baha'is maintain a personal loyalty and willingness to submit to the authority of the Centre of the Covenant (which was 'Abdu'l-Baha during his ministry, and later Shoghi Effendi and the Universal House of Justice). That authority was only lightly and seldom invoked by 'Abdu'l-Baha, usually only in administrative and organisational matters, although it was on occasions also invoked on doctrinal and theological questions (for example, 'Abdu'l-Baha's categoric refutation of the trend among some Western Baha'is to identify him with Christ, Stockman 1995: 207-8). In this way, the maximum possible freedom was given to the Baha'is to think and act in culturally and individually distinctive ways - to develop diverse narratives - while at the same time preventing the community from fracturing and splitting into sects due to the collisions between the different narratives. In this way it was possible to balance the modernist trend towards unity with the post-modernist trend towards diversity and differentiation.

It was for this reason that 'Abdu'l-Baha emphasized the Covenant so much in his writings both to the Baha'is of the East and of the West. He calls the Covenant the 'strong fortress', the 'pulsating artery in the body of the world', that which is able to 'stir and move the hearts of humanity', that through which 'the sun of reality will shine' and the 'clouds of mercy will pour down' (*Covenant* 1950: 71-73). Emphasizing the role of the Covenant in maintaining unity, he states:

> Today no power can conserve the oneness of the Bahá'í world save the Covenant of God; otherwise differences like unto a most great tempest will encompass the Bahá'í world. It is evident that the axis of the oneness of the world of humanity is the power of the Covenant and nothing else. Had the Covenant not come to pass... the forces of the Cause of God would have been utterly scattered and certain souls who were the prisoners of their own passions and lusts would have taken into their hands an axe, cutting the root of this Blessed Tree. Every person would have pushed forward his own desire and every individual aired his own opinion! ('Abdu'l-Baha 1993: 51)

Conclusion

The world at the end of the nineteenth and beginning of the twentieth century was only just beginning to become conscious of itself as an entity. Increasing travel and improved communications were just starting to make people think of the 'world as a single place' (Robertson 1992: 182-84). But in the mind of 'Abdu'l-Baha, this was already a reality. He could see it, and he wrote about it, as the future towards which human beings were groping. In his leadership of the Baha'i community, he sought to make the Baha'i community into a unified body that would exemplify the sort of globalized world that he envisioned - not one of uniformity or the cultural domination of nation over others but a unity overlying a full expression of human individual and social diversity. His aim was thus not that of a Westernization - something that some in the Middle East were strongly advocating. This is perhaps best demonstrated by the stance that he took over the issue of the veiling of women. For Westerners, this was an important point, a touchstone for the modernization of the societies in the Islamic East. When the American Baha'i women pushed for the advance of the process of unveiling among the Iranian Baha'i women, 'Abdu'l-Baha advised against pushing forward too rapidly with this, in the knowledge that other social advances could be endangered by the violent opposition it would create, and he believed that the purely superficial benefit it offered was not worth it. Instead he advocated the far more radically deeper measure of advancing education among the Iranian Baha'i women, knowing that this would push forward the programme of globalization more effectively (Momen 2005).

It may be said that 'Abdu'l-Baha's strategy in his leadership of the Baha'i community was to push the Baha'i community deliberately and systematically towards globalization: firstly by asserting the reality and normativeness of globalization in his writings; and secondly by diversifying the Baha'i community, geographically, ethnically, racially and culturally, and then orchestrating increasing social interactions among the Baha'i communities, thus pressing upon them the reality of the globalized nature of the world in which they lived and creating a culture of globalization in the Baha'i community. In this way, he raised in the consciousness of Baha'is the idea that they were part of a global community and that this global community was an example of the reality enshrined in the concept of globalization formulated in Baha'u'llah's dictum: 'The earth is but one country and mankind its citizens' (1983: 250, No. 117). At the same time he guarded against the contention, conflict and division that would be caused by the clash of cultures and mentalities resulting from the bringing together of different types of peoples by emphasizing the doctrine of the Covenant, which tied each individual Baha'i in a bond of personal loyalty to himself as the final arbiter in all disagreements and disputes.

References

'Abdu'l-Bahá (1945). *Foundations of World Unity*. Wilmette, Ill.: Baha'i Publishing Trust.

'Abdu'l-Bahá [n.d.]. *Iranian National Baha'i Archives photocopied series of Baha'i scriptures*. Tonbridge, Afnan Library: vols. 16, 52, 85, 87.

'Abdu'l-Bahá (1967). *Paris Talks*. London: Baha'i Publishing Trust.

'Abdu'l-Bahá (1978). *Selections from the Writings of 'Abdu'l-Bahá*. Haifa: Baha'i World Centre.

'Abdu'l-Bahá (1982). *The Promulgation of Universal Peace*. Wilmette, Ill.: Baha'i Publishing Trust.

'Abdu'l-Bahá (1993). *Tablets of the Divine Plan*. Wilmette, Ill.: Baha'i Publishing Trust.

Bahá'u'lláh (1983). *Gleanings from the Writings of Bahá'u'lláh*. Wilmette, Ill.: Baha'i Publishing Trust.

Bahá'u'lláh (1990). *The Hidden Words*. Wilmette, Ill.: Baha'i Publishing Trust (Arabic and Persian numbers given).

Balyuzi, Hasan M. (1971). *'Abdu'l-Bahá: The Centre of the Covenant of Bahá'u'lláh*. Oxford: George Ronald.

Beyer, Peter (1994). *Religion and Globalization*. London: Sage.

Browne, Edward G. (1926). *A Year Among the Persians*. Cambridge: Cambridge University Press.

Cousins, Ewert (1999). The Convergence of cultures and religions in light of the evolution of consciousness, *Zygon* 34: 209-19.

The Covenant of Bahá'u'lláh (1950). Manchester: Baha'i Publishing Trust.

Dawson, Lorne (1998). The Cultural Significance of New Religious Movements and Globalization: A theoretical prolegomenon, *Journal for the Scientific Study of Religion*, 37: 580-95.

Gail, Marzieh (1987). *Summon up Remembrance*. Oxford: George Ronald.

Mazandaráni, Fádil [n.d.]. *Táríkh-i Zúhur al-Haqq*, vol. 6, photocopy of manuscript in Afnan Library, London.

McLuhan, Marshall and E.S. Carpenter (eds.) (1960). *Explorations in Communication*. Boston: Beacon Press.

McLuhan, M. and Q. Fiore (1967). *The Medium is the Massage*. London: Allen Lane.

Momen, Moojan (1974). *Dr J.E. Esslemont*. London: Baha'i Publishing Trust.

Momen, Moojan (1981). *The Bábí and Baha'i Religions, 1844-1944. Some Contemporary Western Accounts.* Oxford: George Ronald.

Momen, Moojan (1991). The Baha'i Community of Ashkhabad: its social basis and importance in Baha'i history, in S. Akiner (ed.) *Central Asia: Tradition and Change.* London: Kegan Paul International: 278-305.

Momen, Moojan (1999). *The Phenomenon of Religion.* Oxford: Oneworld.

Momen, Moojan (1999-2000). Jamal Effendi and the Early Spread of the Baha'i Faith in India, *Baha'i Studies Review*, 9: 47-80.

Momen, Moojan (2002). Mysticism and the Baha'i Community, *Lights of 'Irfán*, vol. 3. Evanston, Ill.: 'Irfán Colloquia, 2002: 107-20.

Momen, Moojan (2005). The Role of Women in the Iranian Baha'i Community during the Qajar Period, in Robert Gleave (ed.) *Religion and Society in Qajar Iran*, London: Routledge-Curzon: 346-369.

Morrison, Gail (1982). *To Move the World: Louis G. Gregory and the Advancement of Race Unity in America.* Wilmette, Ill.: Baha'i Publishing Trust.

Robertson, Roland (1992). *Globalization: Social Theory and Global Culture.* London: Sage.

Samandar, Kazim (1973). *Táríkh-i Samandar* (ed. 'A. 'Ala'i). Tihran: BNPT 131 B.E.

Scholte, Jan Aart (1996). Beyond the buzzword: towards a critical theory of globalization, in Eleonore Kofman and Gillian Young (eds.) *Globalization: Theory and Practice.* New York: Pinter: 41-57.

Shoghi Effendi (1968). *Baha'i Administration.* Wilmette, Ill.: Baha'i Publishing Trust.

Stauffer, Robert (1997). Petition from the Persian Reformers. http://bahai-library.org/documents/petition.html.

Stockman, Robert (1995). *The Baha'i Faith in America*, vol. 2: Early Expansion, 1900-1912. Oxford: George Ronald.

Vahid-Tehrani, Mehrangiz. [n.d.]. *Biography of Sayyid Hasan Hashimízádih Mutavajjih.* Manuscript in private hands.

Warburg, Margit (1999). Baha'i: A Religious Approach to Globalization, *Social Compass* 46, (1): 47-56.

Whitmore, Bruce (1984). *The Dawning Place.* Wilmette, Ill.: Baha'i Publishing Trust.

CHAPTER 5

The Baha'i Faith and Globalization 1900-1912

Robert H. Stockman

Any effort to study the early twentieth century Baha'i approach to the process now known as globalization is inevitably hampered by the fact that the Baha'is were not using the term. The Baha'i Faith was, however, evolving its own strategies that could be called globalistic, both in terms of the geographical spread of its community and the beliefs and attitudes of its members. `Abdu'l-Baha (1844-1921), the religion's living head, was coordinating the effort based on the principles laid down in the writings of his father, Baha'u'llah (whose works constituted the core of Baha'i scripture). Baha'is (in this paper, the American Baha'is in particular) found a variety of resources related to globalization in their native cultures; some supported the Baha'i Faith's global principles and priorities, while others undermined the Faith's ultimate, global goals.

Globalization in Early Twentieth Century American Christian Perspective

The culture of the early twentieth century American Baha'is witnessed a sort of globalization driven by the technology and social organization of their own branch of the human race, which tied the globe together with telegraph wires, steel rails, shipping lines, and advanced weaponry on its own terms. This globalization was perceived by many Westerners, such as Americans and British, as proving the religious superiority of Christianity, the cultural superiority of the west, and possibly even the racial superiority of the European peoples. In this context, Christian missionaries - active globalizers in their own right

- usually labored both to Christianize and 'civilize'- that is, to Westernize - the so-called benighted heathen that constituted the majority of the inhabitants of the globe. One can find an excellent example of this attitude toward the rest of humanity in the paper that first introduced the Baha'i Faith publicly to a large Western audience. Henry Jessup's 'The Religious Mission of the English Speaking Nations' had as its purpose to describe the 'four elements which make up the power for good in the English speaking race and fit it to be the Divine instrument for blessing the world', in other words, to spread Christianity around the globe. This triumphalist document ends with an example of how the Christ-spirit is working in the heathen world, presumably to leaven it and prepare it for Christ: it quotes Edward G. Browne, the British Orientalist and scholar of the Babi and Baha'i Faiths, about 'the Babi saint, named Behâ Allah' (Jessup 1893: 1125-26).

This attitude of Western superiority, pervasive in the late nineteenth century, had important consequences for the spread of Christianity. Browne himself offered the following observation about the matter:

> I have often heard wonder expressed by Christian missionaries at the extraordinary success of Bahai missionaries, as contrasted with the almost complete failure of their own. 'How is it', they say, 'that the Christian Doctrine, the highest and noblest which the world has ever known, though supported by all the resources of Western civilization, can only count its converts in Mohammedan lands by twos and threes, while Bahaism can reckon them by thousands?' The answer to my mind is as plain as the sun at mid-day. Western Christianity, save in the rarest cases, is more Western than Christian, more racial than religious; and, by dallying with doctrines plainly incompatible with the obvious meaning of its Founder's words, such as theories of 'racial supremacy', 'imperial destiny', 'survival of the fittest', and the like, grows steadily more, rather than less, material. Did Christ belong to a 'dominant race', or even to a European 'white' race? ... The dark skinned races to whom the Christian missionaries go are not fools... they clearly see the inconsistency of those who, while professing to believe that the God they worship incarnated Himself in the form of an Asiatic man - for this is what it comes to - do nevertheless habitually and almost instinctively express, both in speech and action, contempt for the 'natives' of Asia. (Browne 1926, cited in Sprague 1907: 15)

To what extent did the American Baha'is, by the first decade of the twentieth century, possess a different perspective? It cannot be said that they completely lacked the common prejudices of Westerners - *The Bahá'i Faith in America, Volume One* documents that Ibrahim Kheiralla, the founding teacher of the American Baha'i community, taught a belief in the superiority of the Anglo-Saxon race and in the inferiority of Catholicism, Mormonism, and Islam (Stockman 1985: 67-69).

But it appears that various factors mitigated some of the common Western attitudes and myths of superiority. The American Baha'is' prophet was most definitely an Asiatic man, as was his son and the head of the Faith. They had been taught their new religion by Asian missionaries. Their religion was not part of triumphalist Western culture and society; its origin and heartland lay elsewhere. At least some Americans became Baha'is because of their suspicion about the claims of the superiority of Christianity and perhaps partly of claims of superiority of their own culture. Inevitably, the fact that about 95% of their religion's followers - including a few of the most prominent members in the United States - were Iranians also served as an antidote to Eurocentrism.

It should be noted that Baha'is were not the only Americans who rejected the superiority of Christianity. It was a theme in the writings of Emerson and other Transcendentalists as far back as the 1830s, and can be seen in the European Enlightenment much earlier. Americans manifested it in their interest in Swedenborgianism (a mystical and doctrinally heretical Christian teaching) in the early nineteenth century and in Spiritualism in the mid-nineteenth century. Between 1870 and 1920, some thousands became converts to Theosophy, Vedanta Hinduism, and forms of Buddhism. Such conversion often, though not always, accompanied a rejection of Christianity. Madame Helena Petrovna Blavatsky, a co-founder of Theosophy, expressed a virulent intolerance for Christianity, and Henry Steel Olcott, her spiritual partner, actively wrote against Christian missionary efforts in his adopted homeland of India (Prothero 1996: 64, 157). Influential on many Americans who rejected Christianity were voices such as Swami Vivekanada, who traveled across the United States in the 1890s and often engaged in debates with Christian missionaries about the need to reform so-called 'Christian' civilization, rather than 'save' India. But notably different was the positive tone about Christianity in the writings of most Baha'is, versus the criticisms and invective often heard from Blavatsky, Olcott, Vivekanada, and others (against each other, as well as against Christianity). (*ibid.*: 122, 164-67).

In spite of their biases against Christianity, Westerners who adopted Theosophy and Buddhism often retained a strong belief in the cultural superiority of the West. Stephen Prothero's biography of Olcott has as one of its principal themes Olcott's persistent attempt to remake Hinduism and Buddhism in 'modern' and 'liberal' terms. Such efforts appear to be less common or more muted among the Baha'is.

Globalistic Baha'i Teachings

There are many important Baha'i teachings that relate centrally to the concept of globalization. The oneness of humanity, enunciated in Baha'u'llah's early work The *Hidden Words*: 'Know ye not why we created you all from the same dust? That no one should exalt himself over the other' (Baha'u'llah 1992: 29) was itself enough to convince Pauline Hannen, a prominent early twentieth-century Washington D.C. Baha'i, that she had to overcome her prejudices against black people and work for interracial reconciliation. Later writings by Baha'u'llah and `Abdu'l-Baha helped open many Baha'is up to fellowship with peoples of other religions and backgrounds. Iranian Baha'is of Muslim background were breaking down ethnic barriers and interacting with Iran's Jews and Zoroastrians as early as the 1880s. As a result, converts from those groups soon entered the Iranian Baha'i community, and after a generation or two of hyphenated status (such as 'Jewish-Baha'is'; in other words, as partial members of both groups) they became integrated into the majority Iranian Baha'i community. There are also stories about the interaction of Persian and American Baha'is that are illustrative of the desire to mix and integrate. One Persian Baha'i said to Sydney Sprague, an American who became a Baha'i in Paris about 1903, 'I once thought I was polluted if I was obliged to shake hands with a Christian—now I am glad to shake hands with all the world' (Sprague 1986: 28). Presumably the reference to pollution is a comment on the nineteenth century Muslim view that non-Muslims were ritually unclean and thus should not be touched.

There are many anecdotes that can be offered about how converts to the Baha'i Faith overcame cultural restrictions on intercourse with other groups. Sydney Sprague's two books *A Year with the Bahais of India and Burma* and *The Story of the Bahai Movement: A Universal Religion* are filled with examples of Baha'is of Zoroastrian background assisting Baha'is of Muslim background in Bombay, Baha'is of Buddhist background working with Baha'is of Muslim background in Mandalay, of Zoroastrian and Muslim Baha'is nursing a Baha'i of Christian background (Sprague himself) in Lahore.

The Baha'i concept of the oneness of religion (and progressive revelation) is another important factor relating to globalization. This teaching in itself would not be the basis of good relations with people of other backgrounds, however, if it were not coupled with a Baha'i tendency to accentuate the positive. One could, after all, recognize divine commonalities and still stress the differences between religions. Sydney Sprague offered an astute observation of the result of this desire to stress the positive:

> The Bahai propagandist in India has not the difficulty that besets the Christian missionary, that of pulling down; his duty only is to build on to what is already there, for the Bahai teaches that the essence and truths of all religions are one; he sees Hindu, Buddhist, and Mohammedan with the same eye, and he reveres the prophets of each; instead of showing where they were wrong, he shows where they were right... he shows their adherents that a further revelation has come through the teaching of Baha Ullah.... The Bahai does not disdain the prophecies which have come down to us from all religions, but points out that they have all referred to the coming of a great teacher who should establish peace and harmony on the earth (Sprague 1907: 13-14).

Sprague's reference to prophecy is noteworthy. The fulfillment of prophecy was a very important emphasis in the early Baha'i communities worldwide. Because prophecy consists of metaphors and symbols that almost by definition are ambiguous and subject to many interpretations, it provided Baha'is with an important vehicle for emphasizing commonality among the religions. Edward G. Browne's *A Year Amongst the Persians* shows that in 1887-88 Baha'is attempted to convert Browne to the Baha'i Faith - or at least to dialogue with him - through the claim that Baha'u'llah fulfilled biblical prophecy. The fulfillment of biblical prophecy was central to conversion of Americans to the Baha'i Faith in the nineteenth century and remains important to this day. In a sense, one could say that a central Baha'i teaching in the year 1900 was that Baha'u'llah was the return of 'fill in the blank', with the blank being the traditional prophetic figure of each culture and religion. Prophetic interpretation often became a bridge between cultures; Iranian Baha'i communities wrote letters to American Baha'i communities about the fulfillment of biblical texts.

The importance of prophecy appears to have diminished about 1910 when 'Abdu'l-Baha began to stress the social teachings of Baha'u'llah. They provided a set of teachings that not only appealed across religions traditions, but to the non-religious as well. Many of these teachings - such as a universal auxiliary language, reduction of armaments and collective security, and a world government - are clearly globalistic. They provided Burmese, Iranian, and American Baha'is with much more powerful theological and globalistic bonds than swapping accounts of fulfilled prophecies and stories about the life of 'Abdu'l-Baha. In the early 1920s Shoghi Effendi, recognizing this, made it a policy to take the first reasonably comprehensive introduction to the Baha'i Faith (and especially its social teachings) - Esslemont's *Bahá'u'lláh and the New Era* - and commission translations of it into as many languages as possible, thereby giving the Baha'is of the world a common textbook on their Faith.

'Abdu'l-Baha's Approach to Fostering Globalistic Efforts

Much can be said about 'Abdu'l-Baha's efforts to foster globalism. As soon as the Western Baha'is had acquired a basic understanding of their Faith, he immediately sent out inter-ethnic teams of travelling teachers to demonstrate together Baha'i unity. Sydney Sprague was the first; during his second day on pilgrimage in Akka, Palestine, in late 1904, 'Abdu'l-Baha summoned him and said 'I wish you to leave for India to-night'. Sprague was accordingly on a 2 a.m. ferry boat from Akka to Haifa to catch a British steamer to India. He accompanied fifteen Baha'is of Muslim and Zoroastrian background, and since none knew English, he used the voyage to learn Persian. By living with the local Baha'is rather than staying at fancy hotels and clubs catering to foreigners, the Western Baha'is broke down cultural barriers and unspoken taboos about social mixing of the ethnic groups.

'Abdu'l-Baha's instructions to Harlan Ober, who accompanied Hooper Harris and two Persians on a trip to India in 1906, give a further glimpse into his approach. To both men he said, 'Serve the people, speak in the meetings, love them in reality and not through politeness, embrace them as I have embraced you. Even if you should never speak, great good will be accomplished'. In short, 'Abdu'l-Baha wanted the men to behave very differently than the Christian missionaries described by Browne. 'Abdu'l-Baha added that few conversions could be expected from the trip, but that its impact would be great nevertheless (Harris 1907: [n.p.]).

'Abdu'l-Baha's instructions about the Hindu approach to certain theological subjects is also illuminating because of his use of simile, rather than attempting to criticize Hindu doctrine. He said:

> I will now speak to you about India. In India people believe God is like the sea and man is like a drop in the sea, or that God is like the warp and man is like the woof of this coat. But Baha'ís believe that God is like the sun and man is like a mirror facing the sun ('Abdu'l Baha quoted in Kidder 1953-63: 869).[1]

'Abdu'l-Baha was also quick to emphasize the importance of examples of Baha'i sacrifice for each other. One of the most poignant involves Sydney Sprague. In Lahore, Sprague caught typhoid fever and nearly died. All over India, the Baha'is prayed for his recovery. Two Baha'is nursed him devotedly until they were exhausted. A third, a Zoroastrian Baha'i named Kai Khosroe, travelled up from Bombay to help them, but four days after his arrival he caught the cholera and died within twenty hours. His death was seen as a sacrifice for Sprague's life:

> 'He was a humble shopkeeper,' they said, 'and had no ability to teach, but you are able to go about and teach great multitudes; he could only give his life to serve the Cause of God, and he was glad to do it.' Noble Kai Khosroe, you will always be remembered as the first Oriental friend to give his life for a Western Bahai brother (Sprague 1986: 52).

Those are Sprague's words. But 'Abdu'l-Baha echoed them in a tablet to Sprague:

1 Quoted in Elizabeth Kidder *et al.* Harlan Ober, in *The Bahá'í World,* vol. 13, 1953-63, 869. It should be noted that since these words are not known to have come from a written statement by 'Abdu'l-Baha, they should not be considered part of the Baha'i sacred writings.

Thou didst laud and extol... the self-sacrificial Kay-Khusraw. Thy comments are indeed just. Bethink thee, how vast is the distance that separates thy country from the land of Kay-Khusraw! And yet how profound the influence of the Bahá'í spirit, that it hath moved this Easterner to lay down his life for thee, who art a Westerner! How real the love, and how true the sense of affinity with humankind! Happy indeed are those who have come to know the true potency of this love! ('Abdu'l-Baha 1916: 656).[2]

Activism

Activism is the tendency to view religion more from the point of view of organizations and efforts to do good deeds than from the point of view of prayer, contemplation, and the mystic life. Both activist and quietist tendencies have always existed in religions. Philip Schaff, a Swiss theologian and historian who emigrated to America in the mid nineteenth century, captured the tendency of American religion toward activism when he said that 'American Christianity... is more Petrine than Johannean; more like busy Martha than like pensive Mary, sitting at the feet of Jesus' (Schaff 1961: 95). Activism tends to be this-worldly, whereas the contemplative side of religion is more other-worldly.

In the American context, activism was manifested in the democratic nature of congregational organization, in the numerous committees and voluntary organizations associated with local churches, and in the hundreds of national social organizations to foster Sabbath observance, temperance, sale of Bibles, organization of Sunday schools, and other social and religious improvements. In the nineteenth and early twentieth centuries Americans were seen by European observers as obsessed with this side of religion. But the activistic side of religion has steadily expanded in importance and is now an important aspect of globalization, which stresses religious competition in the marketplace of ideas and in the doing of good deeds, and more generally such traits as self-expression and creation of a civil society.

2 'Abdu'l-Baha to Sydney Sprague, translated by the Research Department of the Baha'i World Centre in 1987. The original translation was made by Ameen Fareed in June 1906 and published in *Tablets of Abdul-Baha Abbas,* 3 vols. (Chicago: Bahai Publishing Society 1916), III, 656 (translation data found in Thornton Chase Papers).

The American Theosophist Henry Steel Olcott was central to introducing activistic ideas to Sri Lankan Buddhism in the late nineteenth century, and the British influence on India was one reason for the rise of the Brahmo Samaj, Arya Samaj, and other Hindu organizations for social development (institutions Olcott influenced as well) (Prothero 1996: 86-115, 134-136). One of Olcott's principal criticisms of the religious practices of the South Asians was their passivity and lack of concern about organization. Thus he criticized his former pupil and friend, Dharmapala, as a 'poor man of business' who exhibited 'ignorance of the business methods by which only can one carry on social reforms to practical results' (*ibid.*: 165).

While it is difficult to assess the role of the American Baha'is in fostering activism in the Baha'i communities of Asia, it tentatively appears that their role was in encouraging and strengthening an activistic tendency that already existed in the Baha'i Faith rather than introducing such a tendency to the community.[3] Thus when American Baha'is arrived in Mandalay they found the local Baha'is had already set up a 'Young Men's Bahai Association', no doubt modelled after a YMCA founded by Protestant missionaries and Olcott's Young Men's Buddhist Associations. In Kungjangoon, a Baha'i village in the Irrawaddy River delta, American Baha'is found a Baha'i clinic.

But perhaps the best examples are in Iran. The Baha'is had established the Tarbiyat School for Boys in 1897, before any contact with American Baha'is. However, it was the 1908 arrival of Sydney Sprague to serve as headmaster that helped modernize and Westernize the school, and the arrival of four American Baha'i women in Iran between 1909 and 1911 helped foster the establishment of the Tarbiyat School for Girls, the opening of a Baha'i-operated clinic that eventually evolved into Mithaqiyyih Hospital, and stimulated thinking about the emancipation of women in the Iranian Baha'i community. Charles Mason Remey, who visited both Iran and Burma during his round the world trip in 1910, put the matter this way:

3 This is not the place to explore whether Baha'u'llah's writings are activistic because of direct western influence on his thought, whether revelation can exist completely independently of the culture into which it comes, or whether latent and unrecognized tendencies toward activism in Baha'i culture were released by contact with Westerners.

There is as much in the East for the Occidental as there is in the West for the Oriental... Our friends of the Orient are rich in the love and unity of the Cause. We, upon the other hand, are full of initiative force and activity. It is necessary that both should combine forces and work together, each strengthening the other. In reality, the East and the West are very dependent one upon the other.... The Bahais in Turkistan, India and Burma, as well as in other countries, are also facing the educational problem, and they, too, need our assistance.

By assistance I mean our cooperation in starting these enterprises.... They do not need our money to support their institutions.... The Bahais of the East represent the most progressive of the people. They are prosperous.... The way in which I feel we can best serve is through helping the friends there to inaugurate and start needed good works (Remey 1910: 2-6).

One is struck by how Remey's words echo the concept of activism, but it is an activism that is also found among the non-American Baha'is, who are 'progressive' and 'prosperous'. Absent is any overt criticism of them.

'Abdu'l-Baha seems to have agreed with Remey's view. He encouraged the Baha'is of the United States to organize the Persian-American Educational Society in 1909, a nonprofit organization that funnelled educational textbooks and other development-related materials to Iran. While Persian Baha'is were sending thousands of dollars in contributions to the United States to help the Americans build the first Baha'i temple in the West, Americans were sending hundreds of dollars in contributions to Iran to help provide scholarships to children wishing to attend the Tarbiyat Schools for Boys and Girls. In this way, lines of mutual support and collaboration were created across the sea, tying the Baha'i communities together.

Conclusion

In summary, in the first decade of the twentieth century, even though it lacked the human resources to make a significant impact on the globalization of human society, one sees the Baha'i religion marshalling its theological, cultural, spiritual, and human resources as best it could to create a truly global religious community, one reflective of its belief in the oneness of humanity and capable of modestly demonstrating to the public its commitment to unity. Decades before the term globalization was coined, the Baha'i Faith was actively pursuing globalistic policies.

References

'Abdu'l-Baha (1916). *Tablets of Abdul-Baha Abbas,* vol 3. Chicago: Bahai Publishing Society.

Baha'u'llah (1992). *The Hidden Words.* Trans. Shoghi Effendi. London: Nightingale Books.

Browne, Edward G. (1926). *A Year Amongst the Persians.* Cambridge: Cambridge University Press.

Chase, Thornton [n.d.]. *Papers, 1898-1912,* Wilmette, Ill.: National Baha'i Archives.

Hooper Harris to William Hoar (copy), 2 February 1907, Thornton Chase Papers, Wilmette, Ill.: National Baha'i Archives.

Jessup, Henry (1893). The Religious Mission of the English Speaking Nations, in Rev. John Henry Barrows (ed.) *The World's Parliament of Religions,* 2 vols. Chicago: Parliament Publishing Co., II: 1125-26.

Kheiralla, Ibrahim (1900). *Behá'u'lláh.* Chicago: I.G. Kheiralla.

Kidder, Elizabeth *et al.* (1970). Harlan Ober, in *The Baha'i World,* vol. 13, 1953-63, Haifa, Israel: Universal House of Justice.

Prothero, Stephen (1996). *The White Buddhist: The Asian Odyssey of Henry Steel Olcott.* Bloomington: Indiana University Press.

Schaff, Philip (1961). America: A Sketch of its Political, Social, and Religious Character, edited by Perry Miller. Cambridge: Harvard University Press.

Remey, Charles Mason (1910). Around the World with Messrs. Remey and Struven, in *Bahai News,* 1, no. 13 (4 Nov. 1910): 2-6.

Sprague, Sydney (1907) *The Story of the Bahai Movement: A Universal Faith,* London: Priority Press.

Sprague, Sydney (1986). *A Year with the Baha'is in India and Burma.* Los Angeles: Kalimat Press.

Stockman, Robert (1985). *The Baha'i Faith in America, 1892-1900: Beginnings,* vol. 1. Wilmette: Baha'i Publishing Trust.

Stockman, Robert (1995). *The Baha'i Faith in America, 1900-12: Early Expansion,* vol. 2. Oxford: George Ronald.

CHAPTER 6

Iranian Nationalism and Baha'i Globalism in Iranian Polemic Literature

Fereydun Vahman

The idea of globalism, one of the central doctrines of the Baha'i Faith, has been extensively invoked in Iranian literature in order to stigmatise this religious movement. Such writings contend that emphasis on world citizenship amounts to disloyalty to Iran and that, for this reason, Baha'is are not sufficiently patriotic. In the context of the intense nationalism that prevailed in Iran from the late nineteenth century onwards, this accusation became an effective weapon for discrediting the Baha'i community.

In a later period, most publications and journals printed by various Islamic movements introduced the Baha'i Faith as a political movement contrived by the imperial powers to weaken Islam and the Islamic identity of Iran.[1]

In an orchestrated campaign, these groups tried to vilify the Baha'is among the Iranian public by branding them as spies and agents of foreign powers, and an enemy within the Iranian Muslim nation.

1 See for example: Anvar, Vadood (1946) *Sākhte-hāye Bahā'īyyat dar dīn va diyāsat,* (Baha'is' innovations in religion and politics) Tehran: Sherkat-e Matbū'āt; Ahmad, A. Morteza (1966) *Tārīkh va naqsh-e sīyāsī-e rahbrarān-e Bahā'ī,* (History and the political role of Baha'i leaders.), Tehran: Dār-ul Kutub al-Islamiyyeh; and journals like: *Ā'in-e Islam, Donyā-ye Islam, Parcham-e Islam, and Nedā-ye Haqq* whose sole aims were to discredit the Baha'i Faith. For the latest, but with the repeated accusations as the previous publications, see 'Abdullāh Shahbāzī', Kānūn-e Bahā'īgarī...', *Jām-e Jam*: 13, August 17, 2003.

None of these polemical publications seriously discuss the teachings of the Baha'i Faith or refute its principles through reason and analysis. Rather, they focus on portraying Baha'is as disloyal Iranians willing to betray their own nation in the interest of foreign elements. Over time, this pattern of indoctrination created an atmosphere of suspicion and even hatred against Baha'is, preparing the way for the violent persecution of this religious community after the establishment of the Islamic Republic in 1979.

The Rise of Nationalism in Iran

The rise of Iranian nationalism had started as early as the beginning of the nineteenth century in reaction to factors such as the humiliation of Iran in the two Perso-Russian wars (1805-1813 and 1826-1828 respectively), the meddling of Russia and Britain in all aspects of Iranian life in the latter part of Qajar rule (1785-1925), the cultural interaction between Iran, Ottoman Turkey, Egypt and India, and the imposing influence of Western ideas. These factors gradually awakened traditionalist Iran and prompted the transformation of a backward and inferior self-conception. Poets and writers tried to portray Iran as a country with a glorious past, a history of grandeur, replete with heroes and just kings, an empire ruling over half the world and for many centuries, a world superpower.

The sentiment is capably captured in Illinois University Professor Dr. Mohamad Tavakoli Targhi's words:

> The newly imagined Iran, constructed of textual traces and archaeological ruins, fashioned a new syntax for reconstruction of the past and the formation of a new national time, territory, writ, culture, literature, and politics. Language, the medium of communication and signification, and the locus of tradition and cultural memory was restyled. Arabic words were purged, 'authentic' Persian terms forged, and neologisms and lexicography were constituted as endeavours for 'national reawakening'. Iran-centred histories displaced dynastic and Islam-centred chronicles. In order to recover from historical amnesia, people reinvented pre-Islamic Iran as a lost utopia with Kayumars as a Persian prophet predating Adam, Mazdak as a theoretician and practitioner of freedom and equality, Kāveh-ye Ahangar [The blacksmith

Kāveh] as the originator of 'national will' (himmat-i millī), and Anushirvan as a paradigmatic just-constitutional monarch' (Tavakoli Targhi 1990: 78).

This trend continued even more forcefully during the reign of Reza Shah (1925-1940) the founder of Pahlavi dynasty who intended to modernise Iran at a rapid pace. He curbed the long-standing influence of the clergy, prohibited the use of the traditional veil *chador* among women by decree, imposed and enforced the use of a semi-European outfit for men as well as a uniform for school children. He also constructed schools for girls and built universities. The nationalistic fever showed itself most emphatically in purging the Persian language of every trace of Arabic, which to some degree curbed Islamic influence in Iranian culture. Zoroastrianism was idealised and praised; and in some periods rumours circulated that the government intended to replace Zoroastrianism as the state religion instead of Islam. These anti-Arab and anti-Islamic sentiments were also reflected in Iranian literature. The works of famous writers like Sadegh Hedayat and Bozorg Alavi are good examples. Heayat's hatred against Arabs and Islam sometimes took on an anti-Semitic character. This nationalist zeal which was felt strongly at the onset of the Constitutional Revolution (1906) continued for a century and even reinforced itself amongst the modern Iranians after the Islamic revolution of 1979. It can be felt clearly not only in Iran but understandingly, also among the Iranian Diasporas in the West.

Country Versus the World?

In such an intense atmosphere of nationalist zeal, the much quoted sentence of Baha'u'llah that 'pride is not for he who loves his country, but for he who loves the [whole] world', was interpreted as evidence of disloyalty and lack of patriotism among Baha'is. It was often the case that in polemical works only the first part of the sentence 'Pride is not for he who loves his country' was quoted and the rest left out (Najafi: 1979: 748).

The British Orientalist E. G. Browne is perhaps one of the first who questioned the patriotism of Baha'is. Commenting on the foregoing statement of Baha'u'llah he writes that it is:

An admirable sentiment, but not, perhaps, one which is likely to be of service to the Persians in this crisis [constitutional revolution of 1906] of their history (Browne 1910: 424).[2]

The following observation of Browne is also of interest; he writes:

I have often asked this question of my Persian friends: 'If a convinced and enthusiastic Baha'i had the choice of seeing Persia a strong and independent country with Islam as the established religion, or a Russian province with Baha'ism as the established religion, which would he choose?' In almost all cases the answer has been that he would choose the second alternative (*ibid.*: 424).

Browne, who had written so much about the persecution of the Babis and the Baha'is, had been well aware of the fact that for his Baha'i acquaintances the decisive element in answering this hypothetical question has not been the choice between an independent or colonised Iran but between living a life under a harsh religious persecution or living in a country with religious tolerance.

Almost a century has transpired since this statement, and Iran is now a strong and independent country with Islam as the established governmental system. As a consequence of human right violations, millions of Iranians have fled the country choosing instead to live the life of a refugee in foreign countries. Still many more would leave if given the possibility without any consideration as to whether they would fall under the rule of America or Australia.

But Browne's statement has made its effect felt during the past century. Polemical writers against the Baha'i Faith, took Browne's statement as the authority assessment of a renowned Orientalist, demonstrating the lack of patriotism in the Baha'i religion. They even went so far as to consider the principle of 'the love of humanity' as treason against Iran, as demonstrated by the following two examples.

Dr. Fereydun Adamiyyat, Professor of History at Tehran University and the author of many books on the history of Qajar Iran, was one of the staunch opponents of the Baha'i Faith and did not miss any

2 The same sentence in Persian repeated in the preface to *Nuqtat-ul Kāf* (edited by Browne) is quoted in a rebuttal work against the Baha'is by Najafi *ibid.*: 749.

opportunity to attack it on the issue of patriotism. One case is his voluminous work on the life of Sepahsalar (1827-1872) Iran's Prime Minister at the time of Nasir al-Din Shah (1848-1896). Discussing the concessions given to the British subject Baron Julius de Reuter, and defending his acts in giving concession to Reuter, he refers to the work of Professor Firuz Kazemzadeh, a Baha'i and at that time Professor of History at Yale. In his book *Russia and Britain in Iran 1864-1914* Kazemzadeh argues that the Shah and Sepahsalar's motives in signing such concessions had been their 'greed', and 'enormous bribes received by Mirza Hosein Khan (Sepahsalar) himself...and others' (Kazemzadeh, 1968: 128).

Adamiyyat attacks Kazemzadeh in a long note, accusing him of being weak in evaluating historical documents, lacking the technique of writing history and absolutely devoid of historical perceptions. He then adds: 'Moreover he [Kazemzadeh] is filled with a bigoted hatred (*kine-ye ta'assob amiz*) against Iran and the Iranians. His hatred against Iran stems from his belief in the Baha'i creed' (Adamiyyat 1977: 328).

Here, we are not discussing Kazemzadeh's qualifications as a historian, or the motives of Sepahsalar in giving concessions to Baron Julius de Reuter.[3] But Adamiyyat's note on Kazemzadeh shows how being a Baha'i is tantamount to hatred against Iran.

Another example is from a sizable 800 pages rebuttal work called *Baha'ian* (the Baha'is) written against the Baha'is by a cleric Seyyid Muhammad Baqir Najafi (Najafi, *ibid*.: 751). Unlike other publications of its kind Najafi, as he claims, has tried to use a logical method for revealing the truth (=falsnesse) of the Baha'i religion. One chapter of his book is devoted to the lack of patriotism among the Baha'is. In this chapter he portrays Baha'is as Zionists as well as Zionist and Israel spies in the Arab and African Islamic countries. Based on the documents which are produced in the book he argues that the teaching of 'unity of humankind' is intended to destroy the love of country and to condition Baha'is to serve the interest of foreign powers.

3 About concessions given to the British at the time of Sepahsalar see also: Taimuri, Ibrahim (1978) He writes that 'Sepahsalar increased the influence of the British and before long gave away to them, almost for nothing, all the vital sources [of Iran's economy].

His documents are either quotations from the rebuttal books of his kind, or quotations from Arabic newspapers reporting the decisions of the conferences of the 'Organisation of Islamic Countries' calling the Baha'is the spies of Israel. No need to say that such resolutions are all passed on the behest and lobbying of the representatives of the Islamic Republic of Iran.

But he has also produced a document from a Baha'i publication. The document in question which, according to the author teaches Baha'i youths to detest their country, is in the form of a facsimile, taken from one of the old issues of *Ahang-e Badi'* the Journal of the Baha'i Youth of Iran. It is a poem entitled 'Divine Melodies', as translated below:

I do not know where I have been born,
But I know well that my country is the world
Wherever I live, I do not feel a stranger,
Whether in Egypt, Peru or Finland.
God created the world and Man created the small cities.
God created Man, and Man created the differences of races.
Let me tell you: to me we all are one,
Whether we come from India, England or China.
I do not feel enmity towards you,
But with a heart full of love I stretch my hands towards you,
Because love of humanity is a precious pearl,
It repels the hatred and calls us to sing cheerful songs of Unity.

(*Ahang-e Badi* 1973: 32)

A New Allegation

These allegations of Baha'is disloyalty were reinforced by yet another contention, namely the suggestion that the Babi and the Baha'i Faiths were essentially created by Russian and British imperialists. This suggestion was easily embraced by Iranians and their penchant for intrigue. Indeed it became one of the most widespread and accepted rumours against the Baha'is.

In his article in *Encyclopaedia Iranica* on 'conspiracy theory' the author Dr. Ahmad Ashraf writes:

Conspiracy theories in Persia, are a complex of beliefs attributing the course of Persian history and politics to the machinations of hostile foreign powers and secret organizations...Particularly since the beginning of the 20th century Persians from all walks of life and all ideological orientations have relied on conspiracy theories as a basic mode of understanding politics and history (Ashraf 1993: 138).

The author then divides conspiracy theories in modern Persia into two categories: 'those focused on supposed plots by Western colonial powers and those focused on satanic forces believed to have been active against Persia from antiquity to the present' (*ibid.*: 138). Somehow the Babi and Baha'i religions fall into both groups! Ashraf then explains the myth of *siasat-e Englis,* (the policy of the British) a well-known Persian expression, pointing to the belief that since the 19th century almost all political and social events in Iran were stage-managed by the British. Giving some examples he continues with the Babi-Baha'i subject:

The British were also supposed to have meddled in religious matters...encouraging the Babis to rebel in the mid-19th century; instigating pogroms against the Baha'is to force them to collaborate with British agents in return for protection, and urging Jews to become Baha'is so that they could forge closer ties with the families of Persian notables and spy on them (Ashraf 1993: 139).[4]

Under the heading *Conspiracy of the Freemason, Baháís and Zionists* Ashraf writes that (here I only quote the Baha'i section):

Belief in a conspiracy among adherents of the Baha'i Faith is based on a forged document attributed to Prince Dimitri Dolgoroukov (known in Persia as Kinyaz Dálghuroki), the Russian minister in Persia 1263-70/1845-54). It purports to be memoirs in which the prince described how he created the Babi and Baha'i faiths as a way of weakening Shi'ism and Persia as a whole. It was first circulated in Tehran in various forms in the late 1930s and has since been widely cited in Muslim polemics as evidence that the Baha'is were controlled first by the Russians and later by the British or Americans or both. A number of editions of this work have been printed sometimes modified to

4 *Ibid.*: 139. For each of these issues the author gives extensive references to the works by the Iranian authors on the history of 19th- and 20th century Iran.

reflect political developments, although a number of scholars have refuted its authenticity.[5] In the 1970s the relative prosperity of Persian Baha'is and the rumour that their numbers had grown to about 3 million (ten times the actual figure) engendered the belief that they had conspired to 'buy' Persia... Furthermore, as Baha'i world headquarters is located in Haifa, Israel, the Baha'i faith is taken by some to be a Zionist political organization, rather than a religion (Ashraf 1993: 145).

In the Persian version of this article which appeared in *Goft-o-gu* (published outside Iran) Dr. Ashraf writes:

Amir Assadollah Alam the [minister of court of the Shah] was one of the rare Iranian politicians who disbelieved the conspiracy theories and had a logical attitude towards events. Nevertheless he considered the Baha'is, Freemasons and the Jews quite influential in shaping the events of Iran. In his memoirs published long after his death in Washington we read: 'I told the Shah, how it would be possible that a person be a freemason, or think internationalist, being member of CIA or being a Baha'i and still he would like his country?' (*ibid.*: 33).

Some of Iranian scholars consider Dolgoroukov's alleged memoirs an insult against Iranians' intelligence, a reflection among Iranians of a feeling of 'inferiority' in relation to foreigners; memoirs which consider a religious movement coming from the heart of Iranian culture as something fabricated by foreigners.[6]

A translation of a few lines of these memoirs would be sufficient to betray its author's goal:

I then decided to create a new religion, a religion without [the sense of the love of] the country. Clearly, Iran's victories were all due to the patriotism [of its people] and the unity between the religions (*sic.*). I should then make a

5 The scholars such as Eqbal (1949): 148; Kasrawi, (1944): 88-90; Mahmud (1949-54): 143; Minovi (1963): 42-44.

6 See as an example Tavakoli-Targhi (2001): 86. See also Banani (1984): 279-80; For the 'real' memoirs of Prince Dolgoroukov see: Kazemzadeh (1966): 17-24. Also see the answer of the Bahā'i community of Iran (1946) to this forged memoirs pointing out to more than eighty grave historical mistakes.

religion without patriotism and with not too much religion in it (*Sālnāme-ye Khorāsān* 1943: 153).

The Iranian historian Adamiyyat unlike the authors of Dolgoroukov's memoirs had tried to prove that it was the British who created the Babi and Baha'i religions. In his biography on Amir Kabir, the Prime Minister during the first years of the reign of Nasir al-din Shah, he writes that:

Mulla Hussain of Boshruye (the first convert to the Babi religion) was a clever Mulla who lived in Meshed. In order to become influential in politics he approached the British agents, and later on became a close friend of the British spy Arthur Conolly, who in 1830 visited Meshed in the disguise of a merchant. Conolly sent him to a secret mission to Herat (now in Afghanistan). Later on Mulla Hosein went to Kufa (in Iraq) and preached the nearness of the coming of the promised one. After some years he went to Shiraz and instigated Seyyed Ali Muhammad to rise and claim to be the Bab... (Adamīyyat: 217, here quoted in Tavakoli-Targhi *ibid.*: 87).

Adamiyyat had not noticed that at the alleged time of the close friendship between Arthur Conolly and Mulla Hosein (1830), the latter had been only 16 years old. He never put his feet in Herat and at 18 he left Iran with his family to reside in Iraq in order to attend the classes of Seyyid Kazim Rashti the leader of Sheykhi movement.

Baha'i Patriotism

It is worth noting that in the Baha'i writings a balanced patriotism and loyalty to one's nation is praised and celebrated. Iran which is the birthplace of the Baha'i Faith is considered as a 'sacred land' and 'Abdul-Baha has written many prayers for the glory and prosperity of Iran.

Rather than encouraging disloyalty, the Baha'i teachings call for a wider world-embracing loyalty within which, in an age of global interdependence, national interests and aspirations can best be achieved. In one of his writings dated November 28, 1931, Shoghi Effendi the Guardian of the Baha'i Faith, asserts that the purpose of the worldwide Law of Baha'u'llah:

...is neither to stifle the flame of a sane and intelligent patriotism in man's heart, nor to abolish the system of national autonomy so essential if the evils of excessive centralization are to be avoided. It does not ignore, nor does it attempt to suppress, the diversity of ethnical origins, of climate, of history, of language and tradition, of thought and habit, that differentiate the people and nations of the world. It calls for a wider loyalty, for a larger aspiration than any that has animated the human race. It insists upon the subordination of national impulses and interests to the imperative claims of a unified world. It repudiates excessive centralization on one hand, and disclaims all attempts at uniformity on the other; its watchword is unity in diversity such as 'Abdul-Bahá Himself has explained (Shoghi Effendi 1991: 41-42).

Even if this vision of the future was an idea beyond its time in an earlier period of Iranian modern history, and however much it may have been exploited to scapegoat this religious community for political ends, contemporary perceptions of Iran's role on the world stage - especially among the younger generations - reflects a desire to be part of an emerging global community. I believe among this enlightened generation the search for an authentic national identity and the progress of the Iranian nation is not only reconcilable with a broader global consciousness, but that the two are inextricably tied to one another. It is paradoxical that the combination of indigenous Iranian roots and the concept of world citizenship is probably best captured in the Baha'i writings.

References

Adamiyyat, Fereydun (1977). *Andīshe-ye taraqī va hokūmat-e qānūn dar 'asr-e Sepahsālār* (The Idea of Progress and the Rule of Law in the Time of Sepahsalar), Tehran: Khārazmī

'Alam, Amir Assadollah (1992). '*Yad-dāsht-hā-ye 'alam*' (The 'Alam's Diaries). In Alī-Naghī Alīkhāni (ed.) vol. 2, Bethesda: Ibex Publishers.

Anonymous (1943). 'E'terāfāt-e siyāsī-ye Kinyāz Dālghūrokī' (Political confessions of Kinyāz Dālghūrokī), *Sālnāme-ye Khorāsān* (The Year Book of Khorasan), Mashhad: [n. p.].

Ashraf, Ahmad (1993). Conspiracy Theory in Ehsan Yarshater (ed.), *Encyclopaedia Iranica*, vol. 6. Costa Mesa: Mazda Publishers.

Baha'i community of Iran (1946). *Jawābī be resāleh-ye e'terāfāt-e siyāsī-ye*

Kinyāz Dālghūroki, (Answer to the allegations of the booklet: Political confessions of Kinyāz Dālghūroki), Tehran: Mo'asseseye Melli-ye Matbū'āt-e amrī.

Banani, Amin (1984). Religion or Foreign Intrigue: The case of the Babi-Bahā'ī Movement in Iran, in *Proceedings of the Thirty First International Congress of Human Sciences in Asia and North Africa*, Tokyo: Publication of Institute of Eastern Culture.

Browne, E.G. (1910). *Persian Revolution of 1905-1909*. Cambridge: Cambridge University Press.

Eqbal, Abbas (1949). *Yadegār*, vol. 5, No. 8-9.

Kasrawi, Ahmad (1944). *Bahā'īgarī*. Tehran: Peyman Publishers.

Kazemzadeh, Firuz (1968). *Russia and Britain in Persia, 1864-1914*. New Haven, Conn.: Yale University Press.

Kazemzadeh, Firuz (1966). Excerpts from Dispatches Written During 1848-52 by Prince Dolgoroukov, Russian Minister to Persia, in *World Order* I.

Mahmud, M. (1949-54). *Tārīkh-e rawābet-e siāsī-e Iran was Engelīs dar qarn-e nūzdahom-e mīlādī*, (The History of Political Relations between Iran and England in the Nineteenth Century), (8 vols.) vol. VIII, Tehran: Amir Kabir Publishers.

Minovi, Mojtaba (1963). Sharh-e Zendegī-ye man, *Rāhnamā-ye Kitāb* 6/1-2, 1342/1963.

Morteza, Ahmad A. (1966). *Tārīkh va naqsh-e sīyāsī-e rahbrarān-e Bahā'ī*, (History and the Political Role of Bahā'ī Leaders), Tehran: Dār-ul Kutub al-Islamiyyeh.

Mostowfi, Abdullāh (1964), *Sharh-e zendegānī-e man, I* (The story of my life), Tehran: Amir Kabir Publishers.

Najafi, Seyyed Mohamad Baqir (1979). *Bahā'iyān* (The Baha'is), Tehran: Tahūrī.

Sālnāme-ye Khorāsān (1943). E'terāfāt-e siyāsī-ye Kīnyāz Dālghūrokī. Mashhad.

Shoghi Effendi (1991). *The World Order of Bahá'u'lláh: Selected Letters*, Wilmette: Baha'i Publishing Trust.

Taimuri, Ibrahim (1978). *asr-e bī-khabarī yā panjāh sāl istibdād dar Iran, yā tārīkh-e imtiyāzāt-e Iran* (The age of unawareness, or fifty years of dictatorship in Iran, or the history of concessions in Iran). Tehran: Iqbal Publishers.

Tavakoli-Targhi, Mohamad (1990). Refashioning Iran: Language and Culture during the Constitutional Revolution. *Iranian Studies,* vol. 23, Nos. 1-4.

Tavakoli-Targhi, Mohamad (2001). Anti Bahā'īsm and Islamism in Iran 1941-1955, *Iran Nameh, A Persian Journal of Iranian Studies,* Vol. XIX, Nos. 1-2.

Vadood, Anvar 1946. *Sākhte-hāye Bahā'īyyat dar dīn va diyāsat.* (Bāha'īs Innovations in Religion and Politics) Tehran: Sherkat-e Matbū'āt.

Yarshater, Ehsan (ed.) (1993). *Encyclopaedia Iranica,* vol. VI. Costa Mesa: Mazda Publishers.

CHAPTER 7

Global Claims, Global Aims: An Analysis of Shoghi Effendi's *The World Order of Baha'u'llah*

Zaid Lundberg

This paper addresses two main questions:

1. What is Shoghi Effendi's (1897-1957) discourse on 'globalization' and 'globality'?
2. What are the global claims and global aims in his work *The World Order of Bahá'u'lláh?*

Global Missionary Plans

Global missionary plans[1] in the history of the Baha'i Faith are traceable to 'Abdu'l-Baha in 1916-17, but they were unrealized during his lifetime.[2] In *Bahá'í Administration* Shoghi Effendi (1928: 69) urged the Baha'is to spread globally, but the first executed systematic plan had to wait until 1936 when he announced the first 'Seven Year

1 These plans are fourteen tablets that are addressed to the North Americans and published in 1919 as *Tablets of the Divine Plan*, see 'Abdu'l-Baha 1993. The mandate in these tablets is to spread the Baha'i Faith to all the five continents including 120 territories and islands.

2 When 'Abdu'l-Baha passed away in 1921 there were neither National Spiritual Assemblies (NSAs – the nationally and democratically elected governing and administrative body of the Baha'i Faith) nor any administrative order (Hofman 1993: 92), and they numbered only ca. 200,000 followers out of which 90 percent were Iranian (Smith 2000: 138). Geographically, the Baha'i Faith was largely confined to Iran with few followers residing in 35 countries, mainly the Middle East, North America and Europe (Smith 2000: 137-54).

Plan' (1937-44).[3] Subsequently, other national plans were developed.[4] The aim of the second 'Seven Year Plan' (1946-53), however, was to establish local spiritual assemblies in various countries on other continents.[5] None of these plans, however, could be considered global but were either national, continental, or, at the most, international in scope. The year 1951-53 is a watershed in the geographical expansion of the Baha'i Faith. In 1951 Shoghi Effendi coins the noteworthy term 'global crusade' and in 1953 he launches the plan via four 'intercontinental conferences' held on four different continents (1965: 104).[6] Thus, 'The Global Crusade' (1953-63)[7] is considered the first truly *global* missionary plan.[8] Although Shoghi Effendi played an important role in the international expansion of the Baha'i Faith he was the key figure in its early global phase.[9] This paper, however, is not on Shoghi Effendi's global missionary plans

3 This plan was directed to the North Americans to 'establish one local spiritual assembly in every state of the United States and every province of Canada, and to create one centre in each Latin American republic' (Momen 1989: 180).

4 E.g., India/Burma, the British Isles, Germany/Austria, and Australia/New Zealand.

5 Europe and Africa.

6 Africa (Kampala), America (Wilmette), Europe (Stockholm), and Asia (New Delhi).

7 'The Global Crusade' is also known as 'The Ten Year Plan' (Hassall 1994/95).

8 Shoghi Effendi (1971: 152, italics added) writes 'Let there be no mistake. The avowed, the primary aim of this Spiritual Crusade is none other than the conquest of the citadels of men's hearts. *The theatre of its operations is the entire planet.*' Indeed, similar to 'Abdu'l-Baha's global missionary plan, its aim was 'to settle Bahá'ís in every significant territory and island group throughout the world' (Smith 2000: 272). At the beginning of global crusade the Baha'i Faith was found within 128 countries and territories and when Shoghi Effendi unexpectedly passed away in London in 1957 the numerical growth was insignificant but it was established in 254 countries with about 50 NSAs (Rabbani 1969: 391-92).

9 Smith (2000: 137-40) divides the expansion of the Baha'i Faith into three distinct phases: 1) the 'Islamic period' (1844-c.1892); 2) 'Internationalization' (c. 1892-1953); and 3) 'Global expansion' (from 1953). See also Rabbani 1969: 94.

but on his globalization discourse in general and the global claims and aims in his most important doctrinal[10] work – *The World Order of Bahá'u'lláh* – that *preceded* his plans. As such, one purpose of this paper is to retrospectively delineate the global discourse at the basis for such subsequent global mission. It is argued that there is an implicit dialectic in this work where, for example, the Baha'i Faith is defined as a 'world religion' (global claim) while a future 'world commonwealth' (global aim) is envisioned. In order to shed light on this dialectic it is maintained that an Aristotelian[11] causality – his idea of a final or teleological cause – is essential and recurrent. In Aristotle's analysis of causality, all things have a purpose or aim, actualized as various potentials develop over time (Aristotle *Physics* II, 7. See Waterfield 1996). No scholarly work so far has put Shoghi Effendi's writings in globalization[12] and Aristotelian contexts.

Shoghi Effendi, Globalization and Globality

In order to portray Shoghi Effendi's global discourse some terminology needs to be discussed. The term 'globalization' appeared in the English language in 1959 – two years after Shoghi Effendi's death (Schreiter 1997: 5). The term 'globality' is comparatively recent and this paper follows the English sociologist J.A. Scholte's distinction between globality (the condition) and globalization (the trend) (2002:

10 Hofman (1993: 18) states that 'Without deep study of this basic document, no Bahá'í can claim to be truly knowledgeable of his Faith. Indeed, no one can have a deep, authentic knowledge of the Revelation of Bahá'u'lláh without study of all these expository and exegetical works of the Guardian.' See also footnote 23.

11 Baha'u'llah (1978: 147), 'Abdu'l-Baha (1978: 7; 1981: 15) and Shoghi Effendi (1991: 154) give several references to Aristotle in their writings. It is also significant that Kluge (2000: 3) states that there is an 'Aristotelian substratum or soil of the Baha'í Writings' and that 'the Baha'í Writings re-affirm many of Aristotle's philosophical ideas and methods of studying reality and adapt and develop them to their own unique purpose of laying the philosophical foundations for Bahá'u'lláh's new world order' (Kluge 2002).

12 Descriptions of 'The World Order of Bahá'u'lláh' have been done by e.g., Hatcher and Martin (1989: 127-42), and Lerche (ed.) (1991) has related the Baha'i writings to 'world order studies'.

2, 4). The latter term has during the last decades generated not only a variety of definitions[13] and conceptualizations but great theoretical implications (Robertson 1992; Waters 1995; Scholte 1999, 2002). The idea of something worldwide is inherent, but not exhaustive, to definitions of globalization (Robertson 1992: 8; Stackhouse 2000: 22). Recently there has been an upsurge in cultural dimensions of globalization where religion has an important role (Robertson 1992; Appadurai 1996). Rather than seeing globalization as a one-dimensional concept the American sociologist Arjun Appadurai (1996) prefers five global 'scapes'[14] and the Australian sociologist Malcolm Waters suggests the term 'sacriscapes' for religion (1995: 187). Accordingly, globalization is currently perceived as a multi-dimensional phenomenon (Waters 1995: 14-16; Robertson 2000: 54; Stackhouse 2000: 37-38).

Shoghi Effendi showed great interest in both education and world matters[15] and during his international studies[16] he chose subjects like economics, social sciences, political science and philosophy (Khadem 1999). In 1931 he writes that 'political and economic unification of the world' is 'a principle that has been increasingly advocated in recent times' (1991: 34). The English sociologist Roland Robertson portrays

13 Beck states that 'Globalization has surely been the most used and abused, most seldom defined, probably the most misunderstood, vague and politically effective slogan during the last years and will be during the years to come' (1998: 36, translation mine. Cf. Robertson 2000: 63 and Scholte 2002). Thus, it is no surprise that authors on globalization are neither unanimous regarding its definition (Schreiter 1997: 4) nor do they agree when this process started (Schreiter 1997: 5; Stackhouse & Paris 2000: 8). Beck (1998: 37) mentions various authors and dates: Marx/Wallerstein 15th century; Giddens 16th century; Robertson 1870-1920; and Perlmutter 1989. Rifkin (2003: 5) argues that it is traceable to 1944.

14 1) Ethnoscapes, 2) technoscapes, 3) financescapes, 4) mediascapes, and 5) ideoscapes.

15 Rabbani (1969: 177) describes Shoghi Effendi as 'the keenest observer of political events and kept abreast of all happenings'and the 'exactitude with which he compiled statistics, sought out historic facts, worked on every minute detail of his maps and plans was astonishing' (Rabbani 1969: 127-28).

16 The French Jesuit school, Collège des Frères, in Haifa, Catholic Boarding School and Syrian Protestant College (later known as the American University) in Beirut, and Balliol College at Oxford University (1920-21).

globalization as 'the compression of the world and the intensification of consciousness of the world as a whole' and 'the overall process by which the entire world becomes increasingly interdependent, so as to yield a 'single place'' (1992: 8). Robertson (1989: 8) also states that 'We could even go so far as to call the latter a 'world society', as long as we do not suggest by that term that nationally constituted societies are disappearing' (Cf. Scholte 2002: 14, 16). Similarly, Scholte defines globalization as 'the spread of transplanetary - and in more recent times - supraterritorial - connections between people' (2002: 2). Although Shoghi Effendi does not use Robertson's term 'compression', he writes in 1931 that the world is 'contracted and transformed into a highly complex organism by the marvelous progress achieved in the realm of physical science, by the worldwide expansion of commerce and industry', and that 'the fortunes of its races, nations and peoples becoming inextricably interwoven' (Shoghi Effendi, 1991: 47, 59, 198). Similar ideas are found in other early works. In 1939 he writes that 'The world is contracting into a neighborhood' (1990: 87).[17] In 1941 Shoghi Effendi writes of 'the fundamental changes effected in the economic life of society and the interdependence of the nations, and as the consequence of the contraction of the world, through the revolution in the means of transportation and communication' and that:

> The world is, in truth, moving on towards its destiny. The interdependence of the peoples and nations of the earth, whatever the leaders of the divisive forces of the world may say or do, is already an accomplished fact. Its unity in the economic sphere is now understood and recognized. The welfare of the part means the welfare of the whole, and the distress of the part brings distress to the whole (Shoghi Effendi 1980: 122).

The American theologian M.L. Stackhouse writes that globalization 'combines the notion of a worldwide, ordered place of habitation subject to *transformation*' (2000: 22, italics added). In 1931 Shoghi Effendi describes his visions of 'present-day society' that implies 'a change such as the world has not yet experienced' and that it:

17 Cf. Shoghi Effendi (1965: 126) and McLuhan's (1962) term 'global village'.

> calls for no less than the reconstruction and the demilitarization of the whole civilized world - a world organically unified in all the essential aspects of its life, its political machinery, its spiritual aspiration, its trade and finance, its script and language, and yet infinite in the diversity of the national characteristics of its federated units (Shoghi Effendi 1991: 43).

On the theme of transformation Shoghi Effendi further writes of 'so fundamental a revolution, involving such far-reaching changes in the structure of society', and of:

> those epoch-making changes that constitute the greatest landmarks in the history of human civilization. Great and far-reaching as have been those changes in the past, they cannot appear, when viewed in their proper perspective, except as subsidiary adjustments precluding that transformation of unparalleled majesty and scope which humanity is in this age bound to undergo (Shoghi Effendi 1991: 45-46).

Apparently, globalization is portrayed as multi-dimensional involving 'transportation and communication' (communication), 'demilitarization' and 'political machinery' (politics), 'spiritual aspiration' (religion), 'trade and finance' (economics), and 'script and language' (culture). Notice that such a process is 'not only necessary but inevitable, and that its realization is fast approaching' and that the world is 'moving on towards its *destiny*' (1991: 43). Key terms as inevitability, realization, and destiny, coupled with world processes suggest an underlying Aristotelian teleology as well as global aims.

Above Robertson defines globalization in terms of a 'single place' and a 'world society.' Waters (1995: 5) similarly states that in 'a globalized world there will be a single society and culture occupying the planet' that will 'tend towards high levels of differentiation, multi-centricity and chaos'. Above Shoghi Effendi describes 'a world organically unified in all the essential aspects of its life' that is 'yet infinite in the diversity of the national characteristics of its federated units'. Thus, Shoghi Effendi, Robertson and Waters envision not only a 'world society' but emphasize that it will be diverse or heterogeneous. It is apparent that although Shoghi Effendi was unable to utilize the term 'globalization' he is in agreement with modern scholars on the subject that globalization is a:

- multi-dimensional phenomenon
- contraction/compression of the world (increasing inter-dependency)
- major transition/transformation
- move towards a single/world society, yet diversified

In conclusion, it is argued that the first three points depict globalization (the trend) and the fourth point suggests globality (the condition). Conceptualized in this manner Shoghi Effendi's global discourse predates modern authors on globalization with more than half a century.

The World Order of Baha'u'llah

The World Order of Bahá'u'lláh: Selected Letters,[18] written to the North American Baha'i communities during 1929-36, is a significant work since it appeared during a period between an end-phase of administration ('the Administrative Order')[19] and a start-phase of missionary plans (1937-63).[20] It is also noteworthy his wife, Ruhiyyih Rabbani, writes that this work was:

> designed to clarify for the believers the true meaning and purpose of their Faith, its tenets, its implications, its destiny and future and to guide the unfolding and slowly maturing Community in North America and in the West to a better understanding of its duties, its privileges and its destiny (Rabbani 1969: 212).

18 For a short summary of these letters see Smith (2000): 364-65.

19 This can be seen from his correspondence with the North American community, published as *Bahá'í Administration* (1923-33).

20 Bramson-Lerche writes that 'In 1926 Shoghi Effendi began to emphasize the transition from concentrating on developing the administrative institutions to using them to further propagation efforts' and that after Shoghi Effendi had 'established a basic understanding in the American community of the principles of the Bahá'í Administrative Order, he began to explain the principles of the World Order of Bahá'u'lláh' (Bramson-Lerche 1982: 257). It is also noteworthy that Momen and Smith (2003) divide Shoghi Effendi's 'ministry' into two phases: 1) The Development of the Baha'i Administrative Order (1922-c.1937), and 2), The Systematic Spread of the Baha'i Faith (c.1937-63). See also Hatcher and Martin (1989): 68, 167.

Thus, both 'tenets' (claims) and terms like 'purpose', 'destiny' and 'future' (aims) are associated with *The World Order of Bahá'u'lláh,* and where the latter implies an Aristotelian teleology. The sixth letter, 'The Dispensation of Bahá'u'lláh', is relevant since Rabbani (1969: 213, clarification added) states 'I know from his [Shoghi Effendi] remarks that he considered he had said all he had to say, in many ways, in the Dispensation'. Moreover, it is significant that it is referred to as his 'confession of faith' (Hofman 1993: 99) and as a 'doctrinal statement' (Smith 2000: 122). Although such remarks may infer its doctrinal status, they can also be substantiated and corroborated from terms and phrases used throughout *The World Order of Bahá'u'lláh* e.g., 'basic principles', 'essential verities', 'cardinal tenets' and 'fundamentals' (Shoghi Effendi, 1991: 3, 123, 199, 15).[21] The phrase 'fundamental verities and ideals of their Faith' is interpreted as representing both claims and aims. In addition, Shoghi Effendi (1991: 147) refers to 'this general exposition of the fundamental verities of the Faith', and that he has 'endeavored to dissipate... misapprehensions' (Shoghi Effendi 1991: 131).[22] Considering these points this paper concurs with scholars who consider *The World Order of Bahá'u'lláh* a major doctrinal work and therefore a main source for understanding the Faith.[23]

21 Variations of the most common phrases are: 'fundamental verities and ideals of their Faith' (pp. 66, 99, 147, 164); 'root principles' (pp. 99, 116); and 'this cardinal principle' (pp. 116, 151).

22 The two first letters of *The World Order of Bahá'u'lláh* refer to Ruth White, and probably Ahmad Sohrab, who questioned the idea of Administration and seriously attacked Shoghi Effendi's 'Guardianship'. It is noteworthy that Bramson-Lerche (1988: 276, italics added) states that 'White's attack... caused Shoghi Effendi to begn [sic] to synthesize and expound those *doctrines* in the Bahá'í Faith which would lay a solid foundation for *expansion* and give the Bahá'ís a more profound understanding of their religion, especially of the administrative order and world order.' Thus, there is a dialectic between doctrines (claims) and missionary expansion (aims).

23 It is noteworthy that in 1987 a letter written on behalf of The Universal House of Justice (quoted in Bergsmo (1991): 9) writes that 'such well-read and familiar titles as Bahá'í Administration, The World Order of Bahá'u'lláh, The Advent of Divine Justice … [etc] … form part of the primary literature of the Faith.' *The World Order of Bahá'u'lláh* and *The Dispensation of Bahá'u'lláh* are also offered as Internet-based distance-learning courses by the Wilmette Institute (Illinois, USA). See also footnote 10.

Before analyzing the global claims and global aims it is important to briefly consider 'three areas' in *The World Order of Bahá'u'lláh*: 1) the Baha'i Faith, 2) the Administrative Order, and 3) the World Order of Baha'u'llah.[24] Regarding the first point the Baha'i Faith is divided into 'three ages that constitute the component parts of the Bahá'í Dispensation' (Shoghi Effendi 1991: 144). Each age is described significantly as 'the Transitional and Formative period of the Faith', or 'the formative age', which commenced with Shoghi Effendi's own 'ministry' (1922-57) (Shoghi Effendi 1991: 98, 143). This period or age can be seen in contradistinction to the 'heroic age' or 'the Primitive, the Apostolic Age', that starts with the 'Declaration of the Báb' (1844) and concludes with the passing of 'Abdu'l-Baha (1921) (Shoghi Effendi 1991: 52, 89). The formative age or period will, in turn, give rise to 'the Golden Age of the Revelation of Bahá'u'lláh', (Shoghi Effendi 1991: 49, 53) 'that golden millennium', (1991: 74, 156) 'the Most Great Peace', (1991: 19, 69) or 'the Kingdom of God' (1991: 39, 44). Not only is the formative age described as 'transitional', but the *Baha'i Faith* itself is 'in its embryonic state', 'nascent', an 'infant', 'slowly maturing', and 'slowly crystallizing' (Shoghi Effendi 1991: 23, 54, 74, 199).

The *Administrative Order* similarly is 'in infancy', a 'newborn child', 'nascent', 'crystallizing', and in a 'process of slow and steady consolidation' (Shoghi Effendi 1991: 156, 144, 98, 154). This Administrative Order is supposed to give rise to *the World Order of Bahá'u'lláh* also illustrated as 'embryonic', a 'gradual emergence', 'yet unborn' and 'slowly and imperceptibly rising' (Shoghi Effendi 1991: 185, 29, 168, 24). Evidently, a number of organic metaphors portray a process of growth and unfoldment of potentials, implying an Aristotelian teleology (Hatcher and Martin 1989: 184-85). The 'three ages' are also portrayed in an organic metaphor:

The period in which the seed of the Faith had been slowly germinating [the Heroic Age] is thus intertwined both with the one which must witness its efflorescence [the Formative Age] and the subsequent age in which that seed

24 This phrase should not be confused with the title of *The World Order of Bahá'u'lláh*, but is a concept that Shoghi Effendi frequently employs in this work.

will have finally yielded its golden fruit [the Golden Age] (Shoghi Effendi 1991: 144, clarifications added).[25]

Notice the sequence: seed - germinating - efflorescence - fruit. Shoghi Effendi (1991: 155) also uses phrases like 'the organic institutions of this great, this expanding Order'.[26] The relationship between the areas above and the usage of organic metaphors is clearer in the next passage:

> Though the framework of His Administrative Order has been erected, and the Formative Period of the Bahá'í Era has begun, yet the promised Kingdom into which the seed of His institutions must ripen remains as yet uninaugurated (Shoghi Effendi 1991: 168).

Observe that 'the promised Kingdom' is described 'as yet uninaugurated' and similarly, that 'the promised glories of the Sovereignty which the Baha'i teachings foreshadow, can only be revealed in the fullness of time' (Shoghi Effendi 1991: 16). Thus, the full potential of the Baha'i Faith is still to be actualized in the future.

In this brief analysis Shoghi Effendi portrays the Baha'i Faith as dialectically positioned between two great ages or periods and that the 'three Baha'i areas' are seen as part of a slow and, yet steady, evolutionary process that develops organically over time (Shoghi Effendi 1991: 23, 155). Thus, in an Aristotelian teleology, the Baha'i Faith is depicted in a state of formation or transition.[27]

Global Claims[28]

The first area, reviewed above as Shoghi Effendi's discourse on 'globalization' or 'globality', does not directly involve the Baha'i Faith but pertains to 'the world':

25 This interpretation is based on the fact that Shoghi Effendi mentions the 'three ages' in the earlier sentence.

26 For an analysis of Shoghi Effendi's 'Organic Order', see Coe 1993: 25-56. For a discussion on 'organicism', which is one of Pepper's 'Root Metaphors' or 'world hypotheses', see Pepper (1942).

27 For an analysis of this 'transition process' see Bramson-Lerche (1991): 12-41.

28 A difference between a claim and an aim is that the former pertains more to statements that relate to *what is* (the presence), or in Aristotelian terms, what is *potential*. In this context it is closely related to doctrines (although

The World

- 'the world, contracted and transformed into a highly complex organism' (p. 47)
- 'the fortunes of its races, nations and peoples becoming inextricably interwoven' (p. 59)
- 'that universal fermentation which, in every continent of the globe and in every department of human life' (p. 170)
- 'a world of inter-dependent peoples and nations' (p. 198)

Subsequent lists concern the 'three Baha'i areas' discussed above:

The Baha'i Faith

- 'the world-wide Faith' (p. 8)
- 'the international character of the Cause' (p. 9)
- 'the world-wide law of Bahá'u'lláh' (p. 41)
- 'insists upon the imperative **claims** of a unified world' (p. 42)
- 'Baha'u'llah's all-embracing dominion' (p. 47)
- 'their world-embracing Cause' (p. 53)
- 'its world-embracing program' (p. 55)
- 'a far-flung Faith' (pp. 66, 98)
- 'transcends political and social boundaries, which includes within its pale so great a variety of races and nations' (p. 66)
- 'Its world-unifying principles' (p. 73)
- 'the universality of its teachings' (p. 93)
- 'has assimilated varied races, nationalities, creeds and classes' (p. 197)
- 'a Faith established within the jurisdiction of no less than forty different countries' (p. 199)
- 'From Iceland to Tasmania … this world-enfolding System, this many-hued and firmly-knit Fraternity' (p. 201)

---

doctrines may also be related to prophecy in the sense of futurology). An *aim* is more related to purpose, intention, and plan, or in Aristotelian terms, what can be *actualized.* As such, an aim is related to *what will be* (the future). In this context it relates to, anticipates, and precedes, global activities and processes, especially global missionary ideas and plans.

The Administrative Order

- 'the world-wide Administration' (p. 47)
- 'this great, this ever-expanding Order' (p. 155)

The World Order of Baha'u'llah

- 'this world-embracing... Order' (p. 18)

Obviously, the present (1929-36) nature of the Baha'i Faith is described most expressively and little attention is paid to the two 'orders'. It is argued that these are unrealized phenomena ascribed to a future globality.[29]

Another means to describe the global claims is by way of statements that define the Baha'i Faith as a *world* religion. Such statements are seen in the seventh and last letter, 'The Unfoldment of World Civilization', to which a whole section - subtitled 'A World Religion' - is devoted:

> Ceasing to designate to itself a movement, a fellowship and the like - designations that did grave injustice to its ever-unfolding system - dissociating itself from such appellations as Bábí sect, Asiatic cult, and offshoot of Shí'ih Islám, with which the ignorant and the malicious were wont to describe it, refusing to be labeled as a mere philosophy of life, or as an eclectic code of ethical conduct, or even as new religion the Faith of Bahá'u'lláh is now visibly succeeding in demonstrating *its claim* to be regarded as a World Religion, destined to attain, in the fullness of time, the status of a world-embracing Commonwealth, which would be at once the instrument and the guardian of the Most Great Peace announced by its Author (Shoghi Effendi 1991: 196, italics added).

This passage is central, not only because the word 'claim' is employed, but also since the Baha'i Faith is claimed 'a world religion' (global claim) while it is an 'ever-unfolding system', 'destined to attain, in the fullness of time, the status of a world-embracing Commonwealth' (global aim). Consequently, although the Baha'i Faith is described as global, its full global potential, in an Aristotelian teleology, has yet to be actualized in the future.

29 Hatcher and Martin (1985: 135-36, italics added. Cf. pp. 85, 130) writes that 'This World Order obviously does not exist; rather, it is *the goal* towards which the Bahá'í community is striving'.

Global Aims

The third letter, 'The Goal of a New World Order', is pertinent since Shoghi Effendi's secretary referred to it as follows:

> Shoghi Effendi wrote his last general letter to the western friends because he felt that the public should be made to understand the attitude the Bahá'í Faith maintains towards prevailing economic and political problems. We would let the world know what *the real aim* of Bahá'u'lláh was (Compilation 1991, italics added).

Again Shoghi Effendi's economic and political interest is mentioned. Especially noteworthy is his statement that 'It is towards this goal - the Goal of a new World Order ... all-embracing in scope ... that a harassed humanity must strive' (Shoghi Effendi 1991: 34). The wording 'the Goal' is synonymous with aim and the phrase 'all-embracing in scope' is tantamount to global. In other words, it is a global aim and such a description is nowhere clearer than in the last letter, 'The Unfoldment of World Civilization', in particular under the subtitle 'World Unity the Goal':

> Unification of the whole of mankind is the hall-mark of the stage which human society is now approaching. Unity of family, of tribe, of city-state, and nation have been successively attempted and fully established. World unity is the goal towards which a harassed humanity is striving. Nation-building has come to an end. The anarchy inherent in state sovereignty is moving towards a climax. A world, growing to maturity, must abandon this fetish, recognize the oneness and wholeness of human relationships, and establish once and for all the machinery that can best incarnate this fundamental principle of its life (Shoghi Effendi 1991: 202).

A 'globality' ('World unity') is seen as an inevitable and more mature stage in the unfoldment of humanity's collective life depicted as: family - tribe - city - state - nation - world unity. This scheme, together with phrases like 'must strive', 'is now approaching', 'is striving', 'is moving', and 'growing to maturity', and terms like 'inevitable' and 'Unfoldment', conveys an Aristotelian teleology and, coupled with terms like 'World unity', constitute global aims and globality. This idea of 'world unity' is also seen in Shoghi Effendi's concept of a 'world commonwealth' where 'all nations, races, creeds and classes are closely and permanently united, and in which the autonomy of its state members and the personal freedom and initiative of the individuals that compose them are definitely and completely safeguarded' (Shoghi Effendi, 1991: 203). The global aims of this 'world commonwealth', also referred to as 'Bahá'í commonwealth', in the last letter, are listed below (Shoghi Effendi 1991: 7, 18). The list is not limited only to this letter but to the global aims and globality found throughout *The World Order of Baha'u'llah.*

The World

- 'Some form of a world super-state must be evolved' (p. 40)
- 'a world parliament' (p. 40)
- 'a supreme tribunal' (pp. 40, 203)
- 'a world community' (p. 40)
- 'a single code of international law' (p. 40)
- 'an organic change in the structure... a change such as the world has not yet experienced' (p. 43)
- 'a world organically unified in all the essential aspects of its life, its political machinery, its spiritual aspiration, its trade and finance, its script and language', (p. 43)
- 'yet infinite in the diversity of the national characteristics of its federated units' (p. 43)
- 'that transformation of unparalleled majesty and scope which humanity is in this age bound to undergo' (p. 46)
- 'to bring to a climax the forces that are transforming the face of our planet' (p. 170)
- 'This commonwealth … must … consist of: (p. 203)
    - a world legislature
    - a world executive
    - an international force
    - a mechanism of world inter-communication
    - a world metropolis
    - a world language
    - a world script
    - a world literature
    - a universal system of currency, weights and measures

- a world federal system (p. 204)
- a world civilization' (p. 206)

The Baha'i Faith

- 'our Faith … shall evolve … and shall forge ahead … till it embraces the whole of mankind' (p. 23)
- 'The Revelation of Bahá'u'lláh, whose supreme mission is none other but the achievement of this organic and spiritual unity of the whole body of nations' (p. 163)
- 'preparing for the spiritual conquest and the complete redemption of mankind' (p. 195)

The Administrative Order

- 'this Administrative Order – the rudiments of the future all-enfolding Bahá'í Commonwealth' (p. 146)
- 'this Order constitutes the very pattern of that divine civilization which... Bahá'u'lláh is designed to establish upon earth' (p. 152)
- 'the Bahá'í Commonwealth of the future of which this vast Administrative Order is the sole framework' (p. 152)
- 'the implications of this constantly evolving Scheme are more fully understood and its ramifications more widely extended over the surface of the globe' (p. 156)
- 'The central, underlying aim which animates it is the establishment of the New World Order' (p. 157)
- 'For this process is actuated by the generating influence of God's changeless Purpose, and is evolving within the framework of the Administrative Order of His Faith' (p. 195)
- 'as their Administrative Order expands and consolidates itself' (p. 199)

The World Order of Baha'u'llah

- 'a World Order that shall reflect... the Abhá Kingdom' (p. 46)
- 'a new order destined to overshadow all mankind' (p. 52)
- 'the New World Order destined to embrace in the fullness of time the whole of mankind' (p. 144)
- 'that World Order, the establishment of which must signalize the Golden Age of the Cause of God' (p. 161)

- 'This New World Order... involves no less than the complete unification of the entire human race' (p. 162)

The choice of words 'must needs be evolved', 'not yet experienced', 'bound to undergo', 'to bring to a climax', 'till', 'supreme mission', 'preparing for', 'the future', 'designed to', 'constantly evolving', 'underlying aim', 'shall', 'Purpose', 'destined to', and 'in the fullness of time' are all significant. Clearly, in contrast to the list on global claims, the emphasis is on the future. Moreover, the words like 'must', 'bound to', 'designed to', 'shall', 'destined to' all indicate an Aristotelian teleology. Coupled with phrases like 'the whole of mankind', 'the whole body of nations upon earth', 'over the surface of the globe' and 'World Order' the list conveys both global aims and a future globality.

So far the global aims and global claims in *The World Order of Bahá'u'lláh* have been analyzed as two separate categories but they are nonetheless intimately related. Many of the areas discussed above can be found for example in a single passage of 'The Unfoldment of World Civilization':

> The Revelation of Bahá'u'lláh [the Baha'i Faith] whose supreme mission is none other but the achievement of this organic and spiritual unity of the whole body of nations, should, if we be faithful to its implications, be regarded as signalizing through its advent the coming of age of the entire human race. It should be viewed not merely as yet another spiritual revival in the ever-changing fortunes of mankind, not only as a further stage in a chain of progressive Revelations, nor even as the culmination of one of a series of recurrent prophetic cycles, but rather as marking the last and highest stage in the stupendous evolution of man's collective life on this planet. The emergence of a world community, the consciousness of world citizenship, the founding of a world civilization and culture – all of which must synchronize with the initial stages in the unfoldment of the Golden Age of the Bahá'í Era – should, by their very nature, be regarded, as far as this planetary life is concerned, as the furthermost limits in the organization of human society ... (Shoghi Effendi 1991: 163, clarification added).

First of all, Shoghi Effendi states what the 'supreme mission' is for the Baha'i Faith. This aim is some form of globality. It further clarifies what the Baha'i Faith is and is not (claims). The role of the Baha'i Faith is associated with the 'evolution of man's collective life on this planet' and 'this planetary life' (global claims and global aims). Four global aims (world community, the consciousness of world citizenship, a world civilization and world culture) are seen to 'synchronize with the initial stages in the unfoldment of the Golden Age'. Shoghi Effendi depicts that the 'Golden Age' has stages and is supposed to 'unfold' suggesting an Aristotelian teleology. Moreover, the idea that 'The emergence of a world community' will coincide with 'the Golden Age of the Bahá'í Era' indicates that globalization and the three Baha'i areas are connected. In another lengthy passage Shoghi Effendi (1991: 170) refers to a 'twofold process'[30] that is part of 'that universal fermentation which, in every continent of the globe and in every department of human life, be it religious, social, economic or political, is purging and reshaping humanity'. This twofold process takes place with 'an accelerated momentum ... transforming the face of our planet'. One process is described as constructive and integrating, the other as disruptive and destructive. The constructive process is associated with the Baha'i Faith and the destructive process is 'identified with a civilization that has refused to answer to the expectation of a new age, and is consequently falling into chaos and decline' or 'this age of transition'. Yet, both Baha'is and 'mankind as a whole' share, in an Aristotelian teleological sense, the same 'destined goal' and 'ultimate consequences'.

Above Stackhouse states that the term globalization 'combines the notion of a worldwide, ordered place of habitation subject to transformation'. Shoghi Effendi frequently employs terms like 'worldwide' and 'order'. Coupled with the idea of the 'three ages', organic metaphors, and recurrent terms like 'unfoldment', 'reconstruction' and 'a twofold process', he also maintains that the world's 'ordered place of habitation' is undergoing an inevitable and radical transformation where the aim is some form of globality ('world unity'). Yet, although such globality is the same for the two processes, Shoghi Effendi makes a subtle, but important, distinction with regard to the actors, the sequence,

30 Although Shoghi Effendi does not refer to 'the Major and Minor Plan of God' (1965, p. 139-40) in *The World Order of Bahá'u'lláh,* he writes about 'God's all-pervasive Will, the shaping of His perfectly and *world-embracing Plan*' (1991: 161, italics added). The major and minor plans illustrate how Shoghi Effendi later envisions the dialectic and correlation between the above-described 'twofold process'.

and ultimate aim of these processes (1991: 162). The latter process, associated with 'the collective efforts of mankind', can only 'hope to achieve anything above or beyond that 'Lesser Peace'' described as a 'political unification of the Eastern and Western Hemispheres' (Shoghi Effendi 1965: 33), or 'political peace between nations' (Smith 2000: 266-67). In contrast, the former process will achieve 'The Most Great Peace' described as:

> a peace that must inevitably follow as the practical consequence of the spiritualization of the world and the fusion of all its races, creeds, classes and nations – can rest on no other basis, and can be preserved through no other agency, except the divinely appointed ordinances that are implicit in the World Order that stands associated with His Holy Name [the Baha'i Faith] (Shoghi Effendi 1991: 162, clarification added).

The actors, processes, and aims can be depicted as follows:

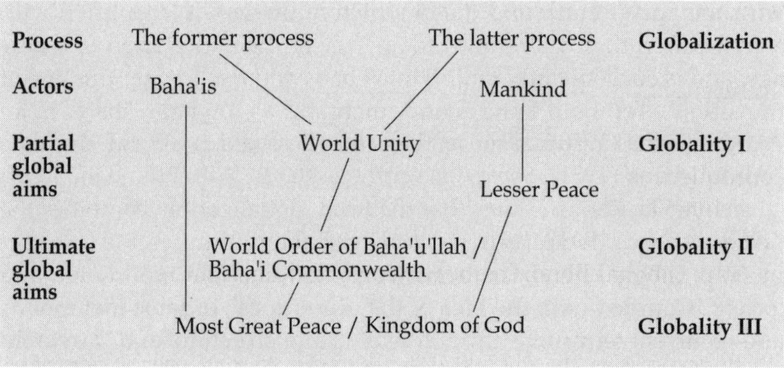

Accordingly, both Baha'is and mankind as a whole are inevitably destined to establish 'world unity' (Globality I), yet the former are only indirectly involved in creating the 'Lesser Peace'. In contrast, the latter are uninvolved in establishing the ultimate global aims, 'the World Order of Baha'u'llah/Baha'i Commonwealth',[31] seen as synonymous

31 Shoghi Effendi (1991: 196, italics added) states 'in demonstrating its claim to be regarded as *a World Religion,* destined to attain, in the fullness of time, the status of *a world-embracing Commonwealth,* which would be at once the instrument and the guardian of *the Most Great Peace* announced by its Author'. More precisely, Shoghi Effendi (1974: 364, italics added) refers to

to 'the world's future super-state', or 'world-civilization'[32] (Globality II), which in turn will inaugurate 'that golden millennium', 'the Most Great Peace/Kingdom of God' (Globality III).[33]

Conclusion

In this brief analysis of Shoghi Effendi's global discourse in general, and his global claims and aims in particular (analyzed in *The World Order of Bahá'u'lláh*), it is clear that even though Shoghi Effendi is a leader of a *religious* community, his discourse on globalization and Globality I includes a range of non-religious dimensions and, is strikingly similar to, and thus predates, modern authors on the subject. Yet, the theological and teleological (Aristotelian) aspects predominate his global discourse and become particularly prevalent in Globality II and III. Retrospectively, it can be argued that it is this discourse that forms the ideological and theological basis for Shoghi Effendi's development and actualization of subsequent global missionary plans.

References

'Abdu'l-Baha (1978). *Tablet to August Forel.* Oxford: George Ronald.

'Abdu'l-Baha (1981). *Some Answered Questions.* Wilmette: Bahá'í Publishing Trust.

'Abdu'l-Baha (1993). *Tablets of the Divine Plan.* http://bahai-library.com/writings/abdulbaha/tdp/.

---

this process as 'the successive stages of *repression,* of *emancipation,* of *recognition* as an independent Revelation, and as a *state religion,* must lead to the establishment of *the Bahá'í state* and *culminate* in the emergence of the *Bahá'í World Commonwealth*'. For a discussion on the relationship between Church and State in a future global Baha'i society, see McGlinn (1995).

32 Shoghi Effendi (quoted in Rabbani 1969: 161) states: 'Our aim is to produce a world civilization ...'

33 Shoghi Effendi (1965: 33, italics added) writes, for example, that 'the Lesser Peace, as foretold by Bahá'u'lláh... must, in the end, *culminate* in the unfurling of the banner of the Most Great Peace, in the Golden Age of the Dispensation of Bahá'u'lláh.' For an analysis of this 'transition process' where the 'Two-fold process', 'Lesser Peace', and 'Most Great Peace' are discussed, see Bramson-Lerche (1991): 12-41.

Appadurai, Arjun (1996). *Modernity at Large: Cultural Dimensions of Globalization* (Public Worlds, vol. 1). Minesota: University of Minnesota Press.

Association for Baha'i Studies (1993). *The Vision of Shoghi Effendi: Proceedings of the Association for Baha'i Studies Ninth Annual Conference,* Nov. 2-4, 1984. Ottawa, Canada: Baha'i Studies Publication.

Baha'u'llah (1978). *Tablets of Bahá'u'lláh Revealed After the Kitáb-i-Aqdas.* Haifa: Baha'i World Centre.

Beck, Ulrich (1998). *Vad innebär globaliseringen? Missuppfattningar och möjliga politiska Svar.* Gothenburg: Daidalos.

Bergsmo, Morten (ed.) (1991). *Studying the Writings of Shoghi Effendi.* Oxford: George Ronald.

Bramson-Lerche, Loni (1982). Some Aspects of the Development of the Baha'i Administrative Order in America, 1922-1936, in M. Momen (ed.) *Studies in Bábí and Baha'i History, vol. 1.* LA: Kalimat Press.

Bramson-Lerche, Loni (1988). Some Aspects of the Establishment of the Guardianship, in M. Moomen (ed.) *Studies in the Bábí & Baha'i Religions, vol. 5.* LA: Kalimat Press.

Bramson-Lerche, Loni (1991). An Analysis of the Baha'i World Order Model, in Charles Lerche (ed.) *Emergence: Dimensions of a New World Order.* London: Baha'i Publishing Trust.

Coe, Roger (1993). An Organic Order: Implications from the Writings of Shoghi Effendi as to the Nature of the World Order of Bahá'u'lláh, in Association: *The Vision of Shoghi Effendi.* Ottawa: Baha'i Studies Publication.

Compilation (1991). *Compilation of Compilations.* Victoria: Baha'i Publications Australia.

Hassall, Graham (1994/95). Baha'i History in the Formative Age: The World Crusade, 1953 - 1963. *The Journal of Baha'i Studies,* 6 (4): 1-21.

Hatcher, W.S. and J.D. Martin (1989). *The Baha'i Faith: The Emerging Global Religion.* San Francisco: Harper & Row.

Hofman, David (1993). Shoghi Effendi: Expounder of the Word of God, in Association: *The Vision of Shoghi Effendi.* Ottawa: Baha'i Studies Publication.

Khadem, Riaz (1999). *Shoghi Effendi in Oxford.* Oxford: George Ronald.

Kluge, Ian (2000). *The Call into Being: Introduction to a Baha'i Existentialism.* http://bahai-library.org/articles/existentialism.kluge.html.

Kluge, Ian (2002). *The Aristotelian Substratum of the Baha'i Writings.* http://www.geocities.com/SoHo/Den/4944/aristotle.html.

Lerche, Charles (ed.) (1991). *Emergence: Dimensions of a New World Order.* London: Baha'i Publishing Trust.

McGlinn, Sen (1995). *Church and State in the World Order of Baha'u'llah.* http://bahai-library.org/unpubl.articles/church.html.

McLuhan, Marshall (1962). *The Gutenberg Galaxy.* London: Routledge & Kegan Paul.

Momen, M. and P. Smith (2003). *Baha'i History.* http://www.northill.demon.co.uk/relstud/history.htm#se.

Momen, Wendi (ed.) (1989). *A Basic Baha'i Dictionary.* Oxford: George Ronald.

Pepper, S.C. (1942). *World Hypotheses: A Study in Evidence.* University of California Press.

Rabbani, Ruhiyyih (1969). *The Priceless Pearl.* London: Baha'i Publishing Trust.

Rifkin, Ira (2003.) *Spiritual Perspectives on Globalization: Making Sense of Economic and Cultural Upheavals.* Woodstock: Skylight Paths.

Robertson, Roland (1987). Church-State Relations and the World System, in T. Robbins and R. Robertson (eds.) *Church-State Relations: Tensions and Transitions.* New Brunswick: Transaction.

Robertson, Roland (1989). Internationalization and Globalization, *University Center for International Studies Newsletter.* University of Pittsburgh, (Spring): 8-9.

Robertson, Roland (1992). *Globalization: Social Theory and Global Culture.* London: Sage.

Robertson, Roland (2000). Globalization and the Future of 'Traditional Religion', in M.L. Stackhouse & P.J. Paris (eds.) *God and Globalization, vol. 1.* Harrisburg: Trinity Press International.

Robertson, R. and W.R. Garrett (eds.) (1991). *Religion and Global Order.* NY: Paragon House.

Scholte, J.A. (1999). *Globalisation: A Critical Introduction.* Basingstoke: Macmillan.

Scholte, J.A. (2002). *What Is Globalization? The Definitional Issue – Again.* http://www.warwick.ac.uk/fac/soc/CSGR/wpapers/wp10902.pdf.

Schreiter, R.J. (1997). *The New Catholicity: Theology between the Global and the Local.* NY: Maryknoll.

Shoghi Effendi (1928). *Baha'i Administration.* NY: Baha'i Publishing Committee.

Shoghi Effendi (1965). *Citadel of Faith: Messages to America 1947-1957.* Wilmette: Baha'i Publishing Trust.

Shoghi Effendi (1971). *Messages to the Baha'i World – 1950-1957.* Wilmette: Baha'i Publishing Trust.

Shoghi Effendi (1974). *God Passes By.* Wilmette, Ill.: Baha'i Publishing Trust.

Shoghi Effendi (1980). *The Promised Day is Come.* Wilmette, Ill.: Baha'i Publishing Trust.

Shoghi Effendi (1990). *The Advent of Divine Justice.* Wilmette, Ill.: Baha'i Publishing Trust.

Shoghi Effendi (1991). *The World Order of Bahá'u'lláh: Selected Letters.* Wilmette, Ill.: Baha'i Publishing Trust.

Smith, Peter (2000). *A Concise Encyclopedia of the Baha'i Faith.* Oxford: Oneworld.

Stackhouse, M.L. and P. Paris (eds.) (2000). *God and Globalization, vol. 1: Religion and the Powers of the Common Life.* Harrisburg: Trinity Press International.

Waterfield, Robin (trans.) (1996). *Aristotle's Physics.* Oxford: Oxford University Press.

Waters, Malcolm (1995). *Globalization.* London: Routledge.

Wilmette Institute: http://wilmetteinstitute.org/.

CHAPTER 8

Baha'i and Ahmadiyya: Globalisation and Images of Modernity

Morten Warmind

Some years ago I was at an Ahmadiyya international gathering, where I was cast in the role of 'benevolent Western scholar'. During a conversation with another participant, whom I later learned was an important person in the movement, I was asked if I knew of any religion which was as modern and international in scope and mind-set as Ahmadiyya. I was supposed, of course, to answer 'no', but instead I ventured with some hesitation to suggest that the Baha'i religion was in certain aspects somewhat similar.

That was most unwise, chiefly because my reply was more impolite than I had intended to be, since my companion knew of the Baha'i religion and did not like it. I was told in no uncertain terms about the dark pitfalls of Baha'i, a religion for world-denying mystics, and the contrasting wonders of Ahmadiyya as the rational, truly modern religion.

The reason I didn't just answer 'no' at the time, was to stress to my companion that I was an uninvolved observer who had other interests than he or the Ahmadiyya movement had. One of my interests was to see for myself how Ahmadiyya functioned in practice as a world religion, uniting people from various cultures. Like Baha'i, Ahmadiyya has a global scope and has spread throughout the globe, but it presents itself differently and has a practice which is very different from Baha'i. It is my opinion that a consideration of the similarities and differences between the two religions may inform the ongoing discussion of globalisation and Baha'i.

The similarities and differences between Baha'i and Ahmadiyya is not a new issue, they are quite often compared to each other by Christian and Muslim detractors. Actually, especially the Muslim opponents of both movements have a tendency to group them together on the basis that they are both founded by false prophets.[1] Also in more objective terms Baha'i and Ahmadiyya have several things in common. Both have an Islamic background, both came into being during the second half of the 19th century, and both are legitimated through claims of prophetic inspiration. Also, from their beginnings both had a global vision and aims of being represented all over the world. Still, they appear quite different in the way they present themselves as global movements; in particular with respect to modernity.[2]

Ahmadiyya

It is useful for this comparison to first outline the origins and history of Ahmadiyya, since those of Baha'i are covered in the introduction to this volume.

Ahmadiyya began in 1889 in Ludhiana, a village in Punjab, with a declaration by a Muslim scholar known as Mirza Ghulam Ahmad. Ahmad declared that a revelation from God had told him that he was the 'Promised One' in each religion: He was messiah for Christians and Jews, the masiodarbahmi for Zoroastrians and Krishna for the Hindus, and he was to collect mankind in one fold and to unite them in one faith (Ahmad 1980, 59). These claims are strikingly similar to the development in Baha'u'llah's claims in the 1860s (MacEoin 1989). It is stressed by the Ahmadis that Ahmad was of Persian descent, and there is certainly a Shi'ite strain in his declaration and in the millenarism which seems to have been part of the movement initially. However, to my knowledge there is no evidence of any inspiration from the Baha'is of Iran. With respect to religious life and practice, the Ahmadis refer consistently to the Quran and hadith and must be said

1 There are several web-sites devoted to this type of discussion, as a search on Google for 'Bahai and Ahmadiyya' will reveal. Each web-site springs from either one position or the other, however, so it is difficult to refer to a single one.

2 I kindly thank my colleague at the Department for the History of Religions, Professor Margit Warburg for her valuable suggestions for this article.

to be Sunnis rather than Shi'ites. They adhere to the oldest of the four Sunni law schools, the Hanafitic school. In fact, there are few doctrinal or practical differences between Ahmadiyya and Sunni Islam, and the Ahmadis present themselves as Muslims.

Like other Muslims, the Ahmadis do not believe that Jesus died on the cross but that he was delivered from the cross to go to heaven. The Ahmadis teach, however, that Jesus (Isa) was delivered from the cross and that he then went to Kashmir where he lived until he was an old man. Even his grave is pointed out. The prominent position of Jesus in Ahmadiyya is special and aroused considerable attention in the West. The special position of Ahmad as the messiah or mahdi who was to rejuvenate Islam and bring it to its perfection is, of course, the most controversial Ahmadi doctrine in the eyes of mainstream Muslims.

Mission and Expansion

It was part of Ahmad's mission that his religion, which was no other religion than true Islam, should be spread to all the world. In the beginning only a few followers joined Ahmad and made the pledge that is still the formal entry into the Ahmadiyya-movement. After some years, the movement gained momentum, and a systematic institutionalised mission, like the one which exists in most of Christendom, was started. One of the ways in which Ahmad spread his message was to compete in debate or prayer with other Muslim scholars and leading religious figures. However, representatives from other religious groups were also challenged and publicity among Westerners was deliberately sought in this way. For example, in the early 1900s Ahmad challenged the famous Christian Scottish-American prophet, John Alexander Dowie, who claimed to be (and dressed up as) a latter day Elijah. Ahmad wrote to several American newspapers that he invited Dowie to a prayer-contest, something which apparently was more common among Muslim religious leaders than Christian, for Dowie declined to take up the challenge. Finally Ahmad publicly predicted that Dowie would die miserably, which he eventually did.[3]

3 This conflict, as well as other similar debates, is treated in Adamson (1991: 256ff). Though the author claims to be impartial, his accounts are clearly very sympathetic towards Ahmad.

The point in this context is not the contest or its results, but the global nature of Ahmad's activities and his reasonably successful playing upon being mentioned in the media. Again, this demonstrates a very different world-view from his contemporary mainstream Pakistani Muslim scholars. At that time, it was certainly unusual for Muslim religious people to envision a systematic Islamic mission in the West, and Ahmadiyya missionaries were among the first to proselytise for Islam in many Western countries. For example, in 1967 Ahmadiyya erected the first mosque in Denmark, the Nusrat Jahan Mosque (Warmind 1991).

Ahmadiyya originally had its centre in Qadian in Punjab, and it is also sometimes known therefore as Qadianism. The formation of Pakistan as a Muslim state in 1947 occasioned the movement of the centre to a little town called Rabwah in Pakistan.

In 1974 the Pakistani government denounced Ahmadiyya as *kafir*, or infidels, and Ahmadis have since then been barred from making the hajj to Mecca. In 1984 anti-Ahmadiyya-proscriptions were passed in Pakistan and parts of the Ahmadiyya body of administration was moved to London, where the 5th khalif, Mirza Masroor Ahmad (elected April 2003) currently resides. Rabwah is still considered the centre of the movement, however.

Baha'i and Ahmadiyya Compared

Several similarities between Baha'i and Ahmadiyya are apparent. The global scope of both religions and their messages of world-unification, are at least superficially identical and have the same origin in a vision of perfecting a global-reaching Islam.[4]

This universalism is a common heritage, which in Europe is originally Hellenistic and can be traced in Neoplatonism, Late Judaism, Christianity and Islam. The one-world idea, which is a combination of religious and political ideas in the outset, is what one could term an inherent globalisation factor prevalent in both Ahmadiyyah and Baha'i.

Another important similarity between Ahmadiyya and Baha'i is the strategy of mission. Both initiated active mission in the West long before mainstream Islam made its entry in Europe and North America. Of course, at that time, there also existed a general obligation among

4 The Bab's global visions in the *Qayyumu'l-Asma* and later writings.

Muslims to spread their religion, but it could reasonably be regarded as dormant in the dominant versions of Islam.[5] The idea of proselytising and sending out missionaries can be seen as the practical side of a global vision. It is also remarkable that both in Baha'i and Ahmadiyya the policy is to encourage the use of the vernacular in the services and the use of translations of the sacred texts in the mission. Both have thus deliberately downplayed the Arabism of Islam, including the position of Arabic as the sacred language above all. This has undoubtedly strengthened the universalistic appeal of both Baha'i and Ahmadiyya (Warburg 1999a).

An important difference between the two is that already at the time of the Bab, Babism and later Baha'i dissociated itself from Islam, and unlike the Ahmadis, the Baha'is see themselves as adherents of an independent religion and not of a true Islam. This doctrinal difference is not arbitrary; as I shall show in the following, it is centred around the issue of the 'right' to announce a new shari'a.

The Problem of the 'Seal'

As any other prophet arising in a Muslim environment, Ahmad had to face the issue of how to legitimise his mission in the light of the famous declaration that Muhammad is the 'Seal of the prophets' (Quran 33:41). Both in Sunni and Shi'i traditions there are prevalent expectations of a prophetic renewer, the mahdi. Ahmadiyya teaches that this renewer is legitimate if he carries the seal of Muhammad. In his capacity as the seal of the prophets, Muhammad is considered by Muslims as the last of the law-giving prophets. Ahmad's position as bearer of the seal obliged him to bring back Islam to its pristine form at the time of Muhammad. In that sense, Ahmadiyya draws upon the millenaristic traditions in Islam.[6] However, Ahmad's title

5 The roughly contemporary Salafiyya-movement can of course be seen as a parallel development inside Islam. It would take some time before it became influential, however. It should also be noted that Muslim missionares were at that time active in other places of the world, notably in Africa.

6 Millenarism is still part of the movement, although it is not as important an aspect as it may once have been. With the institutionalisation of the movement, the millenaristic expectations were reinterpreted. Thus, the fact that Ahmad was eventually followed by a succession of leaders is justified by the Ahmadis with a reference to the original Khalifate.

did not allow him to establish a new religion, i.e. to establish a new shari'a.

It is worth dwelling for a moment on the difference between the way Ahmad justified his mission and how the Bab and later Baha'u'llah coped with the problem of the 'Seal of the prophets'. As discussed above, Ahmad makes clear from the beginning that his religion is no new religion: his mission represents the true, rejuvenated Islam. This is just how the Bab originally saw his mission in the *Qayyumu'l-Asma* from 1844:

> This Religion is indeed, in the sight of God, the essence of the Faith of Muhammad; haste ye then to attain the celestial Paradise and the all-highest Garden of His good-pleasure in the presence of the One True God, could ye but be patient and thankful before the evidences of the signs of God (Taherzadeh 1976: 71).

However, the Bab later (1848) broke with Islam by declaring that he was the Hidden Imam himself. The Bab now stated in his new law book, the *Bayan*, that the day of judgement for the Quran had begun with the Bab's original declaration on 22 May 1844, because Islam had then achieved its perfection (Taherzadeh 1976: 107; Nicolas 1905: 69). These statements allowed the Bab to let his *Bayan* supersede the Islamic shari'a. His break was, however, not absolute in the sense that the Bab, and in particular Baha'u'llah legitimised the Bab's mission by quranic interpretations. Thus, Baha'u'llah argued - more or less in the same vein as Ahmad - that the traditions foretold about the advent of a mahdi, a renewer of the religion. According to Baha'u'llah (1983: 237-247), several of the traditions (hadith) even alludes to the appearance of a renewer who could announce new laws, for example:

> In another passage, it is related of Hádiq, son of Muhammad, that he spoke the following: 'There shall appear a Youth from Baní-Háshim, Who will bid the people plight fealty unto Him. His Book will be a new Book, unto which He shall summon the people to pledge their faith. Stern is His Revelation unto the Arab. If ye hear about Him, hasten unto Him' (Baha'u'llah 1983: 241).

Baha'u'llah also argued that the title of 'Seal of the Prophets' is meaningfully attributed to all messengers of God, not only to Muhammad

(Buck 1995: 55-62). This would include the Bab and the prophet to follow him, i.e. Baha'u'llah himself.

It is not the place here to expound on Baha'u'llah's arguments, which in the end made it possible for him around 1873 to supersede the *Bayan* with his own Baha'i law book, the *Kitab-i-Aqdas*, which thus can be considered the Baha'i shari'a. This is in contrast to Ahmadiyya which does not build on a new shari'a - on the contrary. Ahmadiyya is rather comparable to Babism in 1844-45; both Babism at that time and Ahmadiyya insist on faithfully representing the true, pristine Islam.[7] This comparison is corroborated by the fact that both in early Babism and in Ahmadiyya the concept of jihad has a prominent position. I shall not expound on how the Bab and Baha'u'llah later re-interpreted the doctrine of jihad - reference is made to Lambden elsewhere in this book - but Baha'u'llah specifically forbade jihad in the form of holy war. To my knowledge, jihad has no, or perhaps only a small -, probably philosophical - position in Baha'i. This stands in contrast to Ahmadiyya, where jihad in the form of peaceful mission is salient and is used for this and other activities to strengthen the religion.

This fundamental doctrinal difference between Ahmadiyya and Baha'i concerning a new shari'a or not, has had in my view a profound influence on the way globalisation is coped with.

Born in the Take-off of Globalisation

It is not only an origin in Islamic revival that is shared by Ahmadiyya and Baha'i, but also the historical setting of both religious movements in the late 1800s is very similar. Both movements arose in times of political unrest or even revolution and turmoil at a time when globalisation began to make impact in nearly all parts of the world.

According to the economist Rosabeth Moss Kanter (1995), important indicators of globalisation are *simultaneity*, or the experience of the fact that things apart happen at the same time and that instant communica-

7 There is a striking similarity between Ahmadiyya and Messianic Judaism with respect to their mother creed. Both insist that a prophetic religious innovator has appeared in order to bring back the religion to its true state. In the case of Messianic Judaism the innovator is Yeshua, the prophet called Jesus by the Christians, but in all other respects Messianic Judaism insist on what could be called Orthodox Judaism (Rudolph 1991).

tion is a possibility; *bypass*, or the experience that well established channels for funds, information or power are replaced by new channels; *mobility*, or the ability to move people and goods around as one sees fit. Finally there is *pluralism*, which denotes that at least some people manoeuver in or at least acknowledge several different value-systems at the same time. In the late 19th century all these indicators of globalisation were visible in British South Asia, including the homeland of Ahmad, Punjab. It was a time of an improved infrastructure and new and much faster means of communication, where in particular the telegraph created a hitherto unknown sense of simultaneity. The colonial situation was conducive to a pluralism of values, at least for those who were colonised and forced to reconcile their own values with those of the colonisers. The political changes, industrialisation and urbanisation affecting India in the late 19th century also created new mobility and chances of bypass, at least in a relative sense. As stressed by Roland Robertson (1992: 59) this was a period when a global cultural consciousness emerged. It was a 'modern' or 'new' global awareness - even if it seems hopelessly outdated by now.[8] This historical situation is an additional globalisation factor in the rise of Ahmadiyya, just as the cultural and political environment in the Ottoman Empire where Baha'u'llah lived was influenced by ideas of modernity and internationalism (Cole 1998).

Different Global Images of Modernity

Superficially seen, Baha'is and Ahmadis present themselves rather differently. Baha'i has a modern, or rather Western global aspect compared to Ahmadiyya. It is hard to imagine a conference on Ahmadiyya and globalisation that would not be dominated by bearded males in colourful garb. At least in some ways Ahmadiyya appears to resist the modernising effects of globalisation, compared to Baha'i.[9] Baha'i on the other hand appears to have embraced modernity to such a strong degree that it could almost be called slightly old-fashioned in

8 Literary evidence for the globalisation of the late 19th century can be found in the novel 'Tour du monde en quatre-vingts jours' by the French author Jules Verne, published in Paris in 1873. The new mobility is the theme of the novel.

9 For these see, for instance, Sen McGlinn's paper in this volume.

this day and age of a postmodern disillusion of the grand narratives of modernity.

It is true that there is a good deal of Orientalism in the Western conception of both religions. Both Ahmadis and Baha'is have pictures of impressive bearded men in turbans on their walls as well as words in illegible Arabic calligraphy and a picture of a sacred building in an exotic place. A subtle difference is played out, perhaps, in the fact that the Baha'i building is relatively modern, whereas among the Ahmadis it is the Kaaba in Mecca.

If one looks to the followers of Baha'i and Ahmadiyya, respectively in the West, these similarities and differences are also apparent. The Ahmadi converts I have met describe and see themselves primarily as Muslims. They are converts to Islam through Ahmadiyya. This is obviously connected to the fact that Ahmadiyya very early had an active mission in Europe and the USA and for decades was the only type of Islam with which people in the West had any contact. But the global awareness is only relevant insofar as it can be understood in traditional - or maybe Salafiyya - Islamic terms.[10]

Converts to Baha'i are keenly aware of the global project of Baha'i and often refer to it as one of the main reasons for initially finding Baha'i attractive. Here the global awareness and the idea of unity in diversity are among the key reasons given for conversion (Warburg 1999b).

The question then becomes, why are they so very different? Or why is Ahmadiyya insisting on being Islam and continuing most of the Islamic customs, traditions and beliefs, which are denounced as premodern (or even Medieval) by most Westerners, such as the separation of men and women?

Ahmadiyya wishes all the world to share Islam, a 'value' or a 'commodity' in pretty much the same way as it was in the days of Muhammad. The changes in the doctrines and rituals are minimal and could appear to be made to fit the modern world. There is a more active role for Jesus to accommodate the Christians, and we have a messiah for the Jews, Krishna for the Hindus etc. It seems as if the Ahmadis

10 Salafiyya is an Islamic revival movement founded in the late 19th century. Its goal is to seek back to the roots of the Islamic tradition and to purge what is considered non-Islamic elements in the present beliefs and practices among Muslims.

assume that with these adjustments, Islam surely now can truly be modern and global.

For the Baha'is the goal of one world united in the world order of Baha'u'llah is similar, but still there is a different interplay of ideas in the way in which Baha'i recognises the world. Many of the Muslim ideas are discarded and new 'values' or 'commodities' are brought into play. To an outsider – and to potential converts – the global ideal has become so important for Baha'i that it seems to overshadow (or maybe rather outshine) the other religious contents. Two high-ranking Baha'i authors have, in fact, commented on the Baha'is' engagement in issues that many may find 'political':

> While most people would probably agree that this Bahá'í goal [the unification of the world] is a worthy one, many would regard it as utopian to believe that such an ideal society could ever be actually achieved. Moreover, many people feel that religion should be concerned exclusively with the inner development of the individual, and they are surprised to find a faith that places so great an emphasis on mankind's collective life, on forms of social organisation, and on the achievements of social goals (Hatcher and Martin 1989: 130).

Put very simply it could be claimed that Ahmadiyya conveys traditional Islamic values under an umbrella of globalism, whereas Baha'i appears immediately to be a fairly elaborate set of modern ideas about globality and the unification of the world, with a religious message attached. However, digging deeper into the history of both religions, it appears that a fundamental difference between them is the question of whether they follow a new shari'a or not. The Ahmadis never considered the possibility of superseding the Islamic shari'a – it would undermine the very idea of a return to a true Islam – while the Baha'is could discard the anti-modern traditions of Islam, precisely because they could build on a new shari'a formulated in a time when modernity was present.

References

Adamson, Iain (1991). *Ahmad the Guided One. A Life of The Holy Founder of The Movement To Unite All Religions*. Surrey: Islam International Publications.

Ahmad, Mirza Bashir-ud-din Mahmud (1980) *Invitation to Ahmadiyyat: being a statement of beliefs, a rationale of claims and an invitation, on behalf of the Ahmadiyya Movement for the propagation and rejuvenation of Islam*. London: Routledge & Kegan Paul.

Baha'u'llah (1983). *The Kitáb-i Íqán. The Book of Certitude*. Wilmette: Baha'i Publishing Trust.

[Baha'u'llah] (1988). Law-i-Maq'úd (Tablet of Maq'úd), in [Baha'u'llah], *Tablets of Bahá'u'lláh revealed after the Kitáb-i-Aqdas*: 159-78. Wilmette: Baha'i Publishing Trust.

Buck, Christopher (1995). *Symbol and Secret. Quran Commentary in Baháulláh's Kitáb-i Iqán*, Los Angeles: Kalimat, 1995.

Cole, Juan R.I. (1998). *Modernity and the Millennium: The Genesis of the Baha'i Faith in the Nineteenth-Century Middle East*. New York: Columbia University Press.

Hatcher, William S. and J. Douglas Martin (1989). *The Baha'i Faith: The Emerging Global Religion*. San Francisco: Harper and Row.

Kanter, Rosabeth Moss (1995). *World Class: Thriving Locally in the Global Economy*. New York: Simon and Schuster.

Mac Eoin, D. (1989). Divisions and Authority Claims in Babism (1850-1866), *Studia Iranica*, vol. 18: 93-129.

Nicolas, A.-L.-M. (trans.) (1905). *Le Béyân Arabe. Le Livre Sacré du Bâbysme de Séyyèd Ali Mohammed dit le Bâb*. Paris: Ernest Leroux.

Robertson, Roland (1992). *Globalization. Social Theory and Global Culture*. London: Sage.

Rudolf, David (1991). *Messianic Judaism: Returning to the Religion of Yeshua*. Annapolis: Shulchan Adonai.

Taherzadeh, Habib (ed., trans.) (1976). *Selections from the Writings of the Báb*. Haifa: Baha'i World Centre.

Warburg, Margit (1999a). New Age og gamle dage. Religion og globalisering i dag og i hellenistisk-romersk tid. In Per Bilde and Mikael Rothstein (eds.), *Nye religioner i hellenistisk-romersk tid og i dag*. Aarhus: Aarhus University Press: 39-52.

Warburg, Margit (1999b). Baha'i: A Religious Approach to Globalization, *Social Compass*, vol. 46: 47-56.

Warmind, Morten (1991). Ahmadiyya-Islam, in Tim Jensen (ed.), *Minoritetsreligioner i Danmark – religionssociologisk set.* Copenhagen: Columbus: 41-65.

CHAPTER 9

The Dual Global Field: A Model for Transnational Religions and Globalisation[1]

Margit Warburg

Globalisation is a description of the fact that in these years we are witnessing a rapid internationalisation of the economy aided by innovations and growth in international electronic communications. Globalisation has become a hot topic both inside and outside academia during the last two decades or so.[2] It is deplorable, however that occasionally the topic has become so hot that globalisation is used as a wizard term which explains everything - and hence nothing of scholarly interest.

Despite the popularity and often too inclusive use of the term globalisation I do not want to throw out the baby with the bath water. There is an abundance of empirical facts pointing to the fact that in these years the world experiences a historically unique *increase of scale,* implying an unprecedented global interdependency among peoples and nations (Bergesen 1980; Ferguson 1992; Featherstone and Lash 1995; Scholte

1 This paper is based on my book, *Citizens of the World. A History and Sociology of the Baha'is from a Globalisation Perspective.* Leiden: E.J. Brill (forthcoming).

2 Kanter and Pittinski (1996) reported that the number of articles containing the word globalisation in the title had increased from three to more than a hundred *per year* in the period 1984-1994. In 1998 I surveyed three common sociological data bases (*International Bibliography of the Social Sciences, Sociofile,* and *Social Science Citation Index*) and found that the number of works indexed with the key word 'globalisation' exceeded 1100 in one data base alone (IBSS). Since 1995, the number of works had trebled (Social Science Citation Index).

1996). I agree with Lorne Dawson (1997) that this historical change is 'a qualitatively new state of affairs' which warrants the use of the term globalisation. Earlier historical periods have also been characterised by an increase of scale and therefore have some structural similarity to globalisation. The integration of the cultures around the Mediterranean during the Roman Empire is such a parallel (Tiryakian 1992; Pieterse 1995; Warburg 1999a). However, what distinguishes globalisation from, say, the age of the Roman empire is that cross-cultural interaction between societies as well as between individuals now takes place *on a global scale* and with an unparalleled intensity and simultaneity.[3]

There has been some debate among scholars about the onset of globalisation; however, there seems to be good arguments for tracing the take-off of globalisation back to the heyday of Western imperialism, from around 1870 and well into the twentieth century (Robertson 1992: 60). In this period all parts of the world began to feel the impact of the international economy and for the first time in history instant long-distance communication (telegraph, radio) between people became possible.[4] For the first time in history the major part of the globe came under the hegemony (or at least the dominating influence) of *one* civilisation, that of the West.

3 Rosabeth Moss Kanter (1995: 41-48) emphasises simultaneity as one of four key characteristics of globalisation; the other three being mobility, bypass and pluralism.

4 Instead of emphasising the sharply growing internationalisation of the world economy and the technological innovations characteristic of the period, Robertson lists a number of changes and cultural innovations which he finds are indicative of this take-off phase (and probably more in vein with his declared cultural approach to globalisation): 'Early thematization of 'the problem of modernity.'... The first 'international novels.' Rise of ecumenical movement. Development of global competitions – for example the Olympics and Nobel prizes. Implementation of world time and near-global adoption of Gregorian calendar.' (Robertson 1992: 59). The examples may be illustrative, although some of them are vaguely defined e.g. what is an 'international novel'?. Although some of the examples appear to be well-chosen, the entire list stands, however, as a postulate in the absence of any analytical ties to the major political, historical and technological trends of the period. Despite this criticism I basically agree with Robertson's choice of phases of the historical path of globalisation for the reasons I have given in the text. See Robertson, (1992: 57-60).

In cultural terms globalisation means that nation states, local communities, and individuals around the globe are confronted with a situation of strongly increased, world-wide *relativisation*, to use the term coined by the sociologists of religion, Roland Robertson and JoAnn Chirico (1985). Relativisation means that fundamental values and images are contrasted by a complex of different values and images, and that they - more or less explicitly - are interpreted, debated and acted upon in this context.[5] No community and no individuals can today escape the fact that people are increasingly encountering 'the others' who hold alternative attitudes towards fundamental issues of society and different ways of doing things. Some of these alternatives are attractive, some are repulsive, but they are certainly of growing concern. Since religion deals with fundamental cultural values and images it is clear why Robertson and Chirico centred their discussion around processes of relativisation to account for the resurgence of religion in the modern world (Robertson and Chirico, 1985).

Contrary to popular belief, globalisation theories do not imply simple cultural homogenisation like the earlier 'westernisation' or 'modernisation' theories.[6] In contrast, globalisation may result in cultural *homogenisation* as well as *heterogenisation* through 'an increasingly globe-wide discourse of locality, community, home and the like', to use Roland Robertson's expression (Robertson, 1995: 31).

Religion and Globalisation

Religious organisations all over the world are participating in and affected by globalisation. Peter Beyer (1994: 70-96) has argued that in the face of the challenges of globalisation religious communities may follow one of two options if they wish to continue performing a public role: The liberal or the conservative option. In brief, the liberal option is to embrace particular aspects of the globalisation process, accept pluralism as a consequence of globalisation and hold a positive,

5 I wish to emphasise that relativisation should not be thought of as being confined to mind and speech - it influences the social actor in all respects.

6 The popular 'myth' about 'global cultural homogeneity' as a consequence of globalisation is discussed by Ferguson (1992: 79-82). See also Simpson (1991: 6).

ecumenical attitude towards other religions. The conservative option implies that relativisation and pluralism are seen as negative and must be counteracted by insisting that 'the others' are models of evil and negations of one's own moral codes. Either option must be pursued in the public, especially political, arena, because detachment from this arena will lead to loss of influence on public affairs (Beyer 1994: 93). This may be acceptable to some religious groups, such as Old Order Amish, but certainly not to most religious organisations. As discussed by Rudolph (1997b: 243-261) religious groups are indeed part of civil society, and they are both visible and influential.

Elsewhere I have discussed Baha'i views on and interaction with civil society by applying Peter Beyer's theoretical perspective of liberal versus conservative religious options (Warburg 1999b), and I shall not pursue this theme further here. Instead, I have constructed a model for analysing transnational religious organisations as actors in globalisation. It leans on thoughts conveyed, in particular, by Roland Robertson. The model is called the dual global field, and it will be exemplified with material from my study of the Baha'i religion.

Roland Robertson's Approach to the Study of Globalisation and Religion

Among the students of globalisation, in particular the sociologist of religion Roland Robertson is a significant contributor to the understanding of religion and globalisation.

In a seminal paper he and JoAnn Chirico proposed a world system model to account for the resurgence of religion in the modern world (Robertson and Chirico 1985). Their model was more fully developed in Robertson's monograph from 1992, *Globalization. Social Theory and Global Culture*, and his model of 'the global field' is the basis of my own approach to the study of transnational minority religions in a globalisation perspective, within the framework of the dual global field model.

In their development of what they call the 'Trajectories of Emergence of Humanity' Robertson and Chirico considered *individuals* and *national societies* as the two primary social actors in the globalisation process.[7] This classical sociological issue of individuals versus national society

7 Robertson uses 'individuals' and 'self/selves' interchangeably in his works. I have chosen to use 'individuals', because this term best covers the social actor.

was then extended by including two additional, empirically based constituents of the world, the *world system of societies* and *humankind*. The world system of societies is the system of international diplomacy and its institutions such as the United Nations and other supra-national political bodies. Humankind is the non-institutionalised assembly of close to six thousand million human inhabitants of the earth.

Robertson maintains that in a globalisation perspective these two global entities - world system of societies and humankind - have become of increasing significance for how both individuals and national societies conceive the world. Robertson argues that the outcome of globalisation has been that the identity of individuals is no longer exclusively tied to the national society. They increasingly tend to draw cultural inspiration from other societies or identify themselves with humankind as a universal concept. We may even envisage that a transnational civil society is coming into existence, as argued by Rudolph (1997a). Likewise, in a globalised world the national societies are both politically and with respect to cultural identity heavily related to other national societies and to the world system of societies, i.e. the United Nations and other supra-national political bodies.

Together, individuals, national societies, world system of societies, and humankind constitute a square model with four corners or reference points, as shown on Figure 1.[8] The top section of the model with national societies and world system of societies represents a predominantly societal level, while the bottom section with individuals and humankind represents a humanistic level. The left side symbolises the relation between individuals and national society. The right side stands for the relation between the world system of societies and humankind - a relation which Robertson denotes '*Realpolitik*-humanity

8 The model is that given by Robertson (1992: 27), except that I have modified it on two points: 'Individuals' are used instead of 'selves', cf. note 7 above, and the relativisations involving humankind are unidirectional, from one of the other three corners *to* humankind, but not from it. My reason for this is that only three of the four reference points (individuals, national societies, and world system of societies) represent social *actors* in the true sense of this concept, while the fourth reference point, humankind, is not a social actor, because it is non-institutionalised. In fact, Robertson and Chirico (1985) do consider in a particular sentence whether they should have used one-way or two-way arrows, but although the implications of this choice are far from trivial they are left untouched.

Figure 1. *The global field*

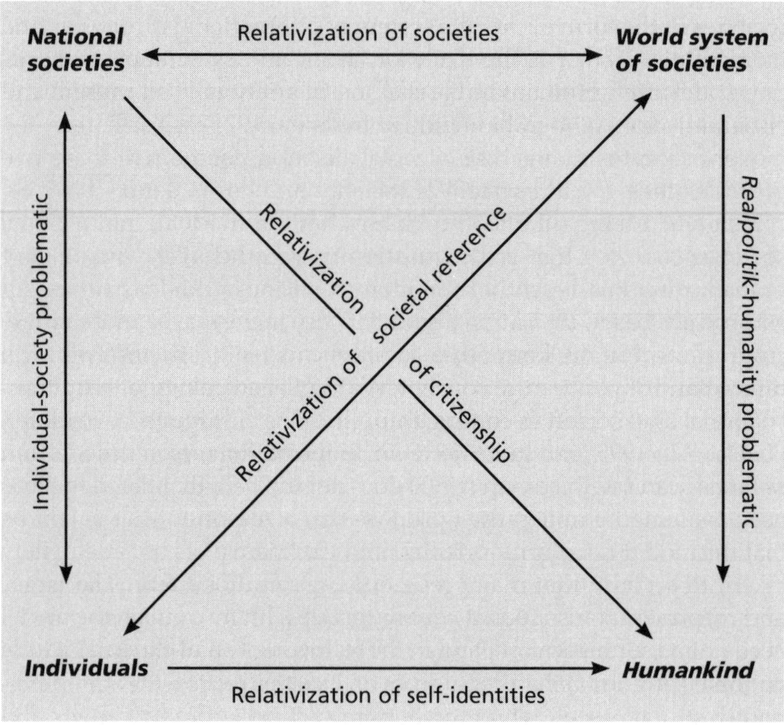

problematic'.[9] These two vertical relations are connected with four processes of relativisation (the horizontal and slanting arrows).

Robertson's global field model is a model of the *dynamics of relativisations* between four major constituents of a globalised world; it is not a model of the *historical path* of globalisation. The diacronic aspect of the model is instead that the contents of the four constituents are historical and change with time; therefore, the relativisations between

9 Robertson does not expound on this term, but he probably wishes to convey the tension in international politics between classic nation-state centred 'realism' and newer 'idealistic' politics (spurred by Western nations in particular) that attempts to reconcile realism with political goals that at the least nominally place the interests of humankind higher than those of the individual states.

'individuals', 'national societies', 'world system of societies', and 'humankind' must also change with time. For example, world system of societies in the form of the UN system is different, more complex and more influential than its predecessor, the League of Nations. Nor does the model attempt to be the basis of a *total* analysis of all present and potential actors of a global field (Robertson 1992: 25-26). Rather, the model facilitates an analysis of how the relativisations may vary in *particular* cases (Robertson 1992: 26).

I should further like to emphasise that the model is not a *theory* of globalisation - hence the question of whether it is true or false needs not be posed - but it should be seen for precisely what it is: An empirically based *model*. As a model it can, however, be more or less *applicable* and to my knowledge its applicability to specific empirical topics has not yet been seriously tested in the sociology of religion.

The lack of interest in empirical applications of Robertson's model is puzzling. In 1995 Jonathan Friedman reviewed Robertson's model and as far as I can see Friedman (1995) does not indicate that the model has been evaluated empirically. I propose that a reason for this might be that the model is majority-oriented and therefore does not adequately take into account that many religious organisations, even the larger ones, represent transnational *minority* groups. In my opinion the model needs some sophistication, and in the following I shall expound a little on this, using the Baha'i religion as an example.

Development of the Dual Global Field

The notion of an 'imagined community' was coined in 1983 by Benedict Anderson (1991) in his analysis of nation states and nationalism. The imagined community *par excellence* is the nation state; however, the concept can be meaningfully extended to communities whose members are residents of many *different* countries but have a feeling of commonness, of sharing a history and a destiny with other members world-wide without having a common national background. They are what I shall call *transnational imagined communities*. Immediately, a number of religious groups leaps to mind: Mormons, Jehovah's Witnesses, Soka Gakkai, and Baha'is to take some of those minority religions which are represented in many countries around the world. In fact, religious groups are among the oldest of the transnational communities (Rudolph 1997a: 1).

Qua their nationality, members of transnational imagined communities are also members of the imagined community of the nation state (or national society in Robertson's terms). This means that in some situations they think and act as national citizens, in other situations as members of the transnational imagined community. This situation of thinking and acting in two *complimentary* modes is characteristic of many minorities and other social sub-groups with a distinct identity. It is interesting that Bryan Turner has specifically noted that the situation of belonging to two different imagined communities may actually become more common with globalisation:

> Globalization brings into question the autonomy and sovereignty of nation-states, and thereby relativizes conventional conceptions and conditions of citizenship participation and motivation. Robertson has shown how the emergence of human rights concerns is a feature of the globalization of citizenship concepts. Recent debates about the instability of the polity through the alienation of social actors have taken the nation-state as their focus, but little research exists about the political commitments of social actors who are also (or primarily) players within a global political framework. If this represents a major shift away from primary loyalties to nation, or state, or party, what will be the nature of political commitment within a global context? How will local and global loyalties be reconciled or combined? (Turner 1992: 317).

In the histories of national minorities the questions posed by Turner have been answered over and over. For the Baha'is loyalty to the nation state is a religious duty: 'In every country where any of this people (i.e. the Baha'is) reside, they must behave towards the government of that country with loyalty, honesty and truthfulness' (Baha'u'llah 1995: 22-23). However, one thing is loyalty, another is commitment, and Turner is probably right in worrying about the possible connection between globalisation and the weakening of the national political fabric.

The transnational imagined community of the five million Baha'is world-wide can be seen as a smaller replica of Robertson's 'global field', but now within a Baha'i context: The 'national Baha'i community', the 'international Baha'i organisations', and 'Baha'is of the World' are the three reference points of the model; the fourth being the individuals.[10]

10 An example of an international Baha'i organisation is the New York based

Figure 2. *The (Baha'i) dual global field*

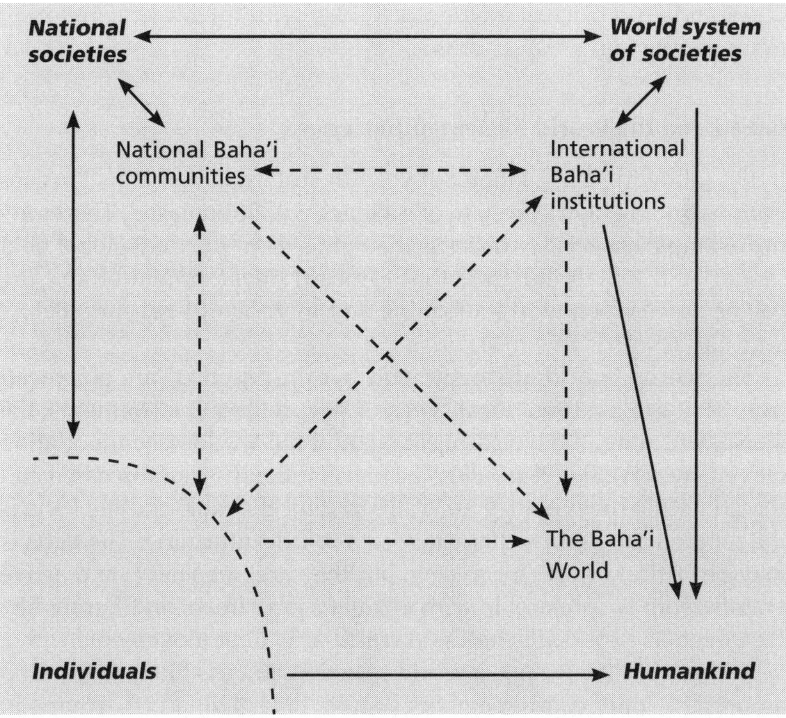

The dual global field model (Figure 2) is adapted to account for Baha'i, but it can be used to describe the relations within most transnational religious minority groups: The outer square is the general global field taken from Robertson, the inner square is the Baha'i global field. These two global fields share the *individuals* who in their relativisations have the ability to switch between the general mode and the Baha'i mode. The two global fields are further connected by processes of *interactions* at the societal level (the two short double arrows in the top of the model) involving the different Baha'i organisations. Finally, an arrow

Baha'i International Community and its branch offices. This organisation has direct reference to the supreme Baha'i leadership, the Universal House of Justice, which is seated in the Baha'i World Centre in Haifa.

points from the international Baha'i organisations to humankind to indicate that the Baha'i leadership addresses humankind with messages and co-ordinates mission activities with a view of converting more people to the Baha'i cause.

Baha'i and the World System of Societies

In the following the relation between the international Baha'i organisations and the world system of societies will be analysed. Therefore, my example especially concerns the *right* side of the dual global field model, and I shall illustrate the historical development of and the balancing between world-affirming and more world-rejecting Baha'i attitudes towards this relation.

The words 'world-affirming' and 'world-rejecting' are borrowed from Roy Wallis' three ideal types of new religious movements, the world-affirming, the world-rejecting, and the world-accommodating movements (Wallis 1984: 9-39). The Baha'i religion is not discussed and placed within the typology by Wallis, but for the rank-and-file Baha'is the religion can best be characterised as world-affirming. The Baha'is may be critical of present society, but they are not zealots and active membership is compatible with ordinary job careers and family life. However, as Roy Wallis notes, in world-affirming movements with a *world-transforming mission* a world-rejecting ethos is likely to develop among the inner cadre members (Wallis 1984: 126). Furthermore, in the case of Baha'i a world-rejecting ethos is in doctrinal compliance with its origin in millenarian Shi'ism, and therefore the religion has the potential of harbouring both world-affirming and world-rejecting attitudes among its adherents.

The Baha'i leadership has regularly commented on developments in the world situation, having a clear notion of the functioning of the international political system. They have done so in *internal* messages addressed to the *national Baha'i communities* and to the *individual Baha'is*. In the last decades the present supreme body of the Baha'i organisation, the Universal House of Justice, has also resumed and intensified the tradition of addressing the public (that is *humankind*) and the governments of the world (that is *world system of societies)* with statements on the Baha'i views of the world order.

The perspective in these messages has oscillated between prevalence of world-rejecting attitudes and of world-affirming attitudes towards civil society - much in response to the general political development in the world. It will be shown that when world-rejecting attitudes were prevalent, the Baha'i leadership turned away from the world system of societies and put this relation on ice. Conversely, when the world-affirming attitudes were dominating, the Baha'is showed a high profile of activism in international *fora* - after World War II, especially within the UN system.

The Historical Development of the Baha'i Global Field

The historical development of the Baha'i religion since its emergence from the messianic Babi movement in nineteenth century Iran can be depicted as a gradual evolution and expansion of the *inner square* of the dual global field model. Ultimately, the goal of the religion is that all of humanity becomes Baha'is. In the model this would mean that the inner square expands until it merges with the outer square in a future world civilisation, called the Most Great Peace.

Babism was a religiously motivated movement *within* a Shi'ite context and worldview, and its emergence had no *direct* connection with globalisation. This changed during the 1860s when one of the Babi leaders, Baha'u'llah, declared that he was a new prophet who should fulfil the promises of the Babi movement. Baha'u'llah was followed by the majority far of the Babis who now began to denote themselves Baha'is. In his capacity of God's manifestation on earth Baha'u'llah began to write letters and statements to various heads of state, in which he explained his own mission and praised or denounced their rule. The first of these letters, the *Suriy-i-Muluk* (Chapter of the Kings) from 1867, was addressed to the world's heads of state collectively, and it was the first Baha'i document relating to the world system of societies (Taherzadeh 1977: 301-36; Cole 1992: 4-10).

World-Rejecting and World-Affirming Attitudes in Baha'i in Relation to World System of Societies

Baha'u'llah's messages to the kings were held in an authoritative voice and were a mixture of general counsels concerning good statesmanship and predictions of chaos and tribulations. The collapse and even the approaching destruction of the world are commonly referred to in several of Baha'u'llah's tablets (Taherzadeh 1977: 310). However, in Baha'u'llah's words, following the 'universal convulsion' a glorious future awaits, and 'the sun of justice will rise from the horizon of the unseen realm' (Taherzadeh 1977: 310). These millenarian themes of destruction and a golden future are a heritage from Babism and continued in Baha'i doctrines.

Baha'u'llah's son and successor, Abdu'l-Baha, repeatedly referred to Baha'u'llah's letters to the kings in speeches given to the public during his extensive travels to the West before World War I (Abdu'l-Baha 1982; Abdu'l-Baha 1995). Abdu'l-Baha's style was, however, less one of doomsday, sulphur and brimstone, and more of a plea for letting humanistic ideals shape the world order. For example, in a short speech on the 5th of November 1912 in Cincinnati, Ohio, Abdu'l-Baha addressed 'the people of Cincinnati and America generally' and ascribed to the United States a pioneering role as 'worthy of raising the flag of brotherhood and international agreement' (Abdu'l-Baha 1982: 388-89). The paragraph continues:

> When this is done, the rest of the world will accept. All nations will join in adopting the teachings of Bahá'u'lláh revealed more than fifty years ago. In His Epistles He asked the parliaments of the world to send their wisest and best men to an international world conference which should decide all questions between the peoples and establish universal peace. This would be the highest court of appeal, and the parliament of man so long dreamed of by poets and idealists would be realized. Its accomplishment would be more far-reaching than the Hague tribunal. (Abdu'l-Baha 1982: 389).

Here, Abdu'l-Baha clearly expressed his generally positive attitude towards the world system of societies, i.e. a world-affirming attitude. This high public Baha'i profile in addressing humankind and the world system of societies was also backed up by formal relations with the international diplomatic system. As early as in 1925 the International Baha'i Bureau was established in Geneva – the city of the League of Nations. It soon acquired some official status vis-à-vis the League of Nations, and attendance at the public sessions of the League was one of the activities of the bureau (Bishop 1937).

A significant change in the official Baha'i attitude towards political involvement can be dated to around 1936 when the Baha'i leader Shoghi

Effendi adopted what was called a policy of 'fallowing'. This meant 'leaving the public field uncultivated by a general propaganda' to await better times (Bishop 1939). Witnessing the rapidly deteriorating world affairs in 1936, Shoghi Effendi had largely pessimistic expectations when he commented in detail on events taking place in the world system of societies, such as the withdrawal of Germany and Japan from the League of Nations (Shoghi Effendi 1991: 188-94). The world-rejecting aspect was in fact pronounced in Shoghi Effendi's characterisation of world politics and the futility of engaging with it:

> What we Bahá'ís must face is the fact that society is disintegrating so rapidly that moral issues which were clear a half century ago are now hopelessly confused and, what is more, thoroughly mixed up with battling political interests. That is why Bahá'ís must turn all their forces into the channel of building up the Bahá'í Cause and its administration. They can neither change nor help the world in any other way at present. If they become involved in the issues the governments of the world are struggling over, they will be lost. (Shoghi Effendi 1976: 31-32).

Abdu'l-Baha's and Shoghi Effendi's somewhat different attitudes towards political involvement in world affairs illustrate how the original millenarian motif in Baha'i had come to shift between world-affirming views of the future society and a world-rejecting concern about the downfall of the present world order. Thus, from 1936 to Shoghi Effendi's death in 1957 the Baha'i religion is an example of how a world-*rejecting* ethos had developed among the inner cadre members of an otherwise world-affirming movement. I cannot go into details here, but it appears that Shoghi Effendi's world-rejecting attitudes were not shared fully by many common Baha'is who maintained a more world-affirming attitude.[11] This is in accordance with Wallis' observation mentioned before.

11 For example, after the outbreak of World War II Shoghi Effendi issued a statement which asked the Baha'is not to assign blame or take sides, even indirectly, in what in internal Baha'i language was referred to as 'the present conflict'. This statement followed the world-rejecting line from 1936, but it caused considerable dissatisfaction among some of the Vancouver Baha'is who could not identify with the official Baha'i position (van den Hoonaard 1996: 259-64).

After World War II the relations with the world system of societies - now represented by the United Nations - were resumed at the organisational level (Smith 1987: 149). The Baha'i International Community was formed in 1948 and it was recognised by the United Nations Economic and Social Council (ECOSOC) as a Non-Governmental Organisation with consultative status in 1970 (Universal House of Justice 1986). This gave the Baha'i International Community a strengthened platform for interaction with the world system of societies, and the Baha'is participated in a considerable number of UN events through the 1970s and 1980s. The Baha'is have been interested in virtually all UN-based activities, in particular questions concerning human rights and the advancement of women.[12]

When studying the internal messages from the Universal House of Justice to the Baha'is of the world there are indications of a gradual move towards a more world-affirming attitude from the late 1970s and onwards. In 1983, for example, the Baha'is were encouraged to give service to what was called 'voluntary non-sectarian organizations' (Universal House of Justice 1996: 611-12). This indicated a break with the previous *de facto* policy of discouraging Baha'is from engaging in non-Baha'i organisations. Later, the Universal House of Justice noted an increasing call upon the Baha'is 'to participate with others in a range of projects associated with governments or with non-governmental organizations' (Universal House of Justice 1992: 99). This is quite far from Shoghi Effendi's view cited above that if Baha'is 'become involved in the issues the governments of the world are struggling over, they will be lost.'

From the mid-1980s the Universal House of Justice also began a more activist policy of addressing governments and the United Nations system in a series of statements on issues of global significance. The latest of these statements is *Turning Point For All Nations* (1995) which was issued on the occasion of the 50th Anniversary of the United Nations in 1995. This document presents a deeply critical review of current world affairs, and it contains a number of specific recommendations for strengthening the UN system. There is no doubt that during the 1990s the Baha'i leadership has decided that the Baha'i

12 In the period 1979-1983, the Baha'i International Community presented 44 statements, reports and other publications to the United Nations. 22 of these addressed human rights, inclusive racial discrimination issues, and nine addressed the advancement of women (de Araujo 1986).

community should be an actor in world affairs, thus adopting a clearly world-affirming attitude.

A Broader Perspective

The Baha'i message of 'world citizenship' and in particular their concern for human rights is characteristic. As Bryan Turner has noted, following Robertson, the emergence of human rights concerns is a feature of the globalisation of citizenship concepts (Turner 1992: 317). These concerns imply that citizens are no more solely the subjects of the state, but that citizens of all the states of the world are endowed with certain rights ranking above the laws and governmental practices of the state they belong to. So, when the Baha'is stress concern for human rights they invariably advocate the formation of a transnational civil society, based on pluralistic principles.

The issue of human rights goes beyond that of a transnational civil society, however. Historically, the modern concept of human rights is linked to the discussions of natural law of the seventeenth and eighteenth centuries, and it was manifested politically in the American Declaration of Independence from 1776 and the French Declaration of Human Rights from 1789. Human rights are therefore not just a set of articles in an international convention which is binding for all states that have ratified it; human rights are ideals that have developed a kind of higher moral status.

James Spickard (1999) observes that today human rights are venerated by both citizens and governments as what he calls 'sacred ideals' prior and superior to ordinary legal and social rules. I would not go as far as Spickard does when he suggests that 'human rights beliefs are essentially religious', but I agree with him that because human rights emphasise the given rights of the individual before the rights of the state, they are bound to collide with the world-view of, for instance, many right-wing Protestants or followers of traditional Islam. Thus, within their logic traditional Muslims argue that in an Islamic state any acceptance of such a human-centred concept of universal human rights would be a denial of the religious supremacy of Allah.[13] This

13 A parallel argument is used by certain right-wing Protestants who attack the concept of human rights because it places the individual human being and not God at the centre.

conflict of world-views has surfaced on many occasions when members of some Muslim groups have attacked the idea of universal human rights for the very reason that they are not based on the Quran. Such groups clearly represent an example of Beyer's conservative option which denies equality with 'the other' and may ultimately lead to a disastrous tribalisation of world society.

Baha'i is one out of many transnational religious organisations that are players on the international field wishing to interact with the world system of societies. Apart from Baha'i, Unification Church, Soka Gakkai, the Mormons, and the Roman Catholic Church are obvious examples. In fact, transnational religious organisations are prominent among the more than five hundred transnational non-governmental organisations (NGOs) which have a consultative status at the UN system.[14]

The ever-changing relationship between the inner global field and the outer, general global field presents leaders and followers of religious organisations with both threats and opportunities. As discussed above, the issue of human rights is an example of such a challenge. For those religious organisations that accept pluralism - at least nominally - the UN system offers an interesting platform, because the UN system *officially* assigns the NGOs a crucial role complimentary to the role of the nation states. This was expressed by the secretary general in connection with the series of world summits[15] and undoubtedly strengthens the influence of these religious organisations on world society, because they obtain international political experience and can by-pass state monopolies with considerable effect.

14 United Nations (1995). Other religious NGOs than Baha'i International Community are for example: Baptist World Alliance, Brahma Kumaris World Spiritual University, a considerable number of Catholic organisations, Conference of European Churches, Greek Orthodox Archdiocese, Lutheran World Federation, Muslim World League, The Salvation Army, Soka Gakkai International, United Nations of Yoga, World Jewish Congress, World Muslim Congress.

15 The significance of the NGOs was emphasised again and again in the preface and the introduction of the concluding report of the series of world summits (United Nations 1997).

Figure 3. *The dual global field*

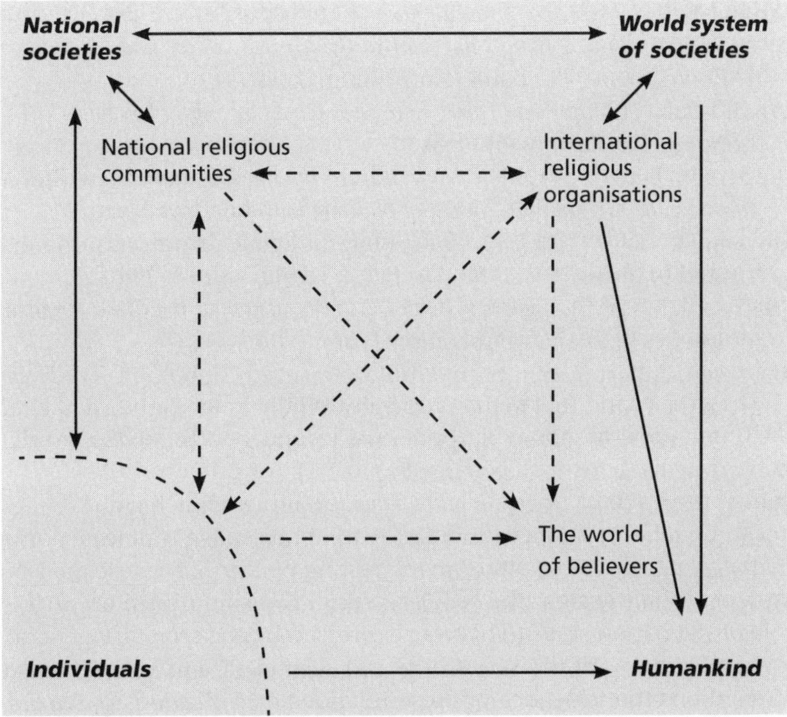

Transnational religious organisations have in common that all four corners of their inner global field exist, i.e. the individuals, the national religious communities, the international religious organisations, and the world of believers (Figure 3). The actions of both leadership and followers of transnational religious organisations and their interactions with other types of social actors can be analysed within the frame of the dual global field model presented here. I have demonstrated this using the historical changes in the interactions between the Baha'i organisation and the world system of societies, because what takes place on this international political arena is a particular manifestation of globalisation and of growing importance for religious organisations that wish to influence the course of the world.

References

Abdu'l-Baha (1982). *The Promulgation of Universal Peace. Talks Delivered by 'Abdu'l-Bahá during His Visit to the United States and Canada in 1912.* Wilmette, Ill.: Baha'i Publishing Trust.

Abdu'l-Baha (1995). *Paris Talks. Addresses Given by 'Abdu'l-Bahá in 1911.* London: The Cromwell Press.

Anderson, Benedict (1991, 2nd rev. edn.). *Imagined Communities. Reflections on the Origin and Spread of Nationalism.* London: Verso.

de Araujo, Victor (1986). The Baha'i International Community and the United Nations 1979-1983, *The Baha'i World*, vol. 18: 396-413.

[Baha'u'llah] (1995). *Tablets of Bahá'u'lláh revealed after the Kitáb-i-Aqdas.* Wilmette, Ill.: Baha'i Publishing Trust.

Bergesen, Albert (1980). From Utilitarianism to Globology: The Shift from the Individual to the World as a Whole as the Primordial Unit of Analysis, in Albert Bergesen (ed.) *Studies of the Modern World-System.* New York: Academic Press: 1-12.

Beyer, Peter (1994). *Religion and Globalization.* London: Sage.

Bishop, Helen (1937). Geneva Scans the European Community, *The Baha'i World*, vol. 6: 130-35.

Bishop, Helen (1939). Geneva Scans the European Community, *The Baha'i World*, vol. 7: 108-13.

Cole, Juan R. I. (1992) 'Iranian Millenarianism and Democratic Thought in the 19th Century', *International Journal of Middle East Studies*, vol. 24: 1-26.

Dawson, Lorne L. (1997). The Cultural Significance of New Religious Movements and Globalization: A Theoretical Prolegomenon. Presented at International Society for the Sociology of Religion Conference, Toulouse, France, July 10.

Featherstone, Mike and Scott Lash (1995). Globalization, Modernity and the Spatialization of Social Theory: An Introduction, in Mike Featherstone, Scott Lash, and Roland Robertson (eds.), *Global Modernities.* London: Sage: 1-24.

Ferguson, Marjorie (1992). The Mythology about Globalization, *European Journal of Communication*, vol. 7: 69-93.

Friedman, Jonathan (1995). Global System, Globalization and the Parameters of Modernity, in Mike Featherstone, Scott Lash, and Roland Robertson (eds.), *Global Modernities*, London: Sage: 69-90.

Hoonaard, Will C. van den (1996). *The Origins of the Baha'i Community of Canada, 1898-1948*. Waterloo: Wilfrid Laurier University Press.

Kanter, Rosabeth Moss (1995). *World Class. Thriving Locally in the Global Economy*. New York: Simon and Schuster.

Kanter, Rosabeth Moss and Todd L. Pittinsky (1996). Globalization: New worlds for social inquiry, *Berkeley Journal of Sociology*, vol. 40: 1-20.

Pieterse, Jan Nederveen (1995). Globalization as Hybridization, in Mike Featherstone, Scott Lash, and Roland Robertson (eds.), *Global Modernities*. London: Sage: 45-68.

Robertson, Roland and JoAnn Chirico (1985). Humanity, Globalization, and Worldwide Religious Resurgence: A Theoretical Exploration, *Sociological Analysis*, vol. 46: 219-42.

Robertson, Roland (1992). *Globalization. Social Theory and Global Culture*. London: Sage.

Robertson, Roland (1995). Glocalization: Time-space and homogeneity-heterogeneity, in Mike Featherstone, Scott Lash, and Roland Robertson (eds.) *Global Modernities*. London: Sage: 25-44.

Rudolph, Susanne Hoeber (1997a). Introduction: Religion, States, and Transnational Civil Society, in Susanne Hoeber Rudolph and James Piscatori (eds.) *Transnational Religion and Fading States*. Boulder: Westview Press: 1-24.

Rudolph, Susanne Hoeber (1997b). Dehomogenizing Religious Formations, in Susanne Hoeber Rudolph and James Piscatori (eds.) *Transnational Religion and Fading States*. Boulder: Westview Press: 243-61.

Scholte, Jan Aart (1996). Beyond the Buzzword: Towards a Critical Theory of Globalization, in Eleonore Kofman and Gillian Youngs (eds.) *Globalization: Theory and Practice*. New York: Pinter: 41-57.

[Shoghi Effendi] (1976). *Principles of Baha'i Administration. A Compilation*. London: Baha'i Publishing Trust.

Shoghi Effendi (1991). *The World Order of Bahá'u'lláh. Selected Letters*. Wilmette: Baha'i Publishing Trust.

Simpson, John H. (1991). Globalization and Religion. Themes and Prospects, in Roland Robertson and William R. Garrett (eds.) *Religion and Global Order. Religion and the Political Order*, vol. IV. New York: Paragon House Publishers: 1-17.

Smith, Peter (1987). *The Babi and Baha'i Religions. From Messianic Shi'ism to a World Religion*. Cambridge: Cambridge University Press and George Ronald.

Spickard, James V. (1999). Human Rights, Religious Conflict, and Globalization. Ultimate Values in a New World Order, *MOST. Journal of Multicultural Societies*, vol. 1. http://www.unesco.org/most/vl1n1spi.htm, 21 June 2000.

Taherzadeh, Adib (1977). *The Revelation of Bahá'u'lláh.* Adrianople 1863-68. Oxford: George Ronald.

Tiryakian, Edward A. (1992). From Modernization to Globalization, *Journal for the Scientific Study of Religion*, vol. 31: 304-10.

Turner, Bryan S. (1992). The Concept of 'The World' in Sociology: A Commentary on Roland Robertson's Theory of Globalization, *Journal for the Scientific Study of Religion*, vol. 31: 311-18.

Turning Point for All Nations. A Statement of Baha'i International Community on the Occasion of the 50th Anniversary of the United Nations (1995). New York: Baha'i International Community.

United Nations (1995). *Directory of Non-Governmental Organizations Associated with the Department of Public Information.* New York: United Nations Department of Public Information.

United Nations (1997). *The World Conferences. Developing Priorities for the 21st Century*, New York: United Nations Department of Public Information.

[Universal House of Justice] (1986). The Baha'i Faith and the United Nations, 1. Summary of the Years 1947-1979, *The Baha'i World*, vol. 18: 393-95.

Universal House of Justice (1992). *A Wider Horizon. Selected Messages of the Universal House of Justice 1983-1992.* Riviera Beach, FL.: Palabra Publications.

[Universal House of Justice] (1996). *Messages from the Universal House of Justice 1963-1986. The Third Epoch of the Formative Age.* Wilmette, Ill.: Baha'i Publishing Trust.

Wallis, Roy (1984). *The Elementary Forms of the New Religious Life.* London: Routledge.

Warburg, Margit (1999a). New Age og gamle dage. Religion og globalisering i dag og i hellenistisk-romersk tid, in Per Bilde and Mikael Rothstein (eds.), *Nye religioner i hellenistisk-romersk tid og i dag.* Aarhus: Aarhus University Press: 39-52.

Warburg, Margit (1999b). Baha'i: A Religious Approach to Globalization, *Social Compass*, vol. 46: 47-56.

Part II

Some Synchronic Themes

CHAPTER 10

Globalization and Decentralization: The Concept of Subsidiarity in the Baha'i Faith

Wendi Momen

The term 'globalization' is used in many different ways. For present purposes, globalization is defined as the process that enables social, economic and political systems and processes, human activities and ideas to take hold and function at an 'international', 'transnational', 'world', 'universal' or 'global' level. Globalization has both positive and negative implications. Some political theorists have identified the need for the creation of global regulatory institutions to enhance the positive aspects of globalization and to mitigate the effects of the negative.

Among these is the proposal put forward by the Bahá'í Faith: the creation of a federated world government which has a range of powers and responsibilities conferred upon it by state actors. The idea of a world government is rejected by many political theorists owing to concerns about the possibility of its unchecked powers, lack of democracy and denial of human rights. The Bahá'í Faith counters these concerns with an array of proposals designed to limit the powers of such a government by effecting the concept of subsidiarity, implementing democratic principles and offering its own principles and practices as a model for upholding human rights and social welfare. This article describes the Baha'i proposals against the backdrop of political theory.

Globalization

The term 'globalization' is now used in so many contexts and by so many groups that it is difficult to know exactly what is meant by it. Different academic disciplines use it differently. It is also 'felt' and experienced differently. Some actively 'participate' in globalization processes while others experience it or are victims, or beneficiaries, of it. It is presently used to describe social phenomena as widely diverse as the activities of transnational corporations and the 'global economy' to spiritual consciousness, to the exportation to rural outposts of western (for which read American) values, pastimes, technologies and solutions to problems, to the proliferation of quasi-global institutions to combat everything from environmental degradation to arms running, to drug and human trafficking and urbanization, AIDS/HIV and to the promotion of defence strategies, a UN rapid reaction force and the proposed Tobin tax to seemly trivial concepts such as global fashion.

Also confusing is the term 'antiglobalization', made 'globally' popular through the demonstrations at the ministerial meeting of the World Trade Organization in Seattle in December 1999, when anti-capitalists were linked with 'a brigade clumsily classified as *antiglobalization* and with agendas that range from saving the earth to defending workers' rights and opposing free trade' (Ratnesar 2001: 25).

Perhaps even more confusing is how to tell the difference between globalization and anti-globalization. What happened in Genoa, despite being called anti-globalization, was an expression of the spirit of globalization, the feeling of rapport and solidarity that people, often well-off, in one place have with people, often disadvantaged, in another.

Thus although within the field of international relations the concept of globalization was at first considered to be only an economic phenomenon, the process of globalization is now affecting related systems such as governance. Globalization may thus now be defined as the process that enables social, economic and political systems and processes, human activities and ideas to take hold and function at an 'international', 'transnational', 'world', 'universal' or 'global' level, terms which are considered interchangeable by some. Another definition of globalization is the growing consciousness of the oneness and interconnectedness of the human family and that the world is a single space. This definition is the focus of the Baha'i teachings and the religion's administrative structures.

Globalization has both positive and negative implications and, in a political and economic sense, a long history. Here is a well-known description of globalization and its effects:

> Modern industry has established the world market. All old-established national industries have been destroyed. They are dislodged by new industries whose products are consumed in every corner of the globe. In place of the old wants, we find new wants, requiring for their satisfaction the products of distant lands and climes... all fixed, fast-frozen relations are swept away; all new-formed ones become antiquated before they can ossify. All that is solid melts into air (Marx and Engels 1848).

In the *Communist Manifesto*, first published in February 1848, a few weeks before revolutions shook much of Europe, Marx and Engels identified globalization as

> ... a revolutionary phenomenon. The triumph of global capitalism had weakened the chains that held human potential in check. Autocratic rulers and priests had seen their power wither away; technology had offered the promise of plenty; great cities had rescued millions from the 'idiocy of rural life'. Trade had diminished the differences and antagonisms between states so that it was possible to dream of a true internationalism. Globalization, in other words, was potentially liberating (Elliott 2001: 30).

It is claimed by some political theorists (e.g. Noberto Bobbio, Jurgen Habermas and David Held) that one of the negative effects of globalization, narrowly defined as the 'growth of unregulated transnational economic activity', has been that it 'undermines the democratic gains won over the last century' (Murphy 2000: 790). The remedy, they suggest, is the

> ... deepening of domestic democratic processes and the extension of democratic forms beyond the nation-state. They champion international institutions both ruled by the people and powerful enough to regulate the global markets in labour, money, goods, and ideas that have expanded so rapidly in recent decades (Murphy 2000: 790).

In addition to the perceived damage to democracy, economic, cultural and ethical damage to largely rural and already disadvantaged communities who are not politically centre stage is popularly seen as the most dangerous outcome of the present economic globalization process. It is this sort of globalization - the damaging sort - that attracts protestors and concerned comment. That the protestors themselves appear to be divided on what the solution might be, is yet another indication of the complexity of the issues and the concept. That protestors actually take advantage of the new globalized world to make their views known is even more ironic and yet points to how far-reaching and deep rooted the globalization process has become. So, for example, while Nye suggests that 'the recent surge in demonstrations is, in part, a reaction to the changes produced by economic integration' he also recognizes that such protest is also 'the result of social globalization, the increased communication across borders, the reduced costs, and the greater ease of individuals and non-governmental organizations (NGOs) in coordinating protests' (Nye 2001: 39) Thus the very fact of globalization has made it

> ... easier to demonstrate against it: the Internet facilitates exchange of protest strategy, the English language's conquest of Europe gives the polyglot protesters a common tongue, the EU's elimination of border controls means activists can more easily hook up with foreign comrades, and free-market competition has slashed the cost of travel throughout Europe (Ratnesar 2001: 26).

Thus globalization is seen as both a problem and a solution, as a cause and a reaction. Few today fail to recognize the globalization of certain problems, the environment, for example. Global warming affects all, but no one suggests that we have yet found global solutions that are workable or institutions capable of addressing the issues. The globalization of markets and the exportation of western methods, ideas and 'remedies' is an inappropriate response to the global problems, but there appears to be a lack of political will or ability either to halt the unregulated and damaging globalization of markets on the one hand or to create appropriate methods and institutions to deal with global challenges such as the environment and international crime on the other.

Responses to Globalization

One reason political theorists such as David Held advocate the creation of global regulatory institutions is because, as Richard Falk says, 'there is little, or no, normative agency associated with this emergent world order: it is virtually designer-free, a partial dystopia that is being formed spontaneously, and in the process endangering some of the achievements of early phases of statist world order' (Falk 1997: 125).

> ... the aggregation of states, what has been called 'a states system', is no longer in control of the global policy process. Territorial sovereignty is being diminished on a spectrum of issues in such a serious manner as to subvert the capacity of states to control and protect the internal life of society, and non-state actors hold an increasing proportion of power and influence in shaping the world order (Falk 1997: 124).

Simply coordinating efforts at the international level has not proved a successful way to address global issues nor have such coordinated efforts been powerful enough to dissuade states and supranational corporations from acting in their own self interest to the detriment of other actors. Hence the creation of more international institutions, reform of the United Nations to give it more 'teeth', a higher level of global governance and world government itself have been proposed as ways to tackle the effects of the proliferation of transnationals that work outside the state system, the problems created by supranational agents such as drug barons and human traffickers, and global environmental concerns such as climate change. At the same time, these proposals suggest that by finding solutions to these problems, the same institutions can also address domestic issues and infrastructure difficulties more adequately, issues such as access to education, fresh water and health and the empowerment of women.

The other side of this is the concern that higher levels of governance, world government and the like, will bring even more problems: that there will be world domination by an evil and self-serving tyrant or, perhaps worse, by one of the present states or religions; that democracy will die; that individual human rights will be completely ignored, never mind the rights of states; that the propensity for arbitrariness will increase; that the right of personal initiative and enterprise will be curtailed; that our property will be expropriated; that there will be a huge international bureaucracy focused on the minutia of daily life that will interfere with how we live our lives; that we will all be taxed heavily to pay for all this; that we will inherit an Orwellian future in which we are all watched and manipulated; and perhaps all of these. Even the report of the Commission on Global Governance backed away from giving support to the concept of a world government on these grounds:

> ... global governance is not global government. No misunderstanding should arise from the similarity of the terms. We are not proposing movement towards world government, for were we to travel in that direction we could find ourselves in an even less democratic world than we have - one more accommodating to power, more hospitable to hegemonic ambition, and more reinforcing of the roles of states rather than the rights of people (Commission on Global Governance 1995: xvi).

Baha'i Response to Globalization: World Government

The Baha'i teachings state that the Baha'i Faith addresses all these issues and proposes a way forward that, Baha'is suggest, will provide workable and practical solutions to all the negative aspects of globalization, preclude the creation of a world tyranny and all its attendant anti-liberal restrictions and foster a consciousness of unity and oneness that will provoke a sense of international collaboration and enable universal peace to be established whilst avoiding the dangers of political over-centralisation. Arising from such political stability and peace, Baha'is state, will be a world better able to focus on overcoming natural disasters and promoting behaviours at the individual and collective levels that eschew criminality and anti-social activity. Baha'is believe that the very tools that are used to invent the mechanisms that will bring peace can also be used to prevent a host of dangers to people from occurring and can be turned into sciences and arts that will benefit humanity. Beyond this, the Baha'i writings suggest that once peace and unity are well-established and a workable government in place, the global economy will change to such an extent that the present gap between wealth and poverty among nations and between people will be compressed, that tax money presently used for defence and the war machine will be put to use for development and that thereby the prosperity of humanity will be increased in general.

Political structures and practices outlined in the Baha'i teachings are set in the context of Baha'i beliefs about the organization of society in its widest sense. At the global level, Baha'i teachings recommend, indeed see as inevitable, a global political order definitely organised, not randomly arrived at, with certain features, e.g. an international executive, parliament and judiciary and associated institutions such as an international standing army or police force, a federalist constitution and democratic elements such as elections by universal suffrage, accountability and collective responsibility; certain responsibilities and tasks, e.g. overseeing the management of the global economy and markets, overseeing the management of the global environment, fixing borders and policing inter-state relations; and certain rights, e.g. taxation (Shoghi Effendi 1991: 40, 203).

The model proffered by Baha'u'llah is a federated world government which has a range of powers and responsibilities conferred upon it by state actors. It is to be brought about by political will, that is, by decision, and is not to be the result of unilateral military or economic action, force or coercion. The decision is to be made by treaty and a constitution is to be established ('Abdu'l-Baha 1990: 64). It is anticipated that world leaders ('rulers and kings', Baha'u'llah 1983: 249) will call and attend a summit to discuss the formation of the world government and conclude the treaty creating it. The agenda items for the summit include creating a 'union of the nations', reducing nationally held armaments, fixing national boundaries, determining how collective security will operate and setting out the principles of international law and how states will relate to one another ('Abdu'l-Baha 1990: 64). The constitution is to be ratified 'by all the human race' ('Abdu'l-Baha 1990: 64), presumably through some sort of referendum or national ballot. Thus the government is to be established from the bottom up, not top down; is to be created, not imposed; has its powers conferred by, not wrested from, state actors. A corollary of this is that states can confer limited powers. However, from the Baha'i perspective, it is not necessary that all state actors agree to form the world government: only a 'certain number' need do so ('Abdu'l-Baha 1990: 64) Exactly how this is supposed to work is not clear.

It is worth pointing out that the government described here is secular, not religious. Baha'is say that they will play no role in its creation, although they support the process, labelling the period in which it is created 'the Lesser Peace'.

The Baha'i teachings posit that the features of the proposed world federal government will be sufficient to counter the natural fears that such an unknown system engenders. Thus, for example, within this system, each state remains sovereign, although some elements of sovereignty are sacrificed to enable the world federal government to operate effectively: the right to make war on others, the right to hold unlimited stocks of arms, the right to act on the international state wholly independently of other actors with impunity (Shoghi Effendi 1991: 40). States are also supposed to give up certain rights to tax their people: Baha'u'llah and his son 'Abdu'l-Baha both deplored the heavy burden of tax imposed by intemperate and war-mongering rulers on their people (see e.g. Baha'u'llah 1983: 250; 'Abdu'l-Baha 1982: 122, 317). A further reason for this may be because any world government requires funding and no doubt a tax would need to be levied to provide this. Further, the constitution is to fix national boundaries ('Abdu'l-Baha 1990: 64), set down international law ('Abdu'l-Baha 1990: 64) and define how relations between and among states are to be conducted ('Abdu'l-Baha 1990: 64). The world government is to operate a form of collective security, requiring the forceful, apparently military, engagement of state actors ('Abdu'l-Baha 1990: 64, Shoghi Effendi 1991: 41) and/or a world police force (Shoghi Effendi 1991: 203).

There are several democratic features of the proposed world government. First, there is a separation of powers into the judicial, legislative and executive branches of government (Shoghi Effendi 1991: 40). The judiciary, a 'world tribunal' is to be elected by the 'peoples and Governments of every nation' and is to be 'composed of members elected from each country and Government' ('Abdu'l-Baha 1967: 155) and thus is to be 'representative of all governments and peoples' ('Abdu'l-Baha 1978: 249). 'Abdu'l-Baha goes into some detail on how this election is to take place ('Abdu'l-Baha 1978: 306). The members of the legislature, the 'world parliament', 'shall be elected by the people in their respective countries' and their election 'confirmed by their respective governments' (Shoghi Effendi 1991: 40). It appears to be the elected legislature, rather than the executive, which is the locus of authority, as its members are called 'the trustees of the whole of mankind' and it is intended that it will 'ultimately control the entire resources of all the component nations' (Shoghi Effendi 1991: 203). The world executive 'corresponds to the executive head or board in present-day national governments' (Shoghi Effendi 1934a). It is not clear whether this is an elected or appointed body or individual.

Other democratic elements include: the autonomy of state members (Shoghi Effendi 1991: 203), individual freedom, freedom to act and 'to take individual initiative' ('Abdu'l-Baha 1978: 302, Shoghi Effendi 1991: 203), freedom of the press 'from the influence of contending governments and peoples' (Shoghi Effendi 1991: 204), equality of people before the law; the equality of women and men; protection of the rights of minorities; freedom of conscience (Shoghi Effendi 1934b; 'Abdu'l-Baha 1980: 87); liberty of thought; the right of speech ('Abdu'l-Baha 1982: 197); and freedom of religion (Shoghi Effendi 1970: 86). Certain other freedoms are implied, as they are guaranteed within the Baha'i Faith itself: freedom from slavery (Baha'u'llah 1992: para 72), freedom of movement and travel (Baha'u'llah 1992: para 131) and so on.

A universal auxiliary language, a single system of weights and measures and a universal currency are to underpin the world federal government and ease communication and trade. Literacy is promoted.

Other aspects of modern democratic government - such as transparency and accountability - are not mentioned in connection with the world government. However, as the Baha'i Faith charges those in government at a national level to have a high standard of personal ethics, it is probable that those functioning at the world level are expected to have these same standards. For example, in speaking of the world tribunal, 'Abdu'l-Baha says that the 'choicest' individuals must be chosen to serve on it ('Abdu'l-Baha 1978: 306), that its members 'should be chosen from among the wisest and most judicious men of all the nations of the world' ('Abdu'l-Baha: 115).

Were there time and space, it would be useful to consider whether the Baha'i teachings on this subject are prescriptive or predictive. Both preclude a diversion into this interesting subject.

Federalism

One concern often levelled against the idea of a world government is that the nation-state will wither away or, at best, become powerless, completely overwhelmed by and under the influence of the world government. Some political theorists consider this the only way forward. This scenario has also been popularized in fiction, in both books and films. The effects of globalization, it is suggested, are so overwhelming that state governments, already struggling to retain vestiges of their sovereignty and power, will be completely absorbed within a global framework and will have nothing to do, everything being centralized within the world government. However, at least in the short term, Nye suggests that this is not likely:

> Global effects are powerful. But they do not enter societies in an unmediated way. On the contrary, they are filtered both by cultural difference, and by domestic political alignment. How global information is downloaded in different countries is a function of domestic politics. In that sense, even in an age of globalization, all politics remains local (Nye 2001: 40).

It is the federal aspect of the proposed world government that provides one of the major safeguards against world tyranny and injustice. 18th century Americans tussled with creating a 'super-state' government that would protect individual and states rights, fearing that a national government would be too powerful and pull everything towards it, just as state actors today wrestle with the need to act globally but protect their interests and those of their citizens. The Americans established a way to distribute powers across a variety of actors, the system of federalism, which 'allotted certain powers [and rights] to the national government and reserved the rest for the states' (Burns 1975: 51). The Baha'i proposal, like many other models, suggests that a federal government of the world will have the same benefits internationally and provide the same protections as the American federal government does for its states and citizens.

The very size of the world, and the magnitude and complexity of tasks facing it, make a federal government, Baha'is suggest, a sensible choice. Again the example of the United States makes this clear:

Under a federal system, local issues do not have to be thrust into the national [or international] arena, thereby making it easier to develop a consensus on national problems.

The size of the United States, with its many diverse cultures, makes it difficult to set national norms for local issues. Our federal system permits these battles to be fought in the state legislatures. There is no need to enforce a single standard on the divergent areas of the nation (Burns 1975: 80).

Thus the Baha'i Faith foresees the establishment of a federated world government as one remedy for the more dangerous aspects of globalization and a positive influence on universal peace and prosperity. At the same time, it advocates the concept of subsidiarity, the 'flip side' of federalism, as a second strand in its political theory.

Subsidiarity

Subsidiarity is the concept that a central authority should perform only those tasks which cannot be performed effectively at a lower level. Subsidiarity

simply means that government should be applied and responsible to the level of society that is appropriate, starting from the individual citizens and leaving to them and their local community as much and as many functions and administration as possible. Nothing should be transferred to another level of government without necessity and even exigency. Mere convenience is not sufficient (Roberts 2001).

The lawyers Grenville Clarke and Louis Sohn, whose seminal work *World Peace through World Law* has influenced a generation of political theorists, underscore the need for subsidiarity in the global system:

The powers of the world organization should be restricted to matters directly related to the maintenance of peace. All other powers should be reserved to the nations and their peoples. This definition and reservation of powers is advisable not only to avoid opposition based on fear of possible interference in the domestic affairs of the nations, but also because it is wise for this generation to limit itself to the single task of preventing international violence or the threat of it... (Clarke and Sohn 1996: xvii).

It is not just a question, therefore, of having a world federal government. Even that government could take upon itself a whole range of powers and responsibilities that would interfere in the functions of the states and individuals. Application of the principle of subsidiarity prevents this. Thus a world government would not take on tasks that lower levels of government could take on and would confine itself to tasks of global import and influence.

The National Spiritual Assembly of the Baha'is of the United Kingdom issued a statement in 1993 succinctly describing the Baha'i concept of subsidiarity:

The basic purpose of local government is to meet the needs of local people and communities, and since these will vary from place to place, the closer that local government is to the people the better. Larger and multi-tiered authorities have a history of remoteness (as much perceived as real) and at least to some extent of bureaucracy.

... Baha'is would see the principle of subsidiarity as embodying something more radical than has been recognised in this debate [on the subsidiarity within the United Kingdom governing structures]. We believe that, wherever possible within the nation, government and service should be local in origin and scope, reflecting the wishes, needs, views, experiences, history and aspirations of local people. That is, it should be as close to the people as possible.

It follows from this that we are in favour of local authorities that deal with as much as can be dealt with: it is necessary to devolve as much authority as possible to the smallest administrative units and leave to larger ones only those matters which need to be dealt with on a larger scale (National Spiritual Assembly UK 1993: 3).

Governing at Sub-Global Levels

The Baha'i Faith posits a federated world government which is dependent for its existence on 'component' (Shoghi Effendi 1991: 203) or member states. There seems to be a presumption that current models of government will continue to operate under the federated global system. There is no attempt to provide a model for government at any level other than the global one. Thus national governments are expected to continue to exist and to govern according to their own constitutions. The form of government of these constituent states is not prescribed in the Baha'i teachings. 'Abdu'l-Baha suggests that they may be 'constitutional or republican, hereditary monarchy or democratic', provided the 'rulers will devote their time to the prosperity of their nations, the legislation of just and sane laws' ('Abdu'l-Baha 1914: 115). However, the Baha'i teachings seem to indicate that some sort of constitutional monarchy is the preferred form at the national level ['just kings', 'Abdu'l-Baha 1990: 20):

Although a republican form of government profiteth all the peoples of the world, yet the majesty of kingship is one of the signs of God. We do not wish that the countries of the world should remain deprived thereof. If the sagacious combine the two forms into one, great will be their reward in the presence of God (Baha'u'llah 1988: 28).

The system of government which the British people have adopted in London appeareth to be good, for it is adorned with the light of both kingship and of the consultation of the people (Baha'u'llah 1988: 93).

Whatever form of national government might be decided upon, national borders are to be fixed by treaty, thereby, Bahá'ís posit, eliminating one source of contention among states. But the prevailing dynamism of the concept of 'unity in diversity' (Shoghi Effendi 1991: 42) is to obviate states from the need to adopt the same forms of government, constitutions or practices and is to work against this tendency, should it exist.

Similarly, the Baha'i teachings expect that there will be governance at all levels of community: city, town and village. For example, 'Abdu'l-Baha provides an outline of how the economics of a village are to operate ('Abdu'l-Baha 1912) - whether this is possible in non-agrarian societies remains to be seen - but it is clear that some form of formal governance would be required and this underscores the principle of subsidiarity:

In brief, from among the wise men in every village a board should be organized and the affairs of that village should be under the control of that board ('Abdu'l-Baha 1912).

The Baha'i teachings are curiously silent on the organization of national and local political institutions (except as they refer to the Baha'i organization itself). 'Abdu'l-Baha in *The Secret of Divine Civilization* does give instruction in the broad principles for the conduct of national government and the values and systems (e.g. education) upon which such government should be based and the leadership skills and qualities required for good government. There is a strong suggestion in this treatise of 'Abdu'l-Baha that one government should learn from another and take what has been found to be of benefit, rejecting what has not ('Abdu'l-Baha 1990: 12, 30, 112).

'Abdu'l-Baha identifies certain features of modern government: 'the setting up of parliaments, the organizing of assemblies of consultation, constitutes the very foundation and bedrock of government' ('Abdu'l-Baha 1990: 17); the rule of law ('Abdu'l-Baha 1990: 17, 38B9); a judicial system which is consistent and universal ('Abdu'l-Baha 1990: 14, 15, 18, 37B8, 100); 'ministers of state and representatives' ('Abdu'l-Baha 1990: 20); suffrage (because elected officials will worry more about their reputations than non-elected ones and will therefore tend to be more just) ('Abdu'l-Baha 1990: 24); using those with good scholarship and education ('spiritual learned') in positions of responsibility ('Abdu'l-Baha 1990: 32ff);a universal education system ('Abdu'l-Baha 1990: 39, 109ff); reliance on 'true' religion ('Abdu'l-Baha 1990: 71, 80ff); the 'free exercise of the individual's rights, and the security of his person and property, his dignity and good name, assured' ('Abdu'l-Baha 1990: 115). Baha'u'llah also provides insights into the characteristics and qualities of good leadership (Baha'u'llah 1988: 127). But, 'Abdu'l-Baha says, government models need not be fixed forever: 'the nonessentials which deal with details of community are changed according to the exigency of the time and conditions' ('Abdu'l-Baha 1982: 169).

However, while the details of local, national and regional governance within the federated world system are not expressly defined in the Baha'i teachings, it is possible to elicit the basic principles of governance from the description of how Baha'i institutions themselves are elected and are to function. It should be pointed out that there is no suggestion in the following that the Baha'i institutions themselves will become the civil government of any community (although there is a point in the development of the World Order of Baha'u'llah, as Baha'is see it, that Baha'i institutions and secular ones will merge – this is, indeed, one goal of the Baha'i Faith and its expansion programme).

How far the principles that govern Baha'i organizations, e.g. Local Spiritual Assemblies, can be written across as models of government for secular organizations such as city councils and national parliaments is unclear. In 1985 the Universal House of Justice suggested that they might be: 'If the Baha'i experience can contribute in whatever measure to reinforcing hope in the unity of the human race, we are happy to offer it as a model for study' (Universal House of Justice 1985). However, Baha'i institutions are not civic authorities (Universal House of Justice 1983).

Thus to the extent that Baha'is themselves consider their institutions to be models for civic governance, it is possible to draw some insights into how Baha'is understand the concept of subsidiarity.

The Baha'i Faith itself operates on a global level and promotes global thinking among its adherents: its highest administrative body is the Universal House of Justice, to which all Baha'is defer; Baha'is undertake global plans of expansion of the religion and are encouraged to travel widely to further the interests of the religion and to promote in themselves a global consciousness. Baha'is from all countries contribute to the international funds of the religion and pay the 'Right of God' to the Universal House of Justice. Baha'is undertake large-scale construction projects, such as the buildings on Mount Carmel, and contribute to international projects of social and economic development and to processes that lead to world peace.

At the same time, Baha'is are organized at the local and national levels: the system of administration for the religion calls for local, national and international elected administrative units – Local Spiritual Assemblies, National Spiritual Assemblies and the Universal House of Justice. In recent years a new, elected, sub-national level of quasi-administration has been introduced in some countries where the Baha'i populations or the complexity of Baha'i administration warrants it: Regional Baha'i Councils. I have in another place ('Governing the People') described these institutions and the democratic elements (and otherwise) which characterize them.

The Baha'i Faith promotes the diversity of cultures and cultural identity and Baha'is are encouraged to develop the cultural diversity of their activities.

The Baha'i teachings warn of the dangers of excessive centralization in governance, which leads to despotism and tyranny, and repudiate attempts at uniformity. One result of subsidiarity is to provide a balance between over-centralization and over-decentralization. This principle is described by Shoghi Effendi in his guidance to National Spiritual Assemblies and their relationship with their substructures:

> ... a unique principle in the administration of the Cause, governing the relations that should be maintained between the central administrative body and its assisting organs of executive and legislative action... The utmost vigilance, the most strenuous exertion is required by them if they wish to fulfil as befits their high and responsible calling, the functions which it is theirs to discharge. They should, within the limits imposed upon them by present-day circumstances, endeavour to maintain the balance in such a manner that the evils of over-centralization which clog, confuse and in the long run depreciate the value of the Baha'i services rendered shall on one hand be entirely avoided, and on the other the perils of utter decentralization with the consequent lapse of governing authority from the hands of the national representatives of the believers definitely averted (Shoghi Effendi 1968: 141-2).

'Abdu'l-Baha suggests that national civil governments will become less centralized, perhaps as the effects of a federal world government are felt:

> It is very evident that in the future there shall be no centralization in the countries of the world, be they constitutional in government, republican or democratic in form. The United States may be held up as the example of future government - that is to say, each province will be independent in itself, but there will be federal union protecting the interests of the various independent states. It may not be a republican or a democratic form. To cast aside centralization which promotes despotism is the exigency of the time. This will be productive of international peace ('Abdu'l-Baha 1982: 167).

Thus the Baha'i Faith promotes, on the one hand, a globalization that is intended to provide universal access to social and welfare benefits that are to uplift the prosperity of humanity and advocates the creation of a world federal government that Baha'is believe will protect and administer it, and is attempting to set in place a model of governing that is based on the ideas of federalism, decentralization, subsidiarity and elements of democracy and democratic process, which, Bahá'ís posit, deal with many of the fears that the prospect of world government engenders.

Conclusion

'Globalization', the process that enables social, economic and political systems and processes, human activities and ideas to take hold and function at a 'global' level, has positive and negative implications. Some theorists suggest that it is necessary to develop some sort of international regulatory institutions to enhance the positive outcomes of globalization and, more important, to mitigate the negative ones. The Bahá'í Faith's response is that a federated world government, based on the principles of democracy and subsidiarity, should be established. In this the Baha'i teachings appear to be both descriptive and prescriptive and also claim to be prophetic. Baha'i scriptures and related works describe what a world government might look like and give some indication of how it might function. Baha'i ideas about the way in which society and government ought to work are coupled with the practices that Baha'is use to govern themselves to present a model of what they consider to be good governance at local, national and global levels. Sometimes described as idealistic, optimist or naive, this model lacks detail for implementation at the international level but Baha'is claim that this is intended, as the state actors themselves are to provide these by negotiation at a summit of world leaders and that the Baha'is themselves will not be instrumental in the government's establishment.

References

'Abdu'l-Baha (1912). Extract from a Tablet to an individual, 4 October.

'Abdu'l-Baha (1914). Selection from *Star of the West* 5: 8 115-17.

'Abdu'l-Baha (1967). *Paris Talks.* London: Baha'i Publishing Trust.

'Abdu'l-Baha (1978). *Selections from the Writings of 'Abdu'l-Bahá.* Haifa: Baha'i World Centre.

'Abdu'l-Baha (1980). *A Traveler's Narrative.* Wilmette, Ill.: Baha'i Publishing Trust.

'Abdu'l-Baha (1982). *The Promulgation of Universal Peace.* Wilmette, Ill.: Baha'i Publishing Trust.

'Abdu'l-Baha (1990). *The Secret of Divine Civilization.* Wilmette, Ill.: Baha'i Publishing Trust.

Baha'u'llah (1983). *Gleanings from the Writings of Bahá'u'lláh.* Wilmette, Ill.: Baha'i Publishing Trust.

Baha'u'llah (1988). *Tablets of Bahá'u'lláh.* Wilmette, Ill.: Baha'i Publishing Trust.

Baha'u'llah (1992). *The Kitáb-i-Aqdas.* Haifa: Baha'i World Centre.

Burns, James MacGregor, J.W. Peltason and Thomas E. Cronin (1975). *Government by the People.* Englewood Cliffs, NJ: Prentice-Hall.

Clarke, Grenville and Louis Sohn (1996). *World Peace through World Law.* Cambridge, Mass: Harvard University Press,

Commission on Global Governance (1995). *Our Global Neighbourhood.* Oxford: Oxford University Press.

Elliott, Michael (2001). The Wrong Side of the Barricades, *Time,* 23 July.

Falk, Richard (1997). State of siege: will globalization win out?, *International Affairs* 3: 1.

Marx, Karl and Friedrich Engels (1948). *Communist Manifesto.*

Murphy, Craig N. (2000). Global governance: poorly done and poorly understood, *International Affairs* 76: 4.

National Spiritual Assembly UK (1993). *Local Government: Unitary Authorities, Subsidiarity and People Power.* November.

Nye, Joseph (2001). Globalisation and Discontent. *The World Today,* 57: 8/9.

Ratnesar, Romesh (2001). Chaos Incorporated, *Time,* 23 July.

Roberts, John (2001). *World Letters.* [n.p.], [n.c.]:152.

Shoghi Effendi (1934a). From a letter written on behalf of Shoghi Effendi to an individual, 17 March.

Shoghi Effendi (1934b). From a letter written on behalf of Shoghi Effendi to an individual, 17 March.

Shoghi Effendi (1968). *Bahá'i Administration.* Wilmette, Ill.: Baha'i Publishing Trust.

Shoghi Effendi (1970). Dawn of a New Day: Messages to India 1923-1957. New Delhi: Baha'i Publishing Trust.
Shoghi Effendi (1991). *World Order of Bahá'u'lláh.* Wilmette, Ill.: Baha'i Publishing Trust.
The Universal House of Justice (1983). Letter to the National Spiritual Assembly of Brazil, 13 April.
The Universal House of Justice (1985). The Promise of World Peace. Haifa: Baha'i World Centre.

CHAPTER 11

The Globalization of Information: Baha'i Constructions of the Internet

David Piff

The present paper is an attempt to discuss some of the sociological dynamics of computer-mediated communication in relation to religious groups. In particular, the paper focuses on the influence of 'newsgroups' - computer aided discussion forums - on the internal dynamics, external relations and public image of religious communities. Computer mediated communication technologies are, of course, integral to the processes of growing international political, economic and social interdependence referred to as globalization. These facilities bring with them the potential to alter factors in the social, cultural and political environments in which religious organizations operate, and affect the ability of these organizations to carry out projects they contemplate enacting on the world stage.

In speaking of the 'globalization of information' I refer to its free flow and easy accessibility across national and other political and social boundaries.

In referring to 'Baha'i constructions' of the Internet, I mean to denote ways in which Baha'i communities, or segments of these communities, have viewed these networked, global communication facilities. The technology is essentially neutral. Depending on how it is used and exploited, what hopes are lodged in it and what rewards or disappointments it delivers, it can and has been seen as a source of benefit or as a threat. These views of the Internet are created and reinforced through social processes, some of which are carried out on the Internet itself.

It should be recognized that the number of individuals actually participating in Baha'i electronic discussion groups is relatively small, constituting a minute fraction of the worldwide Baha'i community.[1] Participants appear to be located mainly in the United States, Canada, Europe, Australia, New Zealand and Japan. Despite their small demographic size, the activities of these groups have become influential factors in lives of participants, and matters of concern to Baha'i institutions.

The 'Promises' and 'Risks' of the Internet

The Baha'i religion consciously promotes the concept 'the earth – one country', and seeks to foster a world without wars, without serious barriers to travel and trade, in which a universal language and an ethic of 'unity in diversity' foster cultural interchange and tolerance. In a well-known passage in one of his 'world order letters' written in 1936, Shoghi Effendi, Guardian of the Baha'i religion, enumerated features of a future 'world commonwealth'. He wrote, 'A mechanism of world inter-communication will be devised, embracing the whole planet, freed from national hindrances and restrictions, and functioning with marvelous swiftness and perfect regularity' (Shoghi Effendi 1974: 203). In the popular discourse of the Baha'i community, this statement is

1 The largest Baha'i-related discussion group is probably BCCA-sponsored *Baha'i-announce*, a moderated group with some 1,800 subscribers from 80 countries. BCCA refers to the *Baha'i Computer and Communications Association*, sponsored by the National Spiritual Assembly of the Baha'is of the United States. In light of a popular view among Baha'is – that the Baha'i leader Shoghi Effendi actually predicted the Internet (see below) – the relatively small proportion of Baha'is participating in online Baha'i discussion groups (a few thousand out of a claimed world population of 5 million adherents) may appear surprising. The fact that the demographic weight of the worldwide Baha'i community resides in the developing world, underrepresented in computer mediated forums, may partially account for this discrepancy. Incidents described in the present paper may have cast a chill over Internet discussion groups and discouraged wider community participation. On the other hand, without further research, it remains unclear whether the proportion of member participation in Baha'i-related online discussion groups differs significantly from that of other religious communities.

seen as a prediction of today's Internet and web technologies, and of the facilitative role such technologies will play in knitting the world together. Members of the Baha'i community sometimes assert that the modern technologies of data processing and telecommunications were brought into being for 'establishing Baha'u'llah's world order' (Piff 2000: 272).[2]

An important feature of the Internet and World Wide Web is the ability of these systems to level the playing field in regard to dissemination of information (including, of course, what could be referred to as 'disinformation' - deliberate falsehoods, exaggerations, rumors). Government agencies, corporations, and a wide variety of public and private institutions have been bedeviled by problems associated with the unprecedented propagation of news and opinion, official and unofficial, fostered by the Internet. The remark by Net political organizer John Gilmore, that 'The Net interprets censorship as damage and routes around it' (Shade 1996: 24) has been borne out in numerous instances. Sociologist Leslie Shade notes that 'The electronic environment raises many problems relative to controlling information and bypassing official channels' and wonders whether it is 'even feasible to prevent access to offensive or potentially illegal newsgroups, given that networks such as Usenet are international in scope' (1996: 24).

Rosabeth Moss Kanter has identified 'bypass' as one of four key trends of globalization: it refers to the availability of multiple optional avenues of communication, a situation that makes it increasingly difficult for traditional guardians to limit or preside over information reaching members of an organization, or of a society at large (Kanter 1995: 45-46; Warburg 2003). Bypass also threatens the ability of leaders to manage the quantity and quality of information from within an organization that reaches the wider society. By providing means for messages to receive additional circulation, the Internet makes public what before had circulated in face-to-face interpersonal settings, been exchanged between friends in private correspondence, or shared in informal discussion circles within a given community.

2 It should be mentioned, at least in passing, that Baha'i splinter groups, internally referred to as 'covenant-breakers' have created their own 'official' web sites, where their views, often clearly contradictory to mainstream Baha'i doctrine, are available to anyone interested. These websites are not discussed in the present paper. The Baha'i covenant doctrine is discussed below.

Beyond this, by allowing widespread circulation of varying viewpoints, the Internet promotes what Kanter terms 'pluralism' within a political, ideological or religious community. Warburg (2003) appropriately recasts the trend as 'multipolarity'. It refers to the tendency of dominant centers of information to give way to several, sometimes competing sources of information and influence (Kanter 1995: 46). Enjoying online access to articles presenting a range of variant opinions, ostensibly identified with the group in question, an outside observer may receive a strong impression that the community does not speak with a single voice on important issues. And to a member of the community, the availability of a range of viewpoints may engender suspicion that their leadership may not 'have it right' and are out of step with the reasonable opinions of some of the community's more thoughtful members.

This situation presents challenges to Baha'i institutions and members of the community. Historically, Baha'i institutions have been at pains to provide specific direction to information presented about the religion, both internally and externally. The most visible instance of this concern is manifested in the community's policy of literature review under which a Baha'i author must submit his or her work to a board appointed by a National Spiritual Assembly, and make any changes requested prior to publication. The purpose of the practice is to assure that the teachings and history of the religion are presented accurately – that is, according to contemporary institutionally sponsored understandings of these matters – and that the material to be published does not in other ways compromise the interests of the Baha'i community. Baha'is understand review to be a temporary measure; 'limited to this stage of (the religion's) development when books published by Baha'is could seriously mislead the public if they too gravely distort its message' (Universal House of Justice 1999b: 6). There is no tradition of internal, self-critical journalism in the Baha'i community – at least not for publication. Baha'i organs of information offer mainly good news about achievements of the community, what amounts to a form of internal public relations. Detailed or thoughtful discussions of community problems are seldom if ever encountered in published Baha'i literature.

This information vacancy is addressed by the informal discourse of the community, a process facilitated by the Internet, and the vacancy may in part account for the enthusiasm with which electronic discussion groups have been embraced in some segments of the community. Given the Internet, it is no longer necessary to print or otherwise duplicate communications in order to get ideas into circulation, and in the Baha'i situation, distribution of information through computer networks to some extent sidesteps editorial controls and institutional review (Warburg 2003).[3]

Counteracting Friendly Damage

Computer mediated communications have blurred the line between publication and conversation. It is impossible to pre-censor every Internet posting made by a Baha'i before it is submitted; efforts at damage control after the fact are sometimes necessary to counteract the effects of particular postings. Apparently well-meant posts to Baha'i discussion lists, or via forwarded email messages, have in recent years initiated actions or disseminated erroneous information potentially embarrassing to Baha'i institutions.

One example, a lobbying effort, briefly carried on in the Bahai-discuss forum in December 1997, to have 'Abdu'l-Baha voted *Time* magazine's 'man of the century' was abandoned following an advisory posted to the same group that the Universal House of Justice was not in favor of the campaign.[4] Another example was an odd message sent around some Baha'i circles at the end of January 2000 alleging that the Baha'i house of worship in Kampala, Uganda, had been taken over by 'rebel forces' at '11.00 p.m. on the 27th of January'. Ugandan Baha'is, the message went on, had 'decided to stay as neutral as possible in this struggle. For this reason they have not resisted the takeover. We must turn to the Concourse on High and pray that this ends in a peaceful way'.[5] A 'hoax' warning about the message was forwarded through Baha'i email lists.

In another instance, a report posted to a U.S. Baha'i 'announce' list

3 This observation is less applicable to moderated than to unmoderated discussion groups.

4 Posting to *Bahai-Discuss* 'Re: FYI (fwd), 1 December 1997'.

5 Email message to author 'FW: [House of Worship Taken over!]' 31 January 2000. 'Concourse on High' is Baha'i terminology for departed holy souls in the afterlife who are deemed capable of influencing events on earth.

gave exciting, and erroneous, details regarding Baha'i participation in a White House meeting conducted by President Clinton, and called attention to enthusiastic responses of other participants to the Baha'is' input at the event. The U.S. National Spiritual Assembly's Office of External Affairs quickly released an email message correcting points of the report. 'The dissemination of such inaccurate information and the attribution of words and thoughts to the participants without any documentation, could', they wrote, 'be embarrassing and even offensive to persons who are mentioned in the posting, which undeservedly presents them in a rather unfavorable light'.[6]

Of course, unwarranted enthusiasm and credulity are not exclusive qualities of Baha'is, or even of religious people generally; such qualities vex society at large as is illustrated by the Internet's ongoing receptivity to virus hoaxes, chain letters, and urban legends.

The Internet undermines attempts at information control, fostering free circulation of opinions. But the flip side of this benefit is the risk that once one has posted a message to a newsgroup, or sent an email message to a friend, one has lost control over it. The message could be forwarded on to any number of other recipients, printed by whoever wants to print it, excerpted or in other ways altered and reposted or even published. Once something has been released to the Net, it could go anywhere, come to anyone's attention, be interpreted in ways unintended by the author, and be preserved indefinitely.

Internet and Community – the *Talisman* Discussion List

The Internet has provided space for creation of Baha'i-oriented discussion groups where some of the more controversial issues of the religion have been freely discussed. Perhaps the most important such group was *Talisman*, whose history, October 1994 – May 1996, marks a watershed in the community's relations to the Internet. This group began as an unmoderated scholarly forum for intellectual discussion of issues of Babi and Baha'i history, doctrine, administration and community life. The list owner was John Walbridge, a Baha'i professor of Near

6 Email message to *NorthWest Baha'is Announce* 'Joyful News from U.S. NSA' 10 March 2000; email message forwarded to author from *Bahai-Tech* 'U.S. National Assembly Corrects Previous Internet Posting' 13 March 2000.

Eastern languages and philosophy at Indiana University. The list was technically hosted by the university and paid for by the 'taxpayers of the State of Indiana'(Walbridge 1994). In other words, the list resided in a secular setting not under the governance of Baha'i institutions.

Interested Baha'is and others subscribed to the list by sending their email addresses to the list owner, and once subscribed, received a copy of each message posted to the list. List rules were minimal: the list owner disclaimed any intention of moderating content and participants were to be 'free to argue for whatever views they wish[ed], provided they [did] so courteously and on the basis of evidence and sound reasoning'. Participants were requested to 'refrain from abusive language, ...ad hominem arguments, accusations of heresy, and other forms of fallacious argumentation' (Walbridge 1994).

The present study does not afford space to fully detail the history of the group.[7] A roster of subscribers from May 1996 listed some 181 members, of who about 65% posted at least one substantive message to the group. Participants included a number of professors and graduate students in the academic fields of history, anthropology, sociology, religious studies, Middle East studies as well as in the hard and life sciences; medical doctors, computing professionals, and engineers. I estimate that almost five million words were posted to *Talisman* during the course of its duration.[8]

It is impossible to do justice to the range of topics discussed or to adequately summarize the often lengthy and substantial conversational threads developed there. More germane to the present paper is the difficulty of adequately describing the rhetorical devices that shaped and maintained the ongoing creation of the *Talisman* community. Further, exploration of the important process of establishing and sustaining an individual persona - a particular 'character' and

7 For a brief published account of *Talisman* see Johnson (1997).

8 I possess a very nearly complete *Talisman* archive, 18 October 1994 - 24 May 1996. By utilizing my computer's 'word count' function I was able to arrive at an overall estimate of some 6.6 million words (about 13,500 printed pages) posted over the life of the group. I reduced this by 25% to exclude the often lengthy computer-generated message 'headers', which remain part of my files but were not actually composed by participants. The interested reader is referred to this URL: http://www-personal.umich.edu/~jrcole/tarc1196.htm, a *Talisman* archive covering the period 1994-96.

'voice' in an electronic, virtual community - and the effect of feedback from other participants on this process - is beyond the scope of this paper.

Talisman members vigorously defended the appropriateness, even the necessity of the activities carried out on the list. However, in a forum that often tested customary boundaries of Baha'i discourse it is not surprising that not all those who signed on to the list felt comfortable with the content and tone of some of the discussions. Offended subscribers sometimes posted vehement farewell messages and left the group. There were recurring objections by some members that the considered opinions and decisions of Baha'i leaders were not being shown appropriate respect. Despite list rules, accusations of disloyalty to the Baha'i covenant were raised against participants in some cases.

The covenant doctrine is central to Baha'i belief. Briefly described, it consists of a set of statements which specify the leadership succession in the religion - from Baha'u'llah to his eldest son, 'Abdu'l-Baha, and from 'Abdu'l-Baha to his eldest grandson, Shoghi Effendi Rabbani and the Universal House of Justice. In Baha'i understanding, these successive centers of the religion possess the power to pronounce authoritatively on aspects of Baha'i belief and teachings, and obedience to them is obligatory for Baha'is. Members of the community who deny any portion of the leadership succession can be declared covenant-breakers, expelled from the community and ordered shunned by all Baha'is. Baha'is see covenant-breaking as being associated with deep character flaws and immorality.[9] In addition to extensive official guidance regarding the covenant and covenant-breakers, a corpus of unofficial gossip and folklore circulates in the Baha'i community regarding them (Piff 2000: 59-70, Piff and Warburg 1998). To hint or suggest, in the course of conversation, that a Baha'i is 'weak in the covenant' or to imply that he or she is a covenant-breaker is to raise suspicions of the gravest kind regarding him or her.

Instances of suspected covenant-breaking are investigated by the International Teaching Centre, with members of the 'protection boards' of the Continental Boards of Counselors sometimes assigned tasks of fact gathering and/or counseling individuals involved.

9 See Taherzadeh (2000: 242-44), National Spiritual Assembly of the Baha'is of Canada (1976: 10-11).

Talisman's *Initial Promise*

From its early days some participants had seen *Talisman* as a potential stimulant to the evolution of the Baha'i community. Many participants spoke of how much they learned from reading and participating in the exchanges, and applauded the openness and honesty of the discourse. One participant cited factors that made *Talisman* 'productive' despite '(or perhaps because of) recurring blow-ups'. These were, he continued,

- A commitment to open discourse that allows participation by everyone...
- A willingness to allow the arguments and themes being explored to work themselves out naturally. My experience with Baha'i consultation is that often at any hint of disagreement, it is shelved. On Talisman it is not.
- It is written... Written works can be thought through much more clearly ... and polished before being submitted. However, the writing can [also] be spontaneous and for immediate effect.
- There can be strong, and sometimes very immediate ... feedback, and from a number of different viewpoints.
- ...As the discussion evolves, one can see the different aspects, both positive and negative, of various intellectual commitments.

'Clearly', he concluded, 'Internet has brought us something entirely new and unexpected. For me, Talisman has been the clearest proof of its revolutionary character'.[10]

Another participant enthusiastically described *Talisman*'s beneficial effects in his own local community (a farm belt city in the United States). He wrote,

> One of the blessings of Talisman for me and for my community has been in the struggle to create a model of openness in the community. ...In [my city] we have monthly Talisman deepenings. It is my job to collect representative ... postings which reflect the main topics under discussion during the preceding month. All viewpoints are included... A few interesting things have happened

10 Posting to *Talisman* 'Re: acad. discourse / cultural style', 10 November 1995.

as a result of these deepenings. One we have more people teaching the Faith than at any time in my ... years here and have had several declarations. Second the level of genuine respect ... and love among the friends is greater than in any time in my 24 years as a Baha'i.

Not all members of his community had embraced the *Talisman* deepenings with enthusiasm. The poster noted that '...a couple of people who were...the naysayers, the professional devils [sic] advocates, the self assured self righteous ones, who of course *knew* what the one true faith was all about' had become relatively inactive.[11] Though many participants were excited at the new approaches to study of the Baha'i teachings made possible by the list, *Talisman* and its discourse were, in this case at least, seen as alienating by some community members.

Talisman and *'Freedom of Information'*

Practices of information control, which, as noted above, are part of Baha'i administrative practice, represented an area where activities on *Talisman* appeared to promise real change. '...This closed-information approach is not long for this world', wrote one member, '(you are seeing it break down on e-mail before your eyes)'.[12] Another member stated, 'I'm convinced the establishment of Shoghi Effendi's vision for a world wide independent media that reports fairly and without undue outside influence has its germination right here on networks like *Talisman*'.[13] During *Talisman*'s final year some Baha'i administrative rights cases in which the National Spiritual Assembly of the Baha'is of the United States was involved were discussed on the list.

Officially, removal of administrative rights is a sanction imposed by National Spiritual Assemblies on individuals for 'gross immorality and open opposition to the administrative functions of the Faith, and disregard for laws of personal status' (Hornby 1994: 50-51). The particulars of situations in which administrative sanctions are applied to

11 Posting to *Talisman* 'acad. discourse / cultural style', 10 November 1995.

12 Posting to *Talisman* 'history and representation', 20 September 1995.

13 Posting to *Talisman* 'PBS and Baha'u'llah's Free Press', 15 January 1996.

Baha'is are normally not published in Baha'i news organs. Ostensibly as a gesture of the 'openness' of Baha'i judicial process which some group participants advocated, several such cases were exposed in detail on *Talisman*. In one instance, a poster asked for confirmation of something he had heard, that a prominent American Indian believer had lost his administrative rights for participating in a traditional healing ceremony that involved the use of peyote.[14] The posting violated group etiquette in that the name of the person involved was used in the subject line of the message, and some group members objected to a breech of privacy. 'Where questions of individual status are concerned', wrote one, 'there are principles of sanctity and concealment of sins which apply as much as the principles of openness and frankness'.[15] While regretting this particular lapse, other group members extolled and valorized the open sharing of information of this kind. One wrote,

> I extend a hearty thanks to ... and ..., strong voices both, for their equally frank and honest letters on the subject of ....'s [administrative] rights. Their unfettered expression of deeply-felt beliefs strikes me as precisely what we developed Talisman to foster.
>
> But let me say this about privacy – I want none of it... Yes, we have developed a tradition of stripping people of their administrative rights in private, without due process, but does that mean we should continue down that path?
>
> ...The next time my administrative rights are threatened ...I want the light of day to shine on that action. I want access to a public, open, and honest proceeding. I want due process, the right to confront allegations directly, and most of all, I want others to feel free to discuss the case.[16]

In the months the followed, winter/spring 1996, letters between several *Talisman* members and Baha'i institutions that described the specifics of administrative rights cases in which they were involved were posted to the group. A member of the Continental Board of Counselors for

14 Posting to *Talisman*, '.....'s rights', 30 September 1995.

15 Posting to *Talisman*, 'RE: Secrecy and Repression', 5 October 1995.

16 Posting to *Talisman* 'Publicly Confronting Injustice', 1 October 1995.

the Americas, also a *Talisman* subscriber, participated in the exchanges by posting relevant correspondence. The public baring of these cases would seem to have had an unsettling influence in both *Talisman* and in the wider Baha'i community.

The Majnun Post[17]

In February 1996 a message accidentally sent out on *Talisman* by Professor Walbridge raised the suspicions of Baha'i institutions and some *Talisman* subscribers. The message seemed to indicate that a particular agenda for change in the community was being discussed, if not pursued, by some members. '*Any* sort of an organization is an absolute nonstarter at this point', Walbridge stated.

> It will just get us all thrown out on our ears, force the decent people to back the scoundrels, and in all [likelihood] push the Faith back into the intellectual ghetto, much like happened after the expulsion of Sohrab. Let's forget it and erase the messages suggesting it.
>
> ...Ditto direct attacks on individuals. Leave them to dig their own graves...
>
> ...We have hit on a winning strategy, I think:

a) Avoid direct confrontations whenever possible.
b) If attacked... indicate that we are prepared to stand our ground and make trouble.
c) Get information and ideas into circulation.
d) Keep the heat on whenever it can be done without direct confrontations.
e) Do not allow ourselves to be painted as bad Baha'is.
f) Give the powers-that-be a graceful way out of their problems.

> They're starting to eat their horses inside the fortress; let's stay safely in the trenches and not jump up and charge the cannons. ...[No] committees, manifestos, or unnecessary martyrs. In particular, now is the time to lay on earnest charm.[18]

17 *Majnun* was the name of a small Baha'i discussion group for which the posting in question was actually intended.

18 *Talisman* posting, 'Majnun: Reality checks' 7 February 1996. Juan R. Cole

Though Dr. Walbridge had vetoed the prospect, the reference to 'any sort of organization' would likely have alerted Baha'i readers that something untoward was afoot. Creation of 'organizations' within the Baha'i community in opposition to its elected and appointed administration is forbidden by the Baha'i covenant doctrine. The message called attention to the case of Ahmad Sohrab, a former secretary of 'Abdu'l-Baha who in April 1929 formed the New History Society in New York as an independent organization to promote the ideals of the Baha'i religion. The Society was seen as a threat to Baha'i unity, and Shoghi Effendi advised the community that the Society was not 'entitled to the cooperation of the Baha'is' (Smith 1987: 124-125). The message's reference to a 'winning strategy' could well have been seen as implying that some *Talisman* members saw themselves as 'fighting the good fight' against legitimately established Baha'i institutions.

This posting was subsequently cited by the Universal House of Justice as having 'revealed' a 'deliberate' plan 'of internal opposition to the Teachings'. They wrote,

> The strategy being pursued has been to avoid direct attacks on the Faith's Central Figures. The effort, rather, has been to sow the seeds of doubt among believers about the Faith's teachings and institutions by appealing to unexamined prejudices that Baha'is may have unconsciously absorbed from the non-Baha'i society... The effect of exposure to such insincerity about matters vital to humanity's well-being is spiritually corrosive (Universal House of Justice 1999b: 6-7).

The Internet as a Zone of Risk

By Spring 1996 rumors alleging that *Talisman* was about to be closed by Baha'i authorities were circulating in the *Talisman* group and in the wider Baha'i community as well. A message forwarded to a *Talisman* subscriber and posted to the list advised,

---

has posted this message at his website under the title, 'A Baha'i Academic strategizes on how to deal with Administrative Tyranny in the Baha'i Faith in the wake of the wrongful deprivation of ...'s administrative rights, rejecting any action such as organizing the would be contrary to the covenant'. For Cole's commentary on the matter see http://www-personal.umich.edu/~jrcole/bahai/1999/majncole.htm.

'Get off the online network -Talisman before you allow yourself to become embarrassed. Talisman grew from a 1970s 'group' of ... Baha'is, who didn't like the way the institutions of the Faith were doing things and wrote and distributed papers etc. For a while there [sic] opinions were published in a magazine ..., then came to the Internet and so the magazine evolved into 'Talisman'. The net-work is monitored by a 'leader' and things have been hotting up on the network the past week or so and one subscriber was 'expelled' (they believe in free speech and questioning things) for his pointing out of some things. The past 48 hours has shown big infighting and so the House may be intervening. Keep away, no matter how interesting you may have found the group...[19]

Despite the 'in the know' tone reflected in the original poster's statement that 'the House may be intervening', I am unable to confirm that the information cited in the message actually originated at the Baha'i World Centre. It could represent unofficial information current there at the time.

There were other examples of negative views of *Talisman*. According to a scholar who wrote to the Universal House of Justice about the matter in a state in the Northeastern U.S.:

Baha'is who were known to participate on Talisman were actively shunned by their fellow believers until the LSA intervened. ...While the LSA is to be praised, the very fact that the situation existed demonstrates the extent to which paranoia has permeated the community (Maneck 1997).

In another instance, a Counselor speaking at a Persian language Baha'i studies conference had, it was reported, 'categorically stated that the Internet has become a place for those suffering from ... deep spiritual illness' (Maneck 1997).

The May 1996 issue of *The American Bahá'í* reported that issues of firmness in the covenant and the Internet had been raised at the U.S. National Baha'i Convention. According to the report, a Counselor had spoken to the convention about the inevitable increase in challenges from outside and within the Faith.

19 *Talisman* posting, 'Fwd: Here's one source of the closure rumours –' 14 May 2000, forwarding a message of 17 April 1996.

> Individual believers have always borne the responsibility to show wisdom in how we speak, he said. When we go outside the established parameters we can hurt ourselves and retard the growth of the Faith.
>
> With the advent of online communications, however, conversation no longer is ephemeral, said [the] Counselor. Errors spread at the touch of a button could be passed along for years, so even more wisdom than ever is required.
>
> He said the National Assembly has shown great restraint and tolerance with electronic expression. But recently a pattern has developed wherein individuals have crossed over the line into questioning the authority of the institutions.
>
> Now it is a Covenant issue, he said. Institutions at some point will have to ask these individuals to reconsider their behavior and at a further point take administrative action (*The American* Baha'i 1996: 15).

Statements like these illustrate concerns of Baha'i leaders that the Internet and Web were realms of risk, where access to negative or oppositional information about the religion was freely available. To say the least, such content painted a view of Baha'i community life and institutional practice grossly at variance to the received self-image of the community and contrary to the picture presented both internally and externally by official spokespersons. By referring to the matter as a 'Covenant issue', Baha'i leaders were attempting to signal the gravity of the matter, stigmatize those involved, alert the faithful and limit the discouraging and destabilizing effect of such information.

In the end, Baha'i institutions did not act directly to close *Talisman* down. But senior Baha'i institutions launched investigations of a few of the more outspoken members of the group. In May 1996, some of these individuals reportedly received telephone calls from a Baha'i official, informing them that they were being investigated by the International Teaching Centre for remarks posted to *Talisman*.[20] A founding mem-

20 *Talisman* posting, 'Facts and Meaning, Constraints on Freedom of Speech', 15 May 1996. I have no direct knowledge of the origins and course of the investigations I have mentioned. However, my understanding is that *Talisman* was monitored by members of senior Baha'i institutions who became concerned at the content and tone of some of the postings to the group. A member of the Continental Board of Counsellors for the Americas was asked to speak to some of the individuals who had authored these postings,

ber of the group renounced his Baha'i membership, a development that had a chilling effect on the group.[21] On 20 May 1996 Professor Walbridge, writing that he believed the 'costs' of continuing the list outweighed its benefits, announced his decision to discontinue it.[22]

*Post-*Talisman *Developments*[23]

A few more recent developments relating to Baha'i Internet discussion groups will be summarized here to bring the narrative more or less up to date. *Talisman* at Indiana University was succeeded almost immediately by *Talisman* at the University of Michigan, a group I was not able to observe. In December 1999 a successor group, *Talisman9*, was established within the Egroups.com hosting domain, now absorbed into Yahoogroups.com. At present there are 239 subscribers to the group. Members must abide by simple rules - no personal flames, no informing on members to Baha'i institutions, and no accusations of heresy.[24] Separately, alt.religion.bahai was established in the Usenet hierarchy in 1997 as a completely unmoderated forum for uncensored discussion of the Baha'i religion; it was succeeded by *talk.religion.bahai* in early January

---

and, apparently, to discuss or at least refer to possible sanctions that could be imposed on them if they did not desist. I have not seen the internal reports and communications that would have grounded and conveyed Baha'i institutions' instructions to investigate the matter. For published accounts, see Johnson (1997), Bacquet (2001) and Cole (2002).

21 *Talisman* posting 'Withdrawal', 3 May 1996.

22 *Talisman* posting, 'The End of Talisman', 20 May 1996.

23 The groups outlined in the present section have pursued *Talisman*'s pattern of open discussion of Baha'i topics. In addition to these, mention should be made of Mark Foster's 'Bahai-studies' list. Dr. Foster, a Baha'i, a *Talisman* participant, and professor of sociology at Johnson County Community College (Overland Park, Kansas), created this list in 1996 as a facility for continuing academic discussion of Baha'i topics. List rules specifically proscribed posts critical of Baha'i institutions. Archives of this list (from1998) are available at http://www.escribe.com/religion/bahaist/.

24 The web address of the group is http://groups.yahoo.com/group/Talisman9/.
In Internet jargon, to 'flame' is to post an email message intended to insult and provoke, directed with hostility at a particular person or people. As a noun the term refers to an instance of flaming (see www.houghi.org/jargon/dictionary).

1999.[25] Among a wide variety of other topics, a more or less ongoing disparagement of Baha'i administrative culture is maintained on these groups, and a hardening of positions against Baha'i institutions can be observed. One can read on these groups of two actions - a legal suit and a formal complaint of violation of privacy - brought by individuals against Baha'i institutions who they believe had wronged them.[26]

In addition, discussion groups have recently been created for individuals who identify themselves as Baha'i believers but remain unconnected with the Baha'i administration. The 'Yahoo Ex-Bahai club' presents itself as a 'friendly forum for those who have left the Baha'i organization or are questioning aspects of Baha'i organizational practice'.[27] The discussion board 'BeliefNet.com' includes a section for 'unenrolled Baha'is' described as 'those who follow Baha'i teaching, but who have opinions and beliefs that may not be officially approved by the Universal House of Justice, and who may not be enrolled members of the Baha'i Faith'.[28]

The effort to create and maintain such spaces can be seen as further

25 Additionally, the *H-Bahai* discussion forum, sponsored by *H-Net* and hosted by Michigan State University, was started up in February 1997 as a list for discussion of scholarly issues and research relating to the Babi and Baha'i religions.

26 The actions in question are 1) a formal complaint to the national Privacy Commissioner brought by a New Zealand woman whose membership in the Baha'i community was revoked in 2000 by the National Spiritual Assembly of that country, alleging that in their dealings with her the assembly had violated that country's privacy act; and 2) a lawsuit brought against a local spiritual assembly in New Mexico in 2001 by a member of the community, alleging the assembly had defrauded and libelled her (see http://www.fglaysher.com/bahaicensorship/NMLawsuit.htm). Both of these matters have now been resolved. In the first, the Privacy Commissioner found no basis for action on his part (see http://home.clear.net.nz/pages/alisonz/strike.htm), and the second, according to Baha'i informants, had been dismissed. The website 'Baha'i Faith and Religious Freedom of Conscience' (http://www.fglaysher.com/bahaicensorship/) has links to documents relating to both cases.

27 See the 'Founder's Message' at http://clubs.yahoo.com/clubs/exbahais.

28 See http://www.beliefnet.com/boards/discussion_list.asp?boardID=23172.

attempts to place participants beyond the reach of the Baha'i organization – a radical form of 'bypass' that may foster maintenance of 'safe' forums for discussions of controversial Baha'i issues, but that may also limit the influence of the discussions on the mainstream Baha'i community. At the same time, by establishing alternative sources of information, these efforts contribute to an appearance of multipolarity and have the potential to erode the religion's officially-promoted image as a harmonious, univocal community.

Internet Apostates

Sociological perspectives on the activities of marginalized members of religious communities and 'apostates' – individuals who have exited organizations in polarized situations and adopted an oppositional stance to the organization – shed light on the events and discourse reviewed here.[29] In a study of apostasy, sociologist David Bromley has identified three types of organization, 'allegiant 'contestant and 'subversive' (Bromley 1998: 21-25). The degree of control over the exit process exercised by the organization, and the social dynamics of the leavetaker's 'career' vary according to the type of organization he or she is exiting.

Allegiant organizations are those that exist in a state of low tension with the surrounding society; their interests 'coincide to a high degree with those of other organizations in their environments'. Internal and external claims are difficult to marshal against allegiant organizations, as such organizations are themselves able to manage the process of settling disputes, enhancing their capacity for self-protection and 'dispute containment'.

Contestant organizations, best exemplified by profit making businesses, exist in a state of 'moderate' tension in relation to external groups, many of which may be direct competitors. Claims are much

29 Instances of similar activities by apostates and/or disaffected members vis-à-vis other religious organizations are too numerous to treat in any detail in the present discussion. An excellent place to begin exploring this issue is the Religious Movements Homepage sponsored by the Department of Sociology of Religion at the University of Virginia (http://religiousmovements.lib.Virginia.edu/). Hundreds of groups are profiled, with summaries of the history, doctrines, and controversies surrounding each and links to websites both official and unofficial.

easier to muster against such organizations than against allegiant ones, and the contestant organization is less able than the allegiant to control the resolution of the claim. Third party adjudicators may be called in to review the case, a situation in which the contestant organization is likely to be guaranteed specific rights, but to lose some measure of control over the outcome.

'Subversive' organizations are those that exist in a state of high tension and 'low coincidence of interests' with organizations in the surrounding milieu. 'Indeed', writes Bromley, "'subversive' is a label employed by opponents specifically to discredit these organizations'. Organizations so labeled are confronted by a 'broad coalition of opponents and few allies'. Some of the more controversial alternative religious movements may illustrate this category. Claims against such organizations tend to proliferate; they may be beset by social control initiatives specifically intended to discredit, contain, suppress, or destroy them. Bromley goes on to theorize that three types of exit roles, defector, whistleblower, and apostate are characteristic, respectively, of the above three types of organization, allegiant, contestant and subversive. For our present purposes, it will not be necessary to further summarize his argument.

In Iran, and in certain other countries in the Moslem world, the Baha'i religion is seen as subversive. Religious and secular authorities actively oppose community activities and individual Baha'is are sometimes at risk of arrest or worse. In the Western world and in some developing countries, the Baha'i religion probably resides somewhere on the continuum between an 'allegiant' and a 'contestant' organization. The religion's stance of 'obedience to government' and 'non-involvement in partisan politics', its participation in United Nations conferences, its fostering of inter-religious dialogue and the absence in its teachings of the sorts of extreme or rigorous practices that have contributed to the stigmatization of some New Religions Movements have meant that in many countries, Baha'is are looked upon as loyal, untroublesome, peace loving citizens, and the religion's founding principles seen as of potential benefit to their host societies. Such factors would tend to characterize an 'allegiant' religious organization. On the other hand, in many national communities, Baha'is are actively attempting to win converts (to the express displeasure, at times, of local religious authorities) an aspect of a 'contestant' posture vis-à-vis the surrounding society and other religious groups.

The Internet has given a voice and means of interconnection to a group of articulate individuals, marginalized in the Baha'i community or no longer members of it, who are willing to alert academics and the public to authoritarian elements and alleged corruption in Baha'i administrative practice and to call attention to what they see as instances of injustice perpetrated by Baha'i institutions. Such 'whistle blowing' activities may succeed in raising the suspicions of organizations in the surrounding society against the Baha'is, and result in some degradation of the religion's public image. As 'allegiant' status is a matter dependent on public perceptions, a tarnished image would expose the Baha'i community to more of the types of confrontations characteristic of contestant or subversive organizations. Baha'is might even be persecuted as a religious group with a program contrary to democratic values.

Additionally, the existence of an ongoing discourse, accessible to interested Baha'is and others, which sustains a continuing criticism of Baha'i administration, may erode the trust of the rank and file in Baha'i institutions. Even if Baha'i apostates make no attempt to create formal organizations (and doing so would, in any case, further undermine their credibility in the eyes of the broader Baha'i community) the presence of their websites and discussion groups create competing loci of information decidedly at odds with official views.

Institutional Responses

In so far as their actions can be observed, Baha'i institutions have adopted a relatively cautious approach in dealing with the Internet. Measures taken include the fostering of moderated discussion groups in which discussions are kept within defined bounds by trusted members, spreading the word in conferences and other community gatherings of the dangers of the Internet, and publishing compilations of 'guidance' regarding the issues at stake.[30] In a few instances, individuals who have used the Internet to propagate information critical of Baha'i institutions have been removed from Baha'i membership. Additionally, various Baha'i speakers have construed the difficulties surrounding the Internet as being part of certain 'mental tests' foreshadowed in statements by 'Abdu'l-Baha as destined to

30 See Universal House of Justice (1999a).

afflict Western Baha'is, a view that may help Baha'is put the matter into perspective.

Broader initiatives launched by senior Baha'i institutions may also play a role in limiting the adverse effects of oppositional discourse on the community. Notable among such initiatives is an 'External Affairs Strategy' announced in September 1994, in which it was envisaged that 'the Faith' could 'begin persuasively to represent itself as a significant global influence promoting the emergence of world peace, gradually overcoming any impression of being merely another sectarian group carrying out propaganda'.[31] This strategy was apparently not formulated in response to challenges posed by the Internet, but it may, if successful, ameliorate such challenges. If Baha'is are able to foster a favorable view of themselves among organizations of the surrounding society, the claims of opponents will seem less credible.

For Baha'is, there is potentially more at stake than just public image. Baha'is believe that the precepts of their religion can bring about world peace, and that if people become acquainted with Baha'u'llah's teachings, they will be positively influenced by them. If, on the other hand, people become convinced that the Baha'is are a group whose program is antithetical to core values of their society, they may decide to actively limit or resist Baha'i propagation.[32]

A second major initiative, given increasing attention in communications of senior Baha'i institutions in recent years is the fostering of 'Baha'i institutes'. These involve close study of basic Baha'i texts by small groups called 'study circles' that learn the fundamentals of Baha'i history and teachings, and are encouraged to engage in local teaching and service projects. The stated aim of the activities is to make Baha'i communities self-sustaining and able to handle anticipated rapid growth in numbers. The 'institute process' was apparently

31 External Affairs Strategy: A paper prepared by an Ad Hoc Committee and approved by the Universal House of Justice for inclusion with a circular letter dated 22 September 1994 written on behalf of the Universal House of Justice to all National Spiritual Assemblies. Quote from page 3.

32 Baha'is allege that progress of the religion in German-speaking Europe was hindered in recent decades by a book by Francesco Ficicchia (1981). According to Baha'i accounts, the book, which portrayed Baha'i history and teachings in an unfavourable light, was seen as authoritative by religious and secular authorities. See Schaefer et al. (2000: 7-8 and passim).

conceived well before the Baha'i community encountered the Internet, but if successful may serve to inoculate Baha'i believers against its undesirable influences.[33]

Summary and Conclusions

The present study has described various ways in which the Baha'i community has viewed the Internet and the facility it offers for instantaneous transmission of and access to information. We have considered three, and adumbrated factors that have contributed to their construction. The writings of Shoghi Effendi, and the vision of the Baha'i religion as embodying the motivating power and organizing principles of a future global civilization has encouraged a view of the Internet as a technology of great promise. Today it assists the propagation and external relations of the Baha'i religion, and is a significant factor in the process of drawing the earth together into one country. Its reach and openness would seem destined to aid in fostering international citizenship. Baha'i agencies all over the world utilize email for instantaneous communications, mount Baha'i scriptures and news on web pages, and sponsor Baha'i discussion lists. However, the ultimate benefits of the technology remain to be seen.

A second view of the Internet is as a place for building a special kind of Baha'i community. The example considered here was *Talisman*, an experiment in creating an area of protected speech where challenging issues of Baha'i life, teachings and history could be explored. *Talisman* offered a dramatic and turbulent example of the excitement and challenges of community building, but it was just one of many Baha'i cyber communities. In ongoing fashion, Baha'is and others interested in the implications of Baha'u'llah's message continue to negotiate the maintenance of virtual communities that bring participants together in shared discursive spaces. In this regard, and despite the example of

33 I have not seen any message or letter from Baha'i administrative agencies assigning Baha'i institutes and study circles a role in community 'protection'. It is interesting, however, that in the United States, Auxiliary Board Members for protection (not propagation) were given oversight over development of these institutes (comment made to author by a former U.S. Auxiliary Board member for protection). I am not informed whether protection boards in other countries were also given this assignment.

Talisman, the Internet has the potential to foster tolerance and openness, and, perhaps, through the consultation of individuals of differing backgrounds and points of view, to develop more fully nuanced, multifaceted and complete understandings of the Baha'i teachings than have been created heretofore.

Finally, as the Internet played host to oppositional discourse, it came to be viewed by both leaders and the general membership as an area of potential risk, an arena in which Baha'i institutions are subjected to persistent derogation, and from which the faithful must be warned.

As the Baha'i Faith emerges more and more onto the world stage, its externally visible profile becomes a matter of increasing importance. At present, online critics of the Baha'i religion appear to lack the numbers and resources to create a serious threat to the religion's public image. At present, in an atmosphere of general public acceptance, at least in the West, Baha'i agencies, authorized spokespersons, and official publications portray and extol positive developments and accomplishments of the community. Marginalized members and former members contest this view in discussion groups and on websites, which, while modest in size, are international in reach and widely accessible. Coverage of the Baha'i religion by major news organizations has been notably positive in recent decades but continuation of this state of affairs is by no means guaranteed. The global interconnectedness of the Internet and World Wide Web increases the stakes of the matter, and the long-term effect of online critics on Baha'i public image, Baha'i self-perception, and even, perhaps, on community existence and livelihood, is as yet unclear.

References

Bacquet, K. (2001). Enemies Within: Conflict and Control in the Baha'i Community. *Cultic Studies Journal*, vol. 18: 109-40.

Bromley, D. (1998). The Social Construction of Contested Exit Roles: Defectors, Whistleblowers and Apostates, in D. Bromley (ed.) *The Politics of Religious Apostasy: The Role of Apostates in the Transformation of Religious Movements.* Westport: Praeger.

Cole, J. (2002). Fundamentalism in the Contemporary U.S. Baha'i Community. *Review of Religious Research,* vol. 43, no. 3: 195-217.

Ficicchia, F. (1981). *Der Baha'ismus. Weltreligion der Zukunft? Geschichte, Lehre und Organisation in kritischer Anfrage.* Stuttgart: Evangelische Zentralstelle fur Weltanschauungsfragen.

Hornby, H. (1994). *Lights of Guidance: A Baha'i Reference File*. New Delhi: Baha'i Publishing Trust.

Johnson, K. P. (1997). Baha'i Leaders Vexed by On-line Critics, *Gnosis* no. 42: 9-10.

Kanter, R. (1995). *World Class: Thriving Locally in the Global Economy*. New York: Simon and Schuster.

Maneck, S. (1997). Letter 10 May 1997 to the Universal House of Justice on the topic of 'Academics on the Internet'. http://internet.susanmaneck.com/.

National Spiritual Assembly of the Baha'is of Canada (1976). *The Power of the Covenant Part Two: The Problem of Covenant-Breaking*. Thornhill: Publications Baha'i Canada.

Piff, D. (2000). *Baha'i Lore*. Oxford: George Ronald.

Piff, D. and Warburg, M. (1998). Enemies of the Faith: Rumours and Anecdotes as Self-definition and Social Control in the Baha'i Religion, in E. Barker and M. Warburg, (eds.) *New Religions and New Religiosity*. Aarhus: Aarhus University Press.

Schaeffer, U., Towfigh, N., and Gollmer, U. (2000). *Making the Crooked Straight: A Contribution to Baha'i Apologetics*. Oxford: George Ronald.

Shade, L. (1996) Is there Free Speech on the Net? Censorship in the Global Information Infrastructure, in R. Shields, (ed.) *Cultures of Internet: Virtual Spaces, Real Histories, Living Bodies*. London: Sage.

Shoghi Effendi (1974). *The World Order of Baha'u'llah*. Wilmette: Baha'i Publishing Trust.

Smith, P. (1987). *The Babi and Baha'i Religions: From Messianic Shi'ism to a World Religion*. Cambridge: Cambridge University Press.

Taherzadeh, A. (2000). *The Child of the Covenant*. Oxford: George Ronald.

The American Bahá'í (17 May 1996).

Universal House of Justice (1999a). *Issues Related to the Study of the Baha'i Faith*. Wilmette: Baha'i Publishing Trust.

Universal House of Justice (1999b). Issues related to the study of the Faith. Letter from the Department of the Secretariat of the Universal House of Justice to All National Spiritual Assemblies, 7 April 1999. *Baha'i Canada*. Rahmat, B.E. 156 (June-July 1999).

Walbridge, J. (1994). Statement describing *Talisman* issued to subscribers (19 October).

Warburg, M. (2003). Religious Groups and Globalisation: A Comparative Perspective, in J. Beckford and J. Richardson (eds.) *Challenging Religion: Cults and Controversies*. London: Routledge.

CHAPTER 12

The Canadian Baha'is 1938–2000: Constructions of Oneness in Personal and Collective Identity

Lynn Echevarria

Globalization theorist Roland Robertson defines globalization, in its basic sense, as involving 'the compression of the entire world on the one hand and a rapid increase in consciousness of the whole world, on the other' (1998a: 29). This consciousness, he argues, is not a corollary to globalisation but rather intrinsic to it (1998b: 376). In this paper I will focus on the second part of Robertson's definition, 'the consciousness of the whole world', and how this consciousness has been nurtured within the Canadian Baha'i community.

Since the inception of the Baha'i Faith the concept of a global community has been vigorously promoted in the teachings of the religion. While this world vision was not immediately understandable to early Canadian Baha'is, it gradually became realized through their engagement with the teachings of their Faith, the social processes of Baha'i community life and the administrative structure of the religion. My analysis of the life histories of Canadian Baha'is shows that an integral aspect of the construction of a Baha'i identity involves the process of incorporating world-mindedness into the self-concept.

Background to the Study

This paper is framed through a sociological perspective and draws upon data from my doctoral research on religion and identity in the Baha'i Faith, conducted in the late 1990s. The sample of twenty people, ages sixty-eight to ninety-three, are from diverse racial and ethnic backgrounds, and live/lived in nine of the Canadian provinces.[1] Additional interviews brought to a total of thirty, the number of people who were interviewed about their Baha'i experience. The people participating in this qualitative study became Baha'is in the 1938 –1950s time period, and so their life stories mirror understandings that have been gleaned and reflected upon over the course of fifty to sixty years.

The life story interviews took place over a three-year period from 1993-1996. The interviews were open-ended, self-directed, and supplemented with a questionnaire only when necessary. In this type of life history, participants speak about their life course at length – from childhood to their present age. This method is different than an interview, which is conducted for a few hours and where the person shares memories about certain events, or gives answers to specific questions.

The stories of the cohort were audiotape recorded and transcribed verbatim.[2] Besides participant observation over the course of many years, I also undertook archival research at the National Baha'i Centre in Toronto, Ontario. Perusing personal correspondence, bulletins, newsletters, official correspondence and minutes of national agencies and committees, enabled me to acquire a broader picture of the 1940s-1960s time period in the National Canadian Baha'i community.

1 The life-history participants of my doctoral study represent various ethnic and immigrant backgrounds, including Hungarian, Jewish-Canadian, Scot, French-Canadian, Black-Canadian, Iranian, and Anglo-Canadian. The religious background of the people in my sample is not as diverse. All of the women came from a Christian background except one who was born into an Iranian Baha'i family, and one who was born into a Canadian Jewish family. The men in the study followed a similar religious background. All of their families were from the main Christian churches, except for three men who came from diverse religious backgrounds such as an Iranian Baha'I, a British spiritualist, and a Thai Buddhist. The age groupings of the women, when interviewed, included two in their late sixties, six in their late seventies, and three in their early nineties. The men were all in their late seventies.

2 Copies of the life narratives were sent to all those participants who wanted them. The length of interviews varied: the longest was 990 tape-recorded minutes or 16.5 hours, the shortest was 135 minutes, or 2.25 taped hours, and the average was 7.5 taped hours.

I chose these people because of their age, and not according to their achievements in the religion or in society. I knew that a few had a reputation of being outstanding in one way or another for their contributions to Canadian society in social and economic development, or to the service of the religion in general. It did not become apparent until later, however, that all these people were very involved in the private and public activities of the religion. In fact, nearly all were avid students of the Baha'i teachings, all were travel speakers and/or lecturers for the Baha'i Faith, many are people of distinguished administrative experience, many are greatly loved and respected within and without the Baha'i community, and all, with two exceptions, were pioneers[3] to other parts of Canada or overseas.

The reader of this paper may have questions about the life-history participants this paper: 'Do these people reflect the range of people in the Baha'i community of the last century, and does this paper reflect the understandings of Baha'is of the present day?' In response, I found, through conducting five full life-history interviews of middle-aged Baha'is that the primary socialization experiences were almost identical in the lives of both the older and the middle-age Baha'is – i.e. engagement with the teachings of the religion, and participation in the social processes of community life deepened the sense of self and religious identity. Any differences would be cultural and historically based – for example, the youth culture that came into the religion in the 1960s, and the changes that occurred within the administrative structure as a result of different goals, plans, and institutions.

As a final word in this introduction I wish to note that, although the short excerpts in this paper do not do justice to the rich accounts of experience transmitted through the life story process, I hope they give the reader some sense of how the Baha'is made meaning of their lives.

3 Pioneering is the term used for a person who volunteers to teach the religion in other places or countries. Usually these people are self-subsistent, except in cases where it is impossible (due to circumstances out of their control) to work in the receiving country. In the case of individuals who intend to travel for the religion or perform these missionary services, they are encouraged to take their families into consultation and consideration, sacrificing if the circumstances dictate, to remain with their families (Shoghi Effendi 1983: 448, 450-1).

An Integrative Global Narrative: The Unifying Concept of Progressive Revelation

'For the first time in human history, self and society are interrelated in a global milieu…', Anthony Giddens observes, 'and this results in 'transformations in self identity' involving every aspect of personal life' as well as the establishment of 'social connections of very wide scope…' (1991: 32). When we consider how religion contributes to this process, James Beckford points out that religions provide: '[M]any of the symbols of common humanity and are therefore implicated in globalization' (2000: 4, 90). Robertson similarly has argued that it is 'a mistake to consider that material-economic forces are the prime mover in the formation of a world as a whole', and that this type of thinking has a 'long history in theology and metaphysical thinking' (1994: 123,131).

The teachings of the Baha'u'llah, in keeping with the traditions of the major world religions, provide a theology that enables people to understand the meaning and purpose of their life. It stands to reason, therefore, that in any examination of the construction of Baha'i consciousness we first need to address fundamental theological concepts.

The concept 'progressive revelation' was referred to by all the Baha'is as very significant to their understanding of religions in the world and their understanding of themselves as Baha'is. According to the Baha'i teachings, humanity has undergone a maturation process guided by God's spiritual teachings revealed through a series of Messengers – the world's principal educators. And further, that God's divine revelation is continuous, progressive, and suited to the requirements of humanity. It is a part of God's eternal covenant to unite humankind and facilitate the advancement of world civilization.[4]

The Baha'is in my study found that the concept of progressive revelation enabled them to 'place' themselves historically within the sometimes-confusing array of world religions. It also gave them a

4 In this regard, the Baha'i writings observe that the maturation of humankind has developed in ever-widening circles of unity – from the family to the tribe, from the city-state to the nation. The next circle or stage in this collective growth, the Baha'i teachings observe, is the 'organization of society as a planetary civilization' (Hatcher & Martin 1985: 76).

means by which to understand the connections and universality of spiritual teachings in all the major world religions. Progressive revelation was an interpretative tool for them to understand religion and civilization on a continuum:

To me I believe in Baha'u'llah because he taught me progressive revelation, to recognize all the founders of all the past [religions] and in the future also.... I was born as Buddhist and didn't believe in God, and being Baha'i I am able to accept God. (Tony Panalaks 1994)

Well, progressive revelation was the main one (teaching)¼that in each age God guides mankind. I always used to think, 'Why would God leave out the Hindus or the Buddhists or the Moslems, or whatever? Why are they heathens?' You know, people would talk about them as if they were bad or evil. (Joanie Anderson 1995)

The important thing...that was the concept of Progressive Revelation. Oh, sure because that's purely a scientific concept. Ruby China said - she gave me the idea, you know, that revelation came in direct proportion to the spiritual capacity of the people! Just like any natural law, or physical law. And I was stumped! That was it! That was the first thing that impacted on me - progressive revelation.... (Bob Donnelly 1994)

Now this one is one that we are very familiar with now. That God is like the sun, Baha'u'llah is one of the more recent reflections of the Sun, and all the different Prophets in between are listed there. Now for me, at that school in that year, and my first year as a Baha'i, that visual depiction of ...progressive revelation, was very easy for me to understand. (Ruth Eyford 1995)

These people indicated that the concept of progressive revelation gave them a feeling of certitude about their connection as Baha'is to people of other religious belief systems. The story of progressive revelation serves as a meta-narrative through which to view humanity's history and evolving religious and global identity.

The Consciousness of Oneness: Building a Vision

While the concept of progressive revelation provided a universal construct for Baha'is to understand the historical evolution and connection of all world religions, it was another theological concept - Baha'u'llah's teaching about the oneness of humanity - that provided an understanding of the potential for unity of the entire human race:

> That feeling of love and, of course peace...the teachings about peace. Yes, progressive revelation was the most important. But ... in that is that all the people in the world were included. You know, they were Black, Japanese, or whatever¼the oneness of mankind. That was very, very wonderful to me because I couldn't see how, if somebody else was a different colour, they should be less important or not be cared about. It really upset me¼. All the teachings seemed so wonderful, the equality of men and women especially, of course. I think a lot of women are attracted to that, and men, too¼and unity, and the love within the Faith, and the love of all humanity. (Joanie Anderson 1995)

This foundational teaching of oneness permeates every Baha'i precept. According to the Baha'i writings: God is one, though the Creator has been given different names; religion is one, each religion is a part of the plan of God for humanity's evolution to a stage of global peace and unity; and, humanity is one - all humanity has been created equal with the 'same God-given capacities' and is as one organic unit in the sight of the Creator (Hatcher & Martin 1985: 75-76).

The theology of oneness is so important to the Baha'i Faith that it is embedded in the sacred symbol of the religion. This symbol is displayed in the homes of believers and worn as a personal adornment in the form of a pendant, pin or ringstone. The symbol is a signifier of belief and affiliation, and has been used by the Baha'is as a means to illustrate the teachings of progressive revelation and 'the three onenesses' (as the Canadian Baha'is liked to describe that spiritual principle).

The symbol is also a mnemonic for Baha'i theology and signifies linkages of oneness for the Baha'is: 'It is an attraction... it is like a picture, it tells a thousand words, it tells the story of the two prophets... the connection between God and man... and you know that's the sort of meaning to it...' (Ethel Martens 1994). Another person said the symbol was a means for introducing the religion: 'It was teaching. Those who saw it were curious, so you would tell them [about] God, mankind and the messengers etc....' (Joanie Anderson 1995). Yet another saw that the symbol and its depiction of the three onenesses was, as she termed it, a 'summary of the whole theology of the Baha'i Faith!' (Aqdas Javid 1994).

Over the course of the last century the oneness concept has been incorporated into the basic and advanced curriculum of Baha'i schools for all ages. Lyrics of a Baha'i children's song, still current and well loved in the1970s, reflects the popularization of this concept in the Baha'i community: 'God is one, man is one, and all the religions agree…If everyone learned the three onenesses, we'd have world unity' (King 1948). Also very popular among the Canadian Baha'is were the statements of Baha'u'llah, '[L]et your vision be world embracing rather than confined to your own selves', and 'the world is but one country and mankind its citizens' (1949: 94, 250). These sayings were memorized and shared with others as an integral part of being a Baha'i. This teaching about oneness provided the Baha'is with the notion of a wider loyalty as world citizens.

The Particular and the Universal: The Work of Shoghi Effendi Rabbani in Building Transnational Identity

While religions provide symbols of common humanity, they also transmit 'particularistic ideas about humanity', and in this manner they 'appropriate and filter the experience of global in local terms' (Beckford 2000: 491). Ursula King articulates the importance of the global to religion as:

> [A] different kind of consciousness which takes into account a new order of complexity wherein the particular and the universal, the local and the regional, interact in quite a new and previously unknown way. There is a search for new identities both transnational and personal...which seeks a new unity and expresses itself in the search for a collective will and for a new global order (1992: 153).

When we consider that the Baha'i religion was brought from Iran to the Western world – a radically different cultural and religious context from the religion's origins – it is useful to examine how the Canadians (1926-1957) were socialized to a Baha'i identity.

In the early part of the last century the infant Canadian Baha'i community was comprised of scattered groups of locally-focused individuals; there was no national community until 1948. Shoghi Effendi Rabbani, the head of the Baha'i Faith, who lived in Haifa Israel, conducted an extensive correspondence with Canadian Baha'is. A study of thirty-nine of his letters to Canada, dated 1926-1957, shows a purposeful process of educating and empowering this young Baha'i community toward an understanding of its potential identity.

The first aspect of Shoghi Effendi's work that we will briefly consider is the articulation of a religious history for the Canadians. In his letters, and in his major book of that time,[5] he refers often to the accomplishments and service of the early North America Baha'is, and also to the early Persian Baha'is. Not only does he advance the idea of a shared religious history between the Baha'is of the East and the rest of the world, he also assigns the Canadians a role in this history. To the Baha'is of North America he gave the appellation the 'spiritual descendants of the dawnbreakers of a heroic age' (Shoghi Effendi 1963: 6). The term 'dawnbreakers' refers to the early Babi and Baha'i believers in Iran who devoted their lives to teaching and travelling, many becoming martyrs, for their newly-adopted Faith.[6] This spiritual appellation was conveyed to a group of people who, in general, had no idea about Iran or its peoples, and knew little about other peoples in the world at that time. We can understand retrospectively that applying the title 'spiritual descendants' to the Canadians could, and indeed did, evoke for them a sense of a spiritual inheritance, a familial legacy from the early believers of their religion.

The second important aspect in the construction of religious identity is the effect of Shoghi Effendi's plans for expansion of the religion. The parochialism of the Canadian Baha'is would change radically as a result of these plans, which were, in and of themselves, a major turning point in the history of the Canadian community, as we shall see.

The Seven Year Plan (1937-1944) was designed to establish govern-

5 See Shoghi Effendi *God Passes By* (Wilmette, Illinois: Baha'i Publishing Trust 1957).

6 This description of spiritual dawnbreakers, was given to the Baha'is of North America in 1939 in *The Advent of Divine Justice*, which describes the potentials and the destiny of the western Baha'i community and the American nation. See Shoghi Effendi *The Advent of Divine Justice* (Wilmette, Ill.: Baha'i Publishing Trust, 1963).

ing councils (assemblies) across Canada and to missionize the religion in North and South America. A description of the initial response of the Canadians reflects the self-focus and inward nature of the Baha'i communities at that time:

> ... [A]nd then the Plan came along and we thought – oh dear we will never do that! How can we have an assembly in every province of Canada, and at the same time have a Baha'i in every country of Latin America. Latin America nobody ever went there! (Audrey Robarts 1994).

Baha'is did, however, respond to fulfil the goals of this plan, and by the time the Ten Year Plan (1953-1963) was introduced, their orientation was much more receptive such that: '[T]hirty-one percent of Baha'is during this time moved more than once, some even as much as ten times' (van den Hoonaard personal communication 1996). The Ten Year Plan was mentioned as very significant by the people in this study. All but two of these people moved to establish new communities, mostly to other countries, during this Plan. Simply put, the Plan changed their lives. It was the catalyst for them to become outer-focused, and it provided them with a mandate for agency:

> I think that, really the Ten Year Crusade was a maturing for the Canadian Baha'i community. And that's when there were Canadians spread all around the world as pioneers. And they still have a wonderful outlook for the world-wide Baha'i community, and outpouring of pioneers from Canada. (Bill Carr 1995)

The act of people moving to other places facilitated a new perspective that the community could/would be a national and, indeed, a global community. This shift in understanding occurred not only for those who moved, but also for their families and Baha'i friends and communities back home.[7] At the same time plans were being given to the Baha'is in other countries to pioneer. One of the Iranian pioneers, who moved to Canada in the 1960s, had this to say about the

7 Shoghi Effendi encouraged the Canadian Baha'is to sacrifice in order to reach the goals which were 'principally national and universal' and to 'centre their complete attention on the obligations of the Ten Year Crusade' (*Messages to Canada*), 43.

compelling effect of Shoghi Effendi's (the Guardian) directives on the Persian Baha'is:

> Oh, the messages of the Guardian was what galvanized the whole society. The Guardian's messages was what really brought all the pioneers to move from Iran and go. There was a time that you wouldn't see a picture of any assembly all across the world without Persians in the middle. What happened – the Guardian made people rise up and pioneer. His letters were just magnificent. We lived for it; we lived to receive letters of the Guardian. It was like a lifeblood for everybody in Iran. That was what galvanized the community and corrected the community. (Aqdas Javid 1994)

The idea of international co-operation in these plans also brought a sense of world solidarity as Baha'is learned that people in other countries were also pioneering. As one person explains: '[W]e combined with the rest of the world, and so our outlook was *out* to pioneering and the fulfilment of the Ten Year Crusade' (Francoise Smith, 1994 emphasis mine).

The shift of thinking that took place in 1953 was facilitated in direct response to the ethic of dispersion Shoghi Effendi had promoted in his plans and directives. It enabled the community to move from an ideological perception of the world as one country to a conscious realization that, as Baha'is, they possessed a transnational identity, both in a Baha'i world community *and* in a global community. This understanding was grounded in personal experience and agency, as we shall now examine.

Pioneering: Cross-Pollinating a Consciousness of World Citizenship

Let us look a little closer at the dimensions of pioneering and its effect on the identity of Baha'is. All of the Baha'is I interviewed responded to the plans of Shoghi Effendi and spent their whole lives engaged in community building. In response to the plans of expansion, all of the Baha'is in my study, except two, became pioneers to such places as South Africa, India, Iceland, French Africa, St. Helena, as well as to many places in Canada. The two people who did not pioneer are of Black-African Canadian heritage. Their life stories parallel the Black experience in Canada from 1920-1960 – lives critically affected by institutionalized racism. This racism constrained their opportunity for higher education or job choice, and thus they were denied the flexibility and mobility to settle in new places and restricted in their life choices. Instead, they devoted their lives to combating racism and working for social change in their secular and Baha'i communities (Echevarria-Howe, 1992).

When pioneering, Baha'is leave their own country and culture, and commit themselves to a new life. This involves 'enlarging and enriching one's circle of association' and the 'expansion of inherited boundaries and norms' (Drewek 1996:166-7). Pioneering was central to their lives - it became a core part of their identity:

Gale Bond, pioneer to Jamaica and the Canadian North (1994): 'I have no idea what would have become of me but I know now from this perspective that the Baha'i Faith gave me a goal a purpose...a conscious purpose.... I was willing to pioneer...'.

Richard Tranter, pioneer to St. Helena and Saskatchewan (1995): 'And then, too, you know, another challenge was to pioneer. Give up my livelihood and go somewhere else to start all over again. You know...I'd spent eighteen years, or so, developing a business and my livelihood, getting well established. Then, all of a sudden, you...you just give that up and you go pioneering. I mean, in those days, you didn't have a job to go. You didn't go out there and look...see if you had a job or anything. You just...I'd never been out west, before. We just sold our business and away we went. Well, some of them [friends] thought we were nuts. Most of them thought we were crazy, but, uh...we knew what we were doing'.

Aqdas Javid, pioneer in Britain and Canada (1994): 'And I am very happy that I pioneered and this is one of the fulfilment of my wishes that as a young girl I wanted to pioneer. And I hope I die in pioneering post!'

Francoise Smith, pioneer in Quebec (1994): 'That's how the Faith could spread so fast. Because people put everything aside and went. That was impressing (sic)'.

Bill Carr, pioneer to Greenland (1995): 'Yes. I think it started with the Ten Year Crusade. I think that really focussed the Baha'i community on the whole world, and then we had all Baha'i friends who had pioneered here or had...pioneered there. We've gone to far-off and exotic places.... So, for me, that was really this bringing into reality that oneness of mankind, and the oneness of the planet, and the oneness of the Baha'i world'.

For these Baha'is, the act of pioneering forever changed the course of their lives and, in turn, expanded their sense of self. In their letters, and the newsletters of the national community, these Baha'is spoke about diverse cultural expressions in the celebration and commemoration of Baha'i events, the local Baha'i history in their new homelands, and how people from other lands applied the Baha'i teachings to their society's needs (Archives National Spiritual Assembly of Canada). As the following excerpts illustrate:

From pioneers living in apartheid South Africa: 'Well you see there was a thing called the Round Robin, which was a pioneer letter, and we got that regularly. You see, as a pioneer those people were very dear to you back home, and so many of them wrote to us'. (Audrey Robarts 1994)

From a pioneer in Greenland: 'We had a Round Robin, published by the New Territories Committee - a branch of the Canadian N.S.A. - and they certainly did their best to keep all the Canadian Baha'i pioneers informed on what was going on'. (Bill Carr 1995)

From pioneers to the Yukon: '...We got some wonderful letters that really encouraged us, especially those first few years. Many people wrote and those letters were just a lifeline.... And then, of course, we got the Canadian Baha'i news, and of course we got the [International News] but the New Territories Committee Bulletin was the thing we just about tore out of each other's hand to read [laughter]. Hardly wait to read it. And you know, other people were in much more isolated places than we were. I wrote individual letters to all kinds of people that first year. We knew an awful lot of Baha'is in different places. We had been a number of places, already. And at summer schools we met people. So I would write them and tell them what it was like'. (Joanie Anderson 1995)

The people from this study, and their many hundreds of fellow pioneers, facilitated over the course of fifty years a 'cross pollination' process by their presence and service in Canada and new homelands. Through their contributions the Canadian Baha'is experienced a growing consciousness of the world community. This was done through the pioneers' stories in extensive personal correspondence and in newsletters to various countries, as I have mentioned, and through talks given on 'travelling-teaching' excursions and visits to conferences in Canada and other countries.[8]

'Living the Life': Development of a World Consciousness Through Study and Service

Reading the spiritual classics and following a traditional spiritual path is no longer enough. Spirituality must be concretely embodied and lived; it must permeate the personal and the political, it must animate our thought, action, and imagination, so that we can work for the transformation of the global community, of the whole world and all life within it. (King 1992: 168)

Social processes in Baha'i community life have an important part to play in orienting the members to a world consciousness. Living a Baha'i life, or 'living the life',[9] is the metaphor most used by the Baha'is to encapsulate what being a Baha'i means to them. It describes a particular pattern of living over a lifetime. As there is no clergy in the religion, or a system of elders, each person has to take on the responsibility to learn about the religion. This learning is made dynamic through a process of individual daily study, prayer, and meditation on the sacred writings and teachings.

As well, people learn to draw upon certain vocabularies of under-

8 There are many letters from pioneers of these times that describe these activities. This correspondence is stored in the National Archives of the Baha'is of Canada, Thornhill, Toronto.

9 The term 'living the life' arises from the following quotation: 'He is a true Baha'i who strives by day and night to progress and advance along the path of human endeavor, whose most cherished desire is to live and act as to enrich and illuminate the world, whose source of inspiration is the essence of Divine virtue, whose aim in life is to so conduct himself as to be the cause of infinite progress. Only when he attains unto such a perfect gift can it be said of him that he is a true Baha'i. For in this holy Dispensation, the crowning glory of bygone ages and cycles, true faith is no mere acknowledgment of the Unity of God, but *the living of a life* that will manifest all the perfections and virtues implied in such a belief' ('Abdu'l-Baha 1960: 25 my emphasis).

standings in order to communicate with others in the same group. Baha'is acquired new perspectives from the Baha'i writings which, as we have spoken about previously, conceptualized humanity as one family and the earth as one home. This learning and sharing took place at informal and formal levels in personal interactions and correspondence, at community gatherings, and in collective study:

> My Baha'i activities, and the people that I met, opened up a whole new world for me...I just learned by observing, by reading...and by my fellow Baha'is asking me to join them in their deepening and social activities. They just sort of took me under their wing and made sure I knew things were going on, that I had the opportunity to attend, and that I understood what I was going to.... Even going to a Feast [community gathering] was a whole new experience. It wasn't like going to church; it wasn't like any other experience I had. It's different from anything you've done before, because there is no other pattern set up exactly like the Baha'i community...where there is so much opportunity for an individual to participate. So much encouragement to be independent in your thinking, and to share your thinking. (Ruth Eyford 1995)

The construction of the self through reading and speaking a language is an integral aspect of the formation of identity, inasmuch as language is critical in providing the images, ideals, and concepts around which a person can articulate their sense of self. The social principles of Baha'u'llah were the key source of this new vocabulary.[10] The principles conceptualize the world as a global community. The Baha'is of my study remember using, in their younger years, a summary of

10 'The oneness of the entire human race, the pivotal principle and fundamental doctrine of the Faith; the basic unity of all religions; the condemnation of all forms of prejudice, whether religious, racial, class or national; the harmony which must exist between religion and science; the equality of men and women, the two wings on which the bird of human kind is able to soar; the introduction of compulsory education; the adoption of a universal auxiliary language; the abolition of the extremes of wealth and poverty; the institution of a world tribunal for the adjudication of disputes between nations; the exaltation of work, performed in the spirit of service, to the rank of worship; the glorification of justice as the ruling principle in human society, and of religion as a bulwark for the protection of all peoples and nations; and the establishment of a permanent and universal peace as the supreme goal of all mankind ...' (Effendi, 1957: 281-82).

twelve of these principles as a means to communicate their beliefs to other people. The principles were printed on white cards that were convenient to carry around in purses and pockets:

> I carried around with me a picture of 'Abdu'l-Baha...on one side of the frame, and on the other, the twelve principles. (Rena 'Millie' Gordon 1995)

> I think the method of teaching, when I first became a Baha'i was to use the twelve basic principles, in one form or another. Sometimes in the Master's Tablets, there's more than twelve but we had twelve standardized principles. And the Baha'is memorized them and they used them in every public talk or spoke on only one of them, or all of them. So, that was really the focus for teaching when I first became a Baha'i. (Bill Carr 1995)

Studying these principles and writings enabled the Baha'is to think about world issues and what solutions the Baha'i teachings provided for them. The life stories of my participants confirm that knowing and sharing the twelve principles, and gradually understanding Shoghi Effendi's diagnosis of world conditions, served to orient and inform their attitudes and actions according to the exigencies of the times. Shoghi Effendi identified current political and religious trends, graphically portraying, for example, 'nationalism, racialism and communism' as the chief impediments to realizing world unification (1967:113). The life-history participants believed that the principles helped them to understand the barriers to achieving world unity, and the solutions to its realization. As one astute participant commented:

> Today you can see what the alcohol is doing, you can see what the drugs are doing, we can see what corruption is doing, we can see what racism is doing, we can see what inequality is doing, what lack of education is doing. And all these principles that Baha'u'llah brought before our eyes...and we saw [the need for] them. (Audrey Robarts 1994)

Through Shoghi Effendi's explanations the Baha'is had the opportunity to understand the rapid social change occurring about them, and their concomitant responsibility to be of service. The process of focusing upon these principles, when teaching others about the religion, assisted in integrating the local/global Baha'i identity into the self-concept:

[W]ell, you see, the Guardian was giving those plans and they were so astounding because we were still in the sinking sand...we didn't see the world condition and how Shoghi Effendi was telling us it. He gave us a picture of the society, the moral condition of it, and what was needed. And we had to teach, and he gave us Plans. (Audrey Robarts 1994)

The Administrative Order: Transforming Principles into Action Locally and Globally

How is the Baha'i Faith different from other religions or high-minded organizations whose outreach and affiliation are worldwide? The difference lies in the administrative order – a system of governing councils worldwide.[11] According to the Baha'i writings and institutions, this system provides the means, the motivation, and the framework to transform spiritual principles of oneness into practice.

In the early years, however, the understanding that there was an individual responsibility in building this order was a big leap in thinking for some of the conservative Canadian Baha'is of the 1930s-1960s. The Canadian community of this era was comprised of many types of people. Some became immediately involved with the administration of the religion, while others did not see the relevance of it. Some understood the concept of a world community, but could not grasp the scope of the vision in the Plans to achieve it. As a perceptive observer from those times commented, there were the 'dreamy Baha'is

11 This institutional system, which Baha'u'llah outlined in his writings, was implemented and developed by 'Abdu'l-Baha. It provides the foundation and the agency that permit the Baha'i community, as the Baha'i writings state to: 'play an effective role in human affairs' (Baha'i World Centre 2001: 58). The system encompasses two kinds of institutions: governing councils called spiritual assemblies, and a protection/propagation board consisting of 'Hands of the Cause', 'Counsellors and their Deputies'. The assemblies are democratically elected by the body of the believers and operate on local, national and international levels. The assembly's duties are oriented to the promotion of the religion and the care, organization and service of the community in their jurisdictions. The protection/propagation boards are an appointed body of individuals who also operate on local, national and international levels. Their duties involve counselling, advising, and encouraging local spiritual assemblies and individuals (Shoghi Effendi 1963).

who were lethargic and timid and [had] no sense of responsibility', the 'sparks' that helped with the Plans and inspired others to work, and 'the steadies' who were 'steadfast' and could be 'relied upon to do the job' (Audrey Robarts 1994).

As the same person notes, understanding that the administrative order would develop into a world-wide global system, and have implication for local Baha'is, was not understood immediately: 'You see, what Baha'u'llah is emphasizing is new. It is not just the salvation of the individual; it is the salvation of the society of the whole globe – the oneness. It was not really glimpsed; there was not enough vision at the time. Everything was quite close up' (Audrey Robarts 1994).

While some people in the 1940s liked the spiritual teachings of the new religion, they were cautious about the social teachings – those that challenged their sense of self and made it necessary to be active in change. There were people described as: 'out of the century' Baha'is, '...those that knew blacks and whites should meet but they hoped it wasn't in their lifetime' (Audrey Robarts 1994). The Baha'i administrative process, however, challenged prejudiced and narrow attitudes and behaviours, because Baha'is were being admonished by Shoghi Effendi and the Baha'i writings to work in groups within the administrative order.

However, when most Canadian cities and rural areas defined themselves as conservatively British or French and marginalized people of other races or ethnicities (Stark and Bainbridge 1985, Bibby 1990), many Baha'i communities were welcoming diversity:

> When I was a boy they were over there and we were over here. We lived in a community that was British and we [the various cultures and races] were all separated. The Baha'i Faith opened our eyes to the world you know. And suddenly we are looking at the whole world instead of our own backyard. (Richard Tranter 1995)

This intermingling of diverse people in a local situation gave the Baha'is a sense of the coming together of the world globally. For example, a Nova Scotian white Baha'i explained that Baha'is in her community in the 1950s, such as African-Canadians, First Nations peoples, and whites, would find themselves working on committees or Spiritual Assemblies together, and would have to overcome their prejudices in order to achieve unity: 'You knew how these people felt because they would say things quite plainly. To follow the Baha'i writings you had to be friendly, courteous, and loving with these people of different cultures and backgrounds. I think that that was a hard thing to do, but I did it' (Audrey Rayne 1994).

The large influx of Native (First Nations) and young people into the Baha'i Faith in the 1960s, and the transference and settlement of Iranians in the 1970s and 1980s, would all serve to greatly diversify the largely immigrant or first-generation Canadians in the Baha'i community. This meant that many Baha'i assemblies and communities have, throughout the past fifty years, experienced working within a microcosm of the global community in their everyday and formal activities. The administrative order was the means, then, through which people were challenged to adopt new attitudes and behaviours towards oneness in their dealings with their fellow members.

It appears, from my study of the stories of early Canadian Baha'is, that there was little understanding of exactly *how* the administrative order would grow, nor how the administration would affect global endeavours. This began to change in the later part of the last century, as a world traveller and educator observes: 'In the beginning many people thought it was idealistic, utopian. They admired us, but that attitude has changed. There are more things that the Baha'is are actually doing – there are schools, we are involved with the United Nations, and they see the growth of the Faith around the world' (Ethel Martens 1994).

Working locally, the Baha'is eventually realized that their efforts were paralleling the efforts of other people in faraway countries. The knowledge that people around the world were working in the administrative order at the same tasks with the same principles, teachings, and orientation of world-mindedness, brought a deep sense of connection to the Baha'is in Canada:

> We all support one another you know…when you go to another part of the world you find people thinking the way that you are. I mean right away – it opens your eyes to the world community. You know that people from different races are thinking the same way that you are. You know that they have the same concerns! (Richard Tranter 1995)

There was also continuity and systematization in the administrative order to the development of a global community through every succeeding Plan, and this was felt as an assurance to the Baha'i communities, as these people observe:

I tell people...that administrative institutions are channels. When developed to the highest level [they] will be the means of establishing the kingdom of God on earth. And that it is an integral part of the spiritual teachings therefore that it is extremely important for us individually and collectively...to develop and deepen our knowledge along all these lines. (Gale Bond 1994)

And the second strength is Baha'i administration it is amazing how you see it coming into shape and is looking after the Baha'i community...And so the instrument for us growing and improving is the Baha'i administration after all. If we didn't have administration of organization how would we...be communicating, how could we be connected? (Aqdas Javid 1994)

Baha'u'llah's brought an Administrative Order that is so unique and so complete in terms of...of a pattern for future society.... I had an appreciation and a love for it. (Ruth Eyford 1995)

Over the years the Baha'is came to understand that the administrative system was the instrument to canalize the efforts and energies of the members. This system, whenever necessary, could create a concentrated focus for Baha'i communities worldwide, nationally, and locally:

But if you have sufficient guidance of an administrative body or from an institution, such as the Hands [of the Cause] or the Counsellors, then you can channel it in such a way that you not only get a real spiritual high but you have a teaching plan to go out to afterwards—so it is not just a nice, life, self-realization project.... (Ted Anderson 1995)

The administrative order was a conduit for directives and news coming from the International Centre, and this was also a means through which Baha'is were socialized to a consciousness of the world as a whole:

But the Baha'i Faith gives you this world vision you know. And you're starting to think about Baghdad in 1963[12]...you know Iran, Persia, the Holy Land, 'Akka. All these new words are coming up and you're starting to think about the whole world. And then finding out about the Faith, things that happened in the Faith in different parts of the world - it opens up your vision. And the Baha'is pioneering out and coming back too and talking about it and things you know. (Richard Tranter 1995)

As historical accounts show, the Baha'is were, over the course of the past one hundred years, gradually trained within the administration to develop, support, and maintain this system. According to their capacity, and using the teachings of Baha'u'llah and the guidance of Shoghi Effendi, they learned, for example, to actualize the Baha'i consultative process, hold democratic elections, uphold the right of the minority in the Baha'i election, and advance and maintain women's equality in the community (van den Hoonaard 1996, Hatcher & Martin 1985). These people also left their country of birth and worked with others in their new homelands within the Baha'i administrative order. They were subject to the same religious teachings, and the news from the Baha'i World Centre; they worked under the umbrella of the same Plans as other Baha'is world-wide; and, they used the same administrative principles Baha'is use globally. In this way the administrative order socialized and moulded all the Baha'is, wherever they lived in the world, to be 'situated universalists' (McMullen 2000).

Concluding Remarks

When we consider the overarching effects of globalization in the last century, we know Baha'is were subject to the rapid social change happening around the world. Their stories reflect their situational geography. For example, they were affected by World War II, trans-Atlantic travel and movement of peoples, the diversity of immigrants arriving in Canada, and the post-war economy, which socialized them to the consumption of global goods and technologies. If and how they were, in turn, influential in promoting a consciousness of the world is a topic of inquiry for other researchers. Nevertheless, what

12 Baghdad, Iraq, was the site chosen for the first Baha'i World Congress 1963, however, due to safety concerns, the venue was changed to London, England (Royal Albert Hall).

stands out as being most important to them are the spiritual concepts they learned from the Baha'i teachings, and their engagement with the social processes and administrative service of Baha'i life. This involvement compelled them to embrace a different way of living and thinking, one that constructed and consolidated their individual and collective identity as people working to overcome nationalist sentiments and racial prejudices.

The Baha'is' nascent understanding of the teaching 'let your vision be world embracing' was quickened by the process of moving out of their home communities, nationwide and worldwide, and by working with diverse peoples within the administrative order. Throughout the course of this service they learned, through adopting, applying, and promoting Baha'i principles, that they were a part of the organic development of a global grassroots movement.

It appears that the Baha'is experienced a cognitive and altruistic shift toward a deeper consciousness of the oneness of humanity, learning to regard themselves as world citizens.

References

'Abdu'l-Bahá (1960, rev. edn.). *The Divine Art of Living: Selections from the Writings of Baha'u'llah and 'Abdu'l-Baha.* Compiled by Mabel Hyde Paine. Wilmette, Ill.: Baha'i Publishing Trust.

Bahá'u'lláh (1949). *Gleanings from the Writings of Bahá'u'lláh.* Birmingham: Templar Printing Works.

Beckford, James A. (2000). 'Start Together and Finish Together': Shifts in the Premises and Paradigms Underlying the Scientific Study of Religion, *Journal for the Scientific Study of Religion,* vol. 38 (4), December: 481-95.

Bibby, Reginald (1990). *Fragmented Gods: The Poverty and Potential of Religion in Canada,* Toronto: Stoddart Publishing Co. Limited.

Couch, Carl (1992). Toward a Formal Theory of Social Processes, *Symbolic Interaction,* 15, No. 2:117-34.

Drewek, Paula A. (1996). *Cross-Cultural Testing of James W. Fowler's Model of Faith Development Among Baha'is: India and Canada.* Ph.D. Thesis. Department of Religious Studies, University of Ottawa.

Echevarria-Howe, Lynn (1992). *Life History as Process and Product: The Social Construction of Self through Feminist Methodologies and Cana-*

dian Black Experience. Masters Thesis, Department of Sociology and Anthropology, Carleton University, Ottawa.

Giddens, Anthony (1991). *Modernity and Self Identity: Self and Society in the Late Modern Age*. Cambridge: Polity Press.

Hatcher, William S. and J. Douglas Martin (1985). *The Baha'i Faith: The Emerging Global Religion*. New York: Harper & Row.

King, Margaret J. (1948). *'God is One', Sing a New Song: Baha'i Songs for Children*. Wilmette, Ill.: Baha'i Publishing Trust, 44.

King, Ursula (1992). The Spiritual, Personal and Political: Religion in Global Persepctive. *Vidyajyoti: Journal of Theological Reflections*. 56, no. 3: 151-169.

McMullen, Michael (2000). *The Baha'i: The Religious Construction of Global Identity*. New Jersey: Rutgers University Press.

Robertson, Roland (1994). Religion and the Global Field, *Social Compass*, 41(1): 121-135.

Robertson, Roland (1998a). Discourses of Globalisation, *International Sociology*, vol. 13: 25-40.

Robertson, Roland (1998b). 'The New Global History: History in a Global Age, *Cultural Values*, vol. 2, Nos. 2 and 3: 368-384.

Shoghi Effendi (1957). *God Passes By*, Wilmette, Ill.: Baha'i Publishing Trust.

Shoghi Effendi (1963, 2nd edn.). *Bahá'í Administration*. New York: Baha'i Publishing Committee.

Shoghi Effendi (1965). *Messages to Canada*. Toronto: National Spiritual Assembly of the Baha'is of Canada.

Shoghi Effendi (1967). *The Promised Day is Come*. Wilmette, Ill.: Baha'i Publishing Trust.

Shoghi Effendi (1983). *Lights of Guidance: A Baha'i Reference File*. Helen Hornby (Compiler) New Delhi: Bahá'i Publishing Trust.

Stark, R. and William Sims Bainbridge (1985). *The Future of Religion: Secularization, Revival and Cult Formation*. Berkeley, Los Angeles, London: University of California Press.

Baha'i World Centre (2001). *Century of Light*. Thornhill, Ontario: Baha'i Canada Publications and Nepean, Ontario: Nine Pines Publishing.

van den Hoonaard, Will C. (1996). *The Origins of the Baha'i Community of Canada 1898 – 1948*. Waterloo: Wilfrid Laurier University Press.

Excerpts from the Life History Participants:
Mr. Ted Anderson 1995
Mrs. Joan (Joanie) Anderson 1995
Mr. William (Bill) Carr 1995
Mr. Bob Donnelly 1994
Mrs. Gale Bond 1994
Mrs. Ruth Eyford 1995
Mrs. Rena (Millie) Gordon 1995
Mrs. Aqdas Javid 1994
Dr. Ethel Martens 1994
Mrs. Audrey Rayne 1994
Mrs. Audrey Robarts 1994
Mrs. Francoise Smith 1994
Mr. Richard Tranter 1995
Mr. Tony Panalaks 1994

CHAPTER 13

Etching the Idea Of 'Unity in Diversity' in the Baha'i Community: Popular Opinion and Organizing Principle[1]

Will. C. van den Hoonaard

'Ye are the fruits of one tree, and the leaves of one branch' is one of the most evocative concepts found in the Baha'i Writings.[2] It appeals to Baha'i of all ages around the world. It has become the signature concept for visual representations of the Baha'i community, and effectively so. The 'Parade of Nations' at the 1992 Baha'i World Congress in New York City, a spectacular ceremonial procession of individuals dressed in native costumes, epitomized the visual diversity of the Baha'i community. To Baha'is, the idea of unity in diversity is central to their teachings, actively promoted in sacred texts and official Baha'i literature, as well as in popular Baha'i discourse. To non-Baha'is, this

1 I thank the following people, in addition to those who have contributed their ideas to my appeals for contributions: Dr Deborah Kestin van den Hoonaard of St. Thomas University, Fredericton, NB, Canada, Mr Cecil E. Cook of South Africa, Zaid Lundberg of Malmö, and Mr David Bowie of British Columbia, Canada. I am also grateful to Dr Margit Warburg for her encouragement.

2 Echoes of the tree analogy (cited earlier) are plentiful in the Baha'i Writings, involving *the drops or the waves of one sea* (Baha'u'llah and Abdu'l-Baha 1955: *159*, 205-6, 306), *the flowers of one* (*ibid.,*: 206, 218, 286-7, 306), *the blossoms of one tree* (*ibid.*: 1955: *75, 158, 159*, 210, 282, 289), *the members of one body* (*ibid.*: *39-40*, 223-4, 228), *the fingers of one hand* (*ibid.*: *39-40*), *the inhabitants of one* (*ibid.*: *79*), *the stars of one heaven* (*ibid.*: 206, 306), *the drops of one river* (*ibid.*: 306), *the rays of one sun* (*ibid.*: 306), *the trees of one orchard* (*ibid.*: 306), or *the blending of many notes 'in the making of a perfect chord'* (Abdu'l-Baha).

quote is likely the most epigrammatic one of all, capturing the essence of Baha'i teachings: the unity of humankind. The ideology of new faiths and new movements constitute a rich source of research (e.g. Carroll 1992; Garner 1996; Miller 2000).

This chapter, however, tackles ideology from a less conventional perspective. Many researchers take upon themselves the task of looking at a new faith's or new social movement's ideology in relation to the wider society. In effect, researchers speak of a 'frame alignment' which is the 'process in which movements make their own assignment of meanings fit the meaning and discourses that people already have' (Garner 1996: 57). By contrast, this chapter explores the relationship between the popular notions of 'unity in diversity' held by Baha'is themselves and what their core, sacred writings say about this term. In many respects, the chapter is about the relationship between the sacred text and the everyday-lived reality of the believers. I intend to explain Baha'i popular opinions about 'unity in diversity,' after which I shall consider secondary Baha'i literature and the core Baha'i literature on the topic.[3] Finally, the chapter concludes with a discussion on the

3 My original intent in developing this chapter was to conduct empirical research in the Canadian Baha'i Community. I had three questions in mind as part of an in-depth interview: the interviewees would, through a process of open-ended questions, allow me to probe the items that they would find important enough to mention, without any prompting on my part. To secure research participants, I placed a research ad in the January 2001 issue of *Baha'i Canada.* I received two responses: one was a thoughtful and interesting first reply to the ad; the other simply reaffirmed the Baha'i importance of 'unity in diversity.' For the second time, I placed a similar appeal in *Baha'i Canada* in January 2003. I had hoped to secure at least 20 interviewees in this manner, but as only three people responded to my research ad – I had to abandon this approach altogether, and I redirected my research to Baha'is in an area near where I live, in Eastern Canada. While in many respects this second approach would at least gain me some interviewees – they all know me and are always interested in my Baha'i research endeavours – I soon discovered that no new or different insights would be forthcoming beyond the popular Baha'i analogies of human diversity.
While these initial approaches proved inadequate in some respects, I did learn, for the most part, that Baha'is do not seem to hold a uniform view on 'unity in diversity'. The present chapter had become more urgent than I had initially realized: surely, there was more to the term than its com-

relevance of the concept as it appears in the Baha'i core literature to our globalizing society.

Baha'i Popular Opinions

Today, Baha'i communities have taken a shine to analogies popularized as unity in diversity, promoting them as widely as possible, informally and formally. A glance at photographs in Baha'i magazines and newsletters confirms the heavy weight Baha'is accord to the tangible meaning of unity in diversity, normally highlighting differences of race, national costume, and tribal or ethnic origin. The term even involves human rights: The seven-year-long program in the Canadian Baha'i Community to promote 'Unity in Diversity' Week (1992-1999) speaks clearly to the issue of human rights (External Affairs 1998) or to the idea of the oneness of humanity (External Affairs 1997). Statistical representation of the Baha'i world community underscores the theme

---

monplace usage, and how did this idea of diversity get etched into the life of the Baha'i community?

Casting my net wider, I solicited the opinions of members of two listservs entitled, 'Bridges' and the 'Sociology' one. The results, while more numerous than what my research ads produced in *Baha'i Canada,* were still meager. The request on 'Bridges' yielded two messages; the 'Sociology' list produced items from seven individuals in Washington (USA), Corsica, Nice, Dublin, Lusaka (Zambia), Hilversum (Netherlands), South Africa, and Cayenne (French Guiana). Finally, I availed myself of the opportunity during my visits to two Baha'i scholarly conferences (Newcastle-upon-Tyne in England, and at Landegg International University in Switzerland), December 2002, to secure the opinions of an additional six Baha'is. Together with the three responses to the ads in *Baha'i Canada,* eighteen Baha'is in all (6 women, 12 men) offered their views on the topic, involving, in all, 9 interviews and 9 email exchanges. I have also made use of earlier listserv discussions, in 1998, on <h-bahai@h-net.msu.edu> and on <educate@johnco. cc.ks.us> to supplement my data. I also used important source and institutional documents including the *World Order* letters of Shoghi Effendi, Guardian of the Baha'i Faith, and a compilation of the Universal House of Justice on cultural diversity (2000 [1997]). I made extensive use of a 1988 monograph produced by the Baha'i Community of Australia, *Integration and Cultural Diversity.* I also used the annual reports of events taking place across Canada between 1992 and 1999 to promote a week in November as 'Unity in Diversity Week'.

of the ethnic and tribal diversity which compose that global community.[4] The Baha'i International Community Office at the United Nations has since the mid-1970s woven 'unity in diversity' into a wide variety of presentations and publications on occasion of its work with international agencies.

In reviewing the opinions gathered from the eighteen research participants, one becomes aware that although the opinions fall generally into at least four separate conceptions of unity in diversity, these conceptions also overlap.[5] Some are directly derived from the Baha'i Writings, while others have gained currency primarily through individual Baha'is' choosing ideas from their own selves or from what the generality of society articulates.

As a cultural concept

The cultural meaning of unity in diversity seems dominant in Baha'i discourse, as the following remarks in a national Baha'i magazine indicate, invoking concepts of tradition, culture, and customs as key ingredients of diversity:

> If the Native believers decide to hold their [Nineteen-Day] Feasts or conferences in the Native **tradition,** or if the French Canadians feel that certain forms of teaching, deepening, or proclamation activities are most suitable to their **culture,** or if the Persian friends [i.e. Iranian Baha'is] decide to hold deepen-

4 The point of the statistical representation of the worldwide Baha'i community was to show its global diversity. In this context, whether the nomenclature of the groups conformed to either anthropological or native uses can be deemed as irrelevant. Similarly, the first enrolment of a member of a particular tribal or ethnic group signifies the diversity of a growing community; who constitutes a member of that group (for example, if he or she has been adopted by that group) is another matter. (There is the case of Mr Benjamin Miller who became the 'first' Baha'i of the Uai tribe in Liberia in 1952; Mr Miller was originally from Cincinnati, migrated to Liberia and was adopted by the Uais (Africa Teaching Committee Records 1952)).

5 While on the whole, a number of the research participants shared opinions on what unity in diversity means, there was one exception, namely the perspective of a 60-year old Iranian Baha'i living in Canada who believes that religion is the centre piece in any discussion in the Baha'i Writings on unity in diversity (Mehrdad N., interview, 5 May 2001)

ing classes in Persian or organize firesides emphasizing hospitality according to Persian **customs,** then all other Baha'is should rejoice..... [I]nwardly we are united at the most fundamental level: our love for Baha'u'llah. (Danesh 1998: 16).

Pauline Rafat also highlights the cultural meaning of unity in diversity when she connects that idea to the 'example of Baha'i communities consisting of different cultures and races,' which 'create misunderstanding, irritation,' etc. (Rafat 1988: 16). In this sense, a number of interview participants, such as James P. who became a Baha'i in Scotland some 22 years ago, first considers that 'different races' have something to do with unity in diversity, but especially bringing in poor people and 'bringing them up to a higher level' (James P., interview 19 April 2002). Ronald W., who has been a Baha'i for 25 years believes that the term encompasses racial diversity 'that's my first thought.' He continues, 'After that, I think of different aspects of diversity, that is financial, intellectual, spiritual' (Simin A., interview, 25 Dec. 2002). For Simin A., an Iranian Baha'i since birth, the 'Parade of Nations' at the 1992 Baha'i World Congress in New York City, was 'an example' of what one means by unity in diversity. She also went to a Baha'i school in India, where she 'experienced diversity' (Simin A., interview, 20 Dec. 2002).

Drawing on metaphors from the physical world is for Sean O. a Baha'i for 29 years since he was 20 years old essential in understanding the Baha'i concept of unity in diversity (Sean O., interview, 20 April 2001). Like in the physical world, society needs diversity to bond its component parts. He uses the example of race relations in the American Baha'i Community where the African-Americans and the whites[6] now prize each other, only after persistent efforts by the Baha'is to develop racial amity. However, for him, unity in diversity entails the survival of differences of cultural minorities in a world civilization. He compares such a world civilization to an orchestra: each instrument has to assert itself, but cannot undermine the orchestra.

In the specific context of a Baha'i community, there are defined limits to diversity, however. Diversity should not contravene the essential principles of the Baha'i Faith. Moreover, the social setting must

6 Such terms as 'African-Americans' and 'whites' are socially-constructed ethnic labels, the uses of which vary over time.

be considered, especially for differences that divide people or that are based on religious, as opposed to cultural practices: if the Baha'i community is the audience (Universal House of Justice, 2000: 106), religious diversity is less acceptable, such as is the case of celebrating Christmas, but if the social setting is wider, involving family members who are Christians, then such diversity takes on a different connotation.

'To make life interesting'

One analogy that is circulating in Baha'i circles compares unity in diversity to an *Indian meal* or a *soup*. Such a meal consists originally of many individual parts. However, the parts lose their distinction as the meal is prepared and cooked: a new flavour is the combined result. There is no question that each ingredient has a function in adding something to the overall taste and 'make it interesting' (Sara T., interview 16 May 2001). 'Life,' says another Canadian Baha'i of Iranian background and one of the few who responded to the research ad in *Baha'i Canada,* 'would be tedious without diversity.' He further states that 'diversity is one of the masterpieces of God' (Omid M., email, 5 February 2001). The cultural meaning of unity in diversity appears to be shifting in very recent times, however. For example, Jan K., a loyal subscriber to a Baha'i listserv, maintains that society at large is entering a stage where diversity is sought after, especially following what he believes youth are saying (Jan K., email, dated, 30 May 2001):

> At the same time I do not need any longer people around me that are just like me, to make me feel more secure. On the contrary: people who are different from me are more interesting and fun than people who are just like me. The more people [who are] like me, ... the more boring life gets. The more individual differences we experience the more fun life gets.

As a means to create harmony

Rosa Q., a 39-year old woman of Indian, Greek, and German background and Baha'i since she was 16, sees unity in diversity as a recognition of the 'harmony between masculine and feminine principles in other words, a balance between women and men' (Rosa Q., interview 27 Dec. 2002). In the same vein, Farhang D. suggests that 'mediation and conflict resolution between divergent interests' is another aspect of unity in diversity (Farhang D., email, 6 May 2001).

Bert R., a Baha'i in French Guiana, explains that unity in diversity conjures up efforts to eliminate prejudice against ethnic groups in his country, although he finds that relational problems, and barriers of education or social might stand in the way of making one feel 'less positive about relating to people' (Bert R., email 27 May 2001). Perhaps in a similar vein, Simin Z. (cited earlier), an Iranian Baha'i, believes that unity in diversity means 'co-existence.' 'In cases where diversity has been a source of disunity,' she says, 'the parties should become tolerant of one another' (Simin Z., interview 20 Dec. 2002).

Individual Differences

Some Baha'is assign a function to the need of establishing 'a mental unity in diversity.'

Rouha Y., for example, claims that our mental perception of the world is like a 'million separate photographs.' By opening up ourselves to diversity, we are able to learn more of how those 'pictures' hang together, relieving the sense of fear that has been part of humanity's collective history (Rouha Y., 29 May 2001). For Evie W., a Baha'i of at least 25 years and living on a remote island in the Atlantic Ocean, unity in diversity is more about bringing people together of 'different talents and capabilities, not necessarily of different cultural backgrounds.' She says, that 'in the real Baha'i community all these facets would be brought out, all contributing to a healthy organism [i.e. society]' (Evie W., interview, 25 Dec, 2002).

When Baha'is refer to the playing of an *orchestra* as an example of diversity, they again emphasize the functionality of the diverse instruments that make the music possible. However, its meaning acquires some depth, because it takes a careful, conscientious, and continuing effort to harmonize orchestrated music, involving intense practice individually, by section, and collectively. It is an all-consuming process. It is noteworthy that although on the surface we seem to be hearing one piece of music, we will still hear the various parts of the orchestra: we simply 'know' and 'hear' when a section of the orchestra is especially strong or weak. The analogy of the orchestra represents a striking model of unity in diversity: all the instruments retain their individuality at the service of the larger good. The 'one voice' of the orchestra is only possible when each 'voice' is heard. The 'Conductor' (i.e. Creator), along with the desire of individuals to be part of the orchestra, is the 'unifying force' (Abdu'l-Baha 1978: 291). In history, dominant groups have come to believe that they should conduct the orchestra, so to speak. To put it bluntly, it is like the bassoon player (or take any instrument of your choice) who decides to lead the orchestra. A world society will surely be one where each instrument takes its rightful place in the orchestra, not in front of it.

Michael L. in England, a Baha'i since 1969, gives a wider scope to the idea of unity in diversity. 'The Baha'i Community,' he says, 'should focus more on unity in diversity in terms of what the idea means, not just the racial thing,' so that eventually the diversity will include scholarship and the arts (Michael L., interview, 19 Dec. 2002). For another long-standing Baha'i, Randy T., it is the following:

> It's one thing to have lofty theories, but they're worth nothing till the rubber hits the road, and that's where institutions and individuals are shaped .... It's not arid and empty talk and concepts, it's the daily reality of self-management, group dynamics and institutional forms that validate rather than stifle variety, it's polycentrism on steroids, hyped up and singing as loud and happily as possible in every musical style on the planet, it's a riotous blend of every flower that can possibly be thriving in every corner of the garden of humanity, and it's every opinion and character finding its place in the mixing bowl of consultation and collaborative decision-making. It's the end of the solitary rugged individual, and the rise of the collective navigation team. (Randy T., email, 19 Dec. 2002)

A reviewer of an earlier version of this chapter even goes as far as suggesting that 'much of what passes for multiculturalism and pluralism strikes me as having 'sectarian tendencies,' (Mark B., email, June 2001) – a term taken from the 1993 (April) annual Ridvan message from the Universal House of Justice:

> Of relevant importance [for the functioning of Baha'i institutions], too, are their resolve to remove all traces of estrangement and sectarian tendencies from their midst, their ability to win the affection and support of the friends under their care... (Universal House of Justice 1993)

Shoghi Effendi, Guardian of the Baha'i Faith, suggests that 'unity in diversity' involves a deeper, intangible diversity that is rooted in the 'diverse shades of thought, temperament and character,' and 'the divergent thoughts, sentiments, ideas, and convictions' of the world's peoples (Abdu'l-Baha, quoted by Shoghi Effendi 1974: 42). It is this particular meaning of the term that Shoghi Effendi draws on when he first uses 'unity in diversity' in the context of social organization. One respondent in my research is one of the very few that echoes this sentiment:

> ... much of the talk of diversity in the Baha'i community is centred in the more obvious of its forms, especially racial .... I came to believe, while teaching at [name of a Baha'i school], that diversity is much more subtle than this, and that an often overlooked area of Baha'i scholarship, with ramifications in an almost formulaic avoidance of popular culture, is in diversity of thought: how does the [Baha'i] Revelation permit, within the confines of Baha'i law, the diversity of thought that often arises from living in a multi-cultural society, one which is highly attuned to and susceptible to a wide variety of social issues? (Wendy C., email 11 Jan. 2001)

Baha'is then express a wide variety of views on the topic of unity in diversity. Some of these popular images are not only powerful among Baha'is, but have also shaped their missionizing literature, Holy Day celebrations, children's classes, and the cultural, and social life of the Baha'i community.

These varied images also suggest a relative unfamiliarity with the notion of unity in diversity. For example, I learned during the data-gathering stage of my research that a Baha'i conference in West Cork, Ireland (9-10 June 2001), entitled, 'Diversity in Unity' still had not produced, within a month of the Conference, a single abstract on the topic related to the theme of the Conference. There are, nevertheless, some other signs: the organizer of a Baha'i workshop in southern Africa indicated, as soon as he had learned of this research, that he would organize a focus group on the topic of unity in diversity, while another believer in southern France promised to engage in some correspondence with me on the topic at a later date. A presentor at a Baha'i summer school in Corsica enquired whether I had any materials to share. It is thus obvious that there is not only a wide variety of opinions on unity in diversity inside the Baha'i community, but there seems to be a degree of unfamiliarity with the concept as available in core Baha'i literature.

Secondary Baha'i Literature

Despite the popularity of the term unity in diversity in Baha'i community life, Baha'i scholarly literature on the topic is rather meagre and none of it has appeared in wider academic publication venues. The literature that does exist, however, reflects, to a large extent, the general opinions held by the Baha'i community. They normally revolve around the theme of multiculturalism or race relations. Michael H. Bond (1998) offers the most complete analysis of the term, a social psychological profile that binds together Baha'i concepts related to unity and diversity and findings in the social-scientific literature. The earliest work is by Christensen (1969) who explored unity in diversity in solving problems in group discussions. There has not been an analysis of the discourse of unity in diversity and how it is etched into the Baha'i community.

There are, moreover, a small number of empirical, published materials that relate to unity in diversity in national Baha'i communities, especially on the theme of race relations. It is not surprising that much of the literature appeared after the arrival of Iranian refugees in Western countries. In Australia, for example, we find the work of Feather *et al.* (1993) on comparing Australian and Baha'i value systems with a special reference to Iranian Baha'is. In the United States, Leonda Keniston (2000) looks at cross-racial friendships in the Baha'i community. D. J. May (1993) considers pluralism and the Baha'i teachings on unity. Michael McMullen (2000) brings in elements of local diversity in the context of a Baha'i community's growth towards a global identity. Richard Thomas' *Racial Unity* (1992) provides both a historical and contemporary study of race relations in the American Baha'i community.[7] In Britain, Moojan Momen (1990) produced a short piece on the integration into the British Baha'i Community of Iranian Baha'is. Hossain Danesh, in Canada, produced a series of articles in *Baha'i*

7 Race relations in the American Baha'i community is usually characterized as 'the most challenging issue', a term designated by the Guardian for this specific use in the United States.

Canada that outlined the challenges facing the Baha'i community with the arrival of Iranian refugees in the country (Danesh 1986a, 1986b, 1986c, 1997, 1998). William Hackborn, a mathematician at Augustana University College (Canada) and van den Hoonaard (1994) looked at ethnic relations in the Baha'i community from the perspective of chaos theory.

Given the wide variety of opinions among Baha'is as well as the emphasis given in the secondary Baha'i literature on multiculturalism and race relations, we may well ask how does the popular usage of the expression of unity in diversity among Baha'is fit with the formal statements of unity in diversity in the Baha'i Writings? Moreover, how does the belief in diversity square with explicit Baha'i statements that we shall have a world where 'ethnic and national differences will all disappear' (Abdu'l-Baha 1982: 46)? How well does the dimension of unity in diversity match the explicit allusions in the writings of Shoghi Effendi to the 'complete unification of the diverse elements that constitute human society' (1967: 122)? What do we make of Shoghi Effendi's references to a vision of 'a world organically unified in all the essential aspects of its life, its political machinery, its spiritual aspiration..., its script and language, involving 'the fusion of all races, creeds, classes, and nations' (*ibid.* 1967: 43, 128)?

Baha'i Core Literature

As evocative as some of these popular analogies are, a scrutiny of the Baha'i Writings and statements by the Guardian and by the Universal House of Justice suggests that these authoritative texts speak to a more fundamental aspect of unity in diversity, namely its relevance for the social organization of society.

The first formal use of the term unity in diversity by Shoghi Effendi occurred in November 1931, when he connected the term to Abdu'l-Baha's phrase of likening humanity to the flowers of a garden (Shoghi Effendi 1974: 41-2). The whole section which he devotes to discussing the term falls after a section that deals with the theme of the 'future Commonwealth of all nations (*ibid.* 1974: 39-41), and occurs before a section that speaks to the 'organic change in the structure of present-day society' (*ibid.* 1974: 42-45). Thus, thematically speaking, the section on 'Unity in Diversity' is bound up with issues of human governance and social structure, as the following extract underscores:

Let there be no misgivings as to the animating purpose of the world-wide Law of Baha'u'llah. Far from aiming at the subversion of the existing foundations of society, it seeks to broaden its basis, to remold its institutions in a manner consonant with the needs of an ever-changing world. It can conflict with no legitimate allegiances, nor can it undermine essential loyalties. Its purpose is neither to stifle the flame of a sane and intelligent patriotism in men's hearts, nor to abolish the system of national autonomy so essential if the evils of excessive centralization are to be avoided. It does not ignore, nor does it attempt to suppress, the diversity of ethnical origins, of climate, of history, of language and tradition, of thought and habit, that differentiate the peoples and nations of the world. It calls for a wider loyalty, for a larger aspiration than any that has animated the human race. It insists upon the subordination of national impulses and interests to the imperative claims of a unified world. It repudiates excessive centralization on one hand, and disclaims all attempts at uniformity on the other. Its watchword is unity in diversity such as Abdu'l-Baha Himself has explained ... (*ibid.* 1974: 41-2)

He touched upon the idea of excessive centralization, linking it clearly to unity in diversity as the 'watchword' and the organizing principle of human governance.[8]

In his efforts to gradually build up the Baha'i administrative system, Shoghi Effendi wove his theme of unity in diversity into so much of his guidance to Baha'is. In his words (on 2 January 1934),

It is not uniformity which we should seek in the formation of any national or local assembly. For the bedrock of the Baha'i administrative order is the principle of unity in diversity, which has been so strongly and so repeatedly emphasized in the writings of the [Baha'i] Cause. Differences which are not fundamental and contrary to the basic teachings of the Cause should be maintained. (Shoghi Effendi 1970: 48)

Within the same year, on 27 December 1934, Shoghi Effendi, in a letter

8 The term 'unity in diversity' does not seem to be derived from Persian. The equivalent term, *vahdat dar kithrat,* is used in Persian literature on mysticism to indicate the unity between the invisible and visible worlds (Email from Iraj Ayman, dated 6 May 2001, to author). The Iranian Philologist Susan Maneck confirms that the term does not appear in the original Persian or Arabic Baha'i texts (Email, 5 May 2001).

written on his behalf, reinforces his use of 'unity in diversity' in the context of having uniformity in essentials:

> He [the Guardian] does not object if there be any differences in these secondary matters, but he feels that he should insist on uniformity in essentials. Diversity in unity–which is so vital and basic a principle of the [Baha'i] Movement –would therefore be maintained. (Shoghi Effendi 1981: 102)

He was reluctant to have national Baha'i communities develop an administrative manual that would govern the affairs of Baha'i communities in a uniform manner, such as when the first American Baha'i pioneers settled in West Africa (Africa Teaching Committee Records 1952).

The emphasis given to social organization as an expression of unity in diversity has become particularly evident in recent statements by the Universal House of Justice and in the development of Baha'i institutions. *The Prosperity of Humankind,* a statement released by the Universal House of Justice in 1995, takes Baha'u'llah's analogy of likening the organization of a planetary society to the human body, and cites 'unity in diversity' as one of the chief organizing principles of such a society (1995: 7). 'Unity in diversity' will 'find full expression,' it says, through the collective coming-of-age of the human race. In many respects, it seems, that 'unity in diversity' is both the enabler and the result of the coming of age.

Discussion

What is striking about the current Baha'i popular discourse and usage of 'unity in diversity' is that it seems rather at variance with the meaning advocated in the writings of Shoghi Effendi or the Universal House of Justice. The former focuses on such tangible qualities of cultural diversity such as dress, language, race, tribe, ethnicity, human temperament, etc. The latter focuses on human governance.

Even though the concept of unity in diversity was articulated as an issue of governance as early as 1931, it took some 35 years before someone spoke about unity in diversity and presented this specific meaning at a Baha'i gathering. Dorothy Ferraby, an Auxiliary Board Member (a member of one of the Baha'i institutions), presented a course on unity in diversity at a Netherlands Baha'i summer school in summer 1966 (*Baha'i News,* Dec. 1966: 8). Even though Ferraby spoke about unity in diversity in the sense of Baha'i governance, the author of the report, however, picked up on the theme of unity in diversity, but spoke of it in terms of 'the ages of those present, from infants to octogenarians, and in the many nationalities,' rather than in terms of governance. It was thus the popular concept of unity in diversity that prevailed in that first published mention, rather in the sense of human governance.

The term appears again the following year, in a display on Race Unity Day in Rarotonga, Cook Islands, entering general Baha'i discourse, now with an exclusive focus on the racial 'diversity of mankind' (*Baha'i News,* Oct. 1967: 7). The Rarotonga report refers to an article on the Baha'i Faith that appears in *Ebony Magazine,* showing 'unity in diversity' (Bennett 1965).[9] By 1977, with the publication of Donald Barrett's article, 'Unity in Diversity' in *World Order Magazine* (Barrett 1977), the term had gained currency in its popular meaning. With societies' withdrawing themselves into ethnic enclaves, *World Order Magazine* decried, in 'Ethnicity: A Counsel of Despair' (1977), the problems of a society driven by ethnic or racial enclaves. In the late 1980s, the collapse of communism and the subsequent wave of dissolving states into smaller entities led the editors of *World Order Magazine* to write about their deepening concern about diversity in another lead editorial, 'Diversity: A Way to Unity' (Fall 1987). There are others, however, who believe that 'each group will first need to become sure of its own capacities, values, abilities, and contributions'– a form of cultural pride – so that each group can relate to others with pride which is a necessary precondition for unity in diversity (Danesh 1998: 6). The popular Baha'i discourse still did not refer to matters of governance implied in the concept of unity in diversity.

With the emphasis placed on the importance of thought and convictions, the Baha'i model of unity in diversity speaks clearly to the varied experience and consequence of diversity as they manifest themselves in the 'divergent thoughts, sentiments, ideas, and convictions' of the peoples of the world (Abdu'l-Baha, quoted by Shoghi Effendi 1974: 42). The Baha'i Writings affirm those experiences as a living reality. It is these experiences, whether collectively or individually, that constitute the diversity in unity.

9 The term, however, does not occur in the *Ebony* article.

The Baha'i concept of diversity extends beyond the tangible superficiality of race, national, linguistic, and ethnic or tribal origins. The formal Baha'i concept of diversity extends to the vast arsenal of human experience that is engendered by such tangibles as language, race, tribe, and ethnicity. Although Baha'i popular culture highlights the tangible attributes of diversity, the Baha'i Writings privilege the intangible dimensions of diversity: the historical experience borne of racial, ethnic, linguistic, and national differences which a decentralized social system must reflect.

Conclusion: Relevance to Globalizing Society

There is an extensive interest in 'unity in diversity' in the generality of society. An Internet search on 'Google' currently (12 March 2003) yields some 254,001 (up from 38,700 in June 2001) results for a search keyed on 'unity in diversity,' involving a broad spectrum of groups engaged with 'unity in diversity': universities, religious groups, research centres, the European Parliament, the United Nations, non-governmental groups, personal websites, biologists, the People's Movement for Racial Healing, and individuals.[10]

In the past 40 years, various social forces have contributed to the mainstay of unity in diversity. During the 1960s, the American civil rights movement laid the groundwork for later legal and social enactments with a focus on human rights. The dreamers of the American 'melting pot' were unsettled by the political machinery to bring minorities into full, democratic partnership, and the minorities themselves, individually and collectively, increasingly protested at the lack of civil rights. While the struggles were offset by legal and political redresses, full partnership in society would remain an - as yet - elusive goal. Carmela Venti's 1997 'Mask American' represents the unease behind the melting pot. The anthropomorphic map reveals the eye, nose, and mouth (of a multicoloured face imposed on a map of the United States) themselves as 'negative space' (Venti 1997: 50), and asks the question: are the inhabitants Americans, ethnics, or hyphenated Americans? The successive waves of movements involving civil rights, multiculturalism, and globalization during the past 40 years or so have, no doubt,

10 Subsequent Google searches may yield different results as criteria for inclusion change in unpredictable ways.

influenced discourse in the Baha'i community on unity in diversity. In some respects, the Baha'i popular concept of unity in diversity is bound within a discursive framework that is culturally and historically specific.

The promotion of multiculturalism during the 1980s in the United States (and in Canada since 1970) was a means to stabilize inter-ethnic/racial relations that gave voice to minorities in a manner that fostered ethnic or racial identity within politically-safe parameters. 'Unity in diversity' had become a half-achieved goal: social, economic, and political institutions have found a place for diversity, while unity still remained a distant, unspoken other half of that goal. As James R. Wilburn has noted, the ascendance of multiculturalism and its inability to produce an equitable society have led serious scholars to develop 'a focus on the pervasive suspicion that this bold, two-centuries-old experiment in free institutions known in America had taken a wrong turn' (Wilburn 1983: vii).

The interest of the Baha'i community seems to run parallel to society's interest in 'unity in diversity.' The first popular use of the term in the Baha'i community occurred in 1966; interestingly, the most complete catalogue of serious non-Baha'i interest in the topic started in 1970.[11] In many respects, the Baha'i popular notion of unity in diversity represents a 'master frame' (Snow and Benford 1988) in the production and maintenance of meanings for Baha'is as they connect to the larger world at this particular moment of time and geography.[12] The Baha'i community, it appears, has taken the idea of 'Ye are the fruits of one tree, and the leaves of one branch' (Baha'u'llah 1971: 218) to heart in visualizing the community both internally and externally, and seems to have taken a practical interest in the topic. Sometimes this interest piggy-backed with accounts on the arrival Iranian Baha'i migrants, sometimes with the serious attention paid by the United States Baha'i

11 Carol L. Birch (1983) lists some 3,021 works on the subject of unity in diversity, from 1970 to 1981, inclusive. No doubt, there must have been works pre-dating this collection, but were of insufficient number to be included in the volume.

12 David A. Snow and Robert D. Benford signify 'framing' (in the study of social movements) 'which denotes an active, processual phenomenon that implies agency and contention at the level of reality construction' (1988: 6).

Community to race relations as 'the most challenging issue,' a term coined to refer to vital importance of resolving the racial issues in that country.

The Baha'i concept of unity in diversity as originally formulated by Shoghi Effendi seems to be finding a home in recent globalizing trends. The popular notions of unity in diversity, visually inspiring and emotionally appealing, might always carry the day, but they seem to be different than the ideas conceived by the Guardian in 1931.

During the past three decades, the processes of devolution, or decentralization, have marked the changes within the Baha'i Community. The creation of Assistants to the Auxiliary Board was one of the early institutional changes in the 1970s, followed by the new Unit Conventions of the 1980s that elect delegates to the National Convention on the basis of much smaller regions. One can see a more striking decentralization by the establishment in the 1990s of 'Regional Baha'i Councils, in an increasingly larger number of countries where the size of the Baha'i population of the size of the country warrants a mid-tier decision-making body (i.e. neither at the local or national level). Whereas first the National Spiritual Assembly appointed its members, it is now the members of local spiritual assemblies that elect members of these Regional Baha'i Councils. So, too, even at the local level, very large Baha'i communities have begun to make room for 'Neighbourhood' Nineteen-Day Feasts. To be sure, the Baha'i Community is still centralized, but mainly in 'primary' matters, and increasingly it has become decentralized when it comes to 'secondary' matters, i.e. issues that do not bear directly on principles found in the Baha'i Writings.

In the larger society, unity in diversity has become a more powerful concept in the 1990s, not as an extension of the workings of civil rights or multiculturalism for that matter, but as an outcome of globalization (see, e.g., Rowntree: 2000). Suddenly, even majorities in national societies have become minorities in a world system. An entire national society could, under the hammer of hegemonic corporations, become a minority. In the face of McDonaldization, even certain manufacturing, organizational, and service processes could now occupy a 'minority' status (Ritzer: 2000). Standardization now affects the global economy on a sufficiently large scale that environmental degradation, the exploitation of children as workers, and the other global ills that we all like to cite are now the norm in our discourse about this economy.

The popular, massive protests against the direction that globalization is taking, as represented in the structure and decisions of the World Trade Organization in Seattle in 1999 and more recently at G-8 meetings in various parts of the world, have given a fresh and meaningful life to the term unity in diversity. Human governance, within this new framework, implies the divestment of centralized and centralizing systems.

With local and national institutions weakened, and even chastised by multinational corporations, debates about new forms of human governance are taking place, from establishing local currencies and alternative money systems (see, e.g., Lietaer: 2000) to establishing an international court adjudicating on matters related to genocide and crimes against humanity. The forces of social integration and disintegration fall on both sides. Some international, global tendencies have a salubrious, diversifying effect; others propel traditional economic and political institutions towards disintegration. Some local efforts have a germ of restoring integration, while others exemplify anarchistic tendencies. Diversity has come to occupy a central role in this debate: it either undermines efforts at standardization or it must be affirmed in the presence of corporations and trade pacts with global ramifications. As Ulf Hannerz, one of the most noted sociologists of our times, affirmed:

> There is now a world culture, but we had better make sure that we understand what this means. It is marked by an organization of diversity rather than by a replication of uniformity. No total homogenization of systems of meaning and expression has occurred, nor does it appear likely that there will be one any time soon. But this world has become one network of social relationships and between its different regions there is a flow of meanings as well as of people and goods. (Hannerz 1987 (cited by Marcus 1998: 51))

The emphasis on decentralization as part of an evolving structure of Baha'i governance reflects the spirit and form of the 'new social movements' that social theorists are speaking of (see, e.g., Bowles and Gintis 1986). Adam refers to 'all of this talk about diversity, plurality, and decentredness' when scholars seek out the new social movements (Adam 1993: 329), without the fall of the meta-narrative, however. There is a worldview - a comprehensive one at that - which, at its heart, like many new social movements, 'recognizes and supports subordinated people' (cf., *ibid.* 1993: 330).

If the Baha'i Writings aver (as I have tried to show above) that diversity is more about 'customs, manners, habits, ideas, opinions and dispositions' (Abdu'l-Baha 1978: 291), than about tangible differences of skin colour, language, or the like, then what matters in a future society is the collective experience of having developed a vaster and more complex range of individual experiences – it is this range of experience that will always be present and will shape the social organization of the global society. One could argue, that given the individual's access to a world ledger of experiences, individual diversity is bound, in fact, to increase. In this light, the Baha'i conception of 'unity in diversity' in the sense of human governance, echoes the needs of the age. Michael Novak, an author of at least eight books on the topic of unity in diversity, speaks of unity in diversity as 'the highest possible attainment of a civilization, a testimony to the most noble possibilities of the human race…' (Dedication in Birch 1983).

There are some interesting perspectives in the Baha'i Writings that put the idea of unity in diversity on its head. Abdu'l-Baha's assertion that 'multiplicity is the greatest factor for coordination' (1978: 291) swivels the concept of unity in diversity, especially when popular conceptions have it that 'diversity needs coordination.' For Abdu'l-Baha, it is coordination that needs diversity. In Abdu'l-Baha's terms, differences 'reinforce' harmony, and diversity 'strengthens' love (1978: 291). Does this mean that we should make a greater effort in appreciating and welcoming diversity? If music needs notes, unity needs diversity.

Another Baha'i statement speaks of the 'diversity of the national characteristics' of states in a federated world as being 'infinite' (Shoghi Effendi 1974: 43). What are the far-reaching implications of such a statement? Is homogeneity finite, by contrast? What does one make of Abdu'l-Baha's assertion that 'a token of diversity is the essence of perfection…' (1978: 219)? Does such a statement carry implicit assumptions about the goal of education, namely to cultivate diversity as a means to achieve perfection?

These possible answers are merely tentative suggestions, not definite. They do, however, strongly suggest that more weight needs to be given to the notion of diversity in the Baha'i Writings and their implications for the life of Baha'i communities and, indeed, for the world as a whole. On an analytical level, a study of concepts found in the Baha'i texts and their relationship to human-lived experiences provides a key to understanding how these concepts are framed in the contemporary world. On an empirical level, we see that when we privilege the *popular* meaning of unity in diversity, we privilege the norms of mainstream, dominant culture. Alternatively, when we adopt unity in diversity as a principle of human *governance,* we know that 'diversity' is as an essential factor as 'unity.' In the former, we 'other,' rather than befriend, members of minorities, i.e. strangers. In the latter, we pay tribute to the phrase of Abdu'l-Baha, to 'call none a stranger' (Abdu'l-Baha 1978: 280) and we touch upon a very fundamental principle of social and institutional interaction and relations that only then will come home to roost in microscoping a globalized world.

References

'Abdu'l-Baha (1978). *Selections from the Writings of 'Abdu'l-Bahá.* Haifa: Research Department of the Universal House of Justice.

'Abdu'l-Baha (1982). *Promulgation of Universal Peace.* Wilmette, Ill.: Baha'i Publishing Trust.

Adam, Barry (1993). Post-Marxism and the New Social Movements, *Canadian Review of Sociology and Anthropology* 30: 316-36.

Africa Teaching Committee Records 1952. Box 1, Folder 1-11, 13 December. Wilmette, Ill.: National Baha'i Archives.

Baha'i Canada. A national news organ of the National Spiritual Assembly of the Baha'is of the Canada.

Baha'i News. A national news organ of the National Spiritual Assembly of the Baha'is of the United States.

Baha'u'llah (1971). *Gleanings from the Writings of Bahá'u'lláh.* Wilmette, Ill.: Baha'i Publishing Trust.

Baha'u'llah & 'Abdu'l-Baha (1955). *The Baha'i Revelation.* London: Baha'i Publishing Trust.

Barrett, Donald M. (1977). Unity in Diversity, *World Order* 12 (2): 9-12.

Bennett, Lerone, Jr. (1965). Baha'i: A Way of Life for Millions, *Ebony Magazine* (April). 7pp.

Birch, Carol L. (ed.) (1983). *Unity in Diversity: An Index to the Publications of Conservative and Libertarian Institutions*. Metuchen, NJ: Scarecrow Press.

Bond, Michael Harris (1998). Unity in Diversity: Orientations and Strategies for Building a Harmonious, Multicultural Society, Keynote address, *Conferences on Multiculturalism: Diversity in Action*. University of Tartu, Tartu, Estonia. 6 May. 24pp.

Bowles, Samuel, and Herbert Gintis (1986). *Democracy and Capitalism*. New York: Basic Books.

Carroll, William K. (1992). *Organizing Dissent: Contemporary Social Movements in Theory and Practice*. Toronto: Garamond Press.

Christensen, Philip R. (1969). *The Unity-Diversity Principle and its Effects on Creative Group Problem Solving: An Experimental Investigation*, B.A. Thesis. Harvard University.

Danesh, Hossain (1986a). The Challenge of Integration, Part 1: The Dynamics of Integration, *Bahá'í Canada* 8 (Oct.): 5, 17.

Danesh, Hossain (1986b). The Challenge of Integration, Part 2: Transforming the Baha'i Community, *Baha'i Canada* 8 (Nov.): 6, 16.

Danesh, Hossain (1986c). The Challenge of Integration, Part 3: Further Considerations, *Baha'i Canada* 8 (Dec.): 8, 18.

Danesh, Hossain (1997). Three Stages of Integration: Part 1, *Baha'i Canada* 9 (Dec.): 15-16.

Danesh, Hossain (1998). Three Stages of Integration: Part 2, *Baha'i Canada* 9 (Jan.): 15-16.

External Affairs (1997). Unity in Diversity Week Offers new Opportunities, *Baha'i Canada* 10 (October): 13-15.

External Affairs (1998). Unity in Diversity Week to Focus on Human Rights, *Baha'i Canada* 11 (October): 17-18.

Feather, N.T., R.E. Volkmer and I.R. Mckee (1993). A Comparative Study of the Value Priorities of Australians, Australian Baha'is, and Expatriate Iranian Baha'is, *Journal of Cross-Cultural Psychology* 23: 95-106.

Garner, Roberta (1996). *Contemporary Movements and Ideologies*, New York: McGraw-Hill.

Hannerz, Ulf (1987). Cosmopolitans and Locals in World Culture. Stockholm, Unpublished manuscript.

Keniston, Leonda Williams (2000). Religion as a Medium for Cross-Racial Friendship Formation: A Study of the Baha'is of the State of Virginia and Washington, D.C. Unpublished paper, 31pp.

Lietaer, Bernard A. (2000). Community Currencies: A New Tool for the 21st Century. http://www.transaction.net/money/cc/cc01.html.

Marcus, George E. (1998). *Ethnography Through Thick and Thin.* Princeton, NJ: Princeton University Press.

May, D.J. (1993). *The Baha'i Principle of Religious Unity and the Challenge of Radical Pluralism.* M.A. Thesis. University of North Texas.

McMullen, Mike (2000). *The Baha'i: The Religious Construction of a Global Identity.* New Brunswick, NJ: Rutgers U.P.

Miller, David L. (2000). *Introduction to Collective Behavior and Collective Action.* Prospect Heights, Ill.: Waveland Press.

Momen, Moojan (1990). The Integration into the British Baha'i Community of Recent Iranian Baha'i migrants, *Baha'i Studies Bulletin* 4: 50-53.

Rafat, Pauline (1998). The Beauty and Challenge of Diversity, *Baha'i Canada* 10 (Oct.): 16-17.

Ritzer, George (2000). *The McDonaldization of Society.* (3rd edn.).Thousand Oaks, CA: Pine Forge Press.

Rowntree, Lester, (ed.) (2000). *Diversity Amid Globalization: World Regions, Environment, Development,* Toronto: Prentice-Hall.

Shoghi Effendi (1967). *The Promised Day Is Come.* Wilmette, Ill.: Baha'i Publishing Trust.

Shoghi Effendi (1970). *Dawn of a New Day.* New Delhi: Baha'i Publishing Trust.

Shoghi Effendi (1974). *World Order of Bahá'u'lláh.* Wilmette, Ill.: Baha'i Publishing Trust.

Shoghi Effendi (1981). *The Unfolding Destiny of the British Baha'i Community: The Messages from the Guardian of the Baha'i Faith to the Baha'is of the British Isles.* London: Baha'i Publishing Trust.

Snow, David A., and Robert D. Benford (1988). Master Frames and Cycles of Protest. Paper presented at the *Workshop on Frontiers in Social Movement Theory.* Ann Arbor: University of Michigan, 8-11 June.

Thomas, Richard W. (1992). *Racial Unity: An Imperative for Social Progress.* Ottawa, On.: Association for Baha'i Studies.

Universal House of Justice (1988). Baha'i Participation in Cultural and Religious Festivals of Other Religions: Letter to the Spiritual Assembly of the Baha'is of Malaysia, dated 26 May 1982. *Baha'i Canada* 9 (Dec.): 17-18.

Universal House of Justice (1993). Ridvan Message. April 21.

Universal House of Justice (1995). *The Prosperity of Humankind.* Haifa: Baha'i World Centre.

Universal House of Justice (2000). Cultural Diversity in the Age of Maturity, *Compilation of Compilations.* Ingleside, New South Wales, Australia, vol. 3: 92-138.

Venti, Carmela (1997). Maps, Metaphor, and Memory: Anthropomorphic Cartography, *Mercator's World.* 2: 50-53.

van den Hoonaard, Will C. (2000). Homogenization is for Milk: Some Baha'i Perspectives on Diversity. Various Baha'i national centres (Hellerup, Denmark) and (Oslo, Norway). Oct.

van den Hoonaard, Will C., and William Hackborn (1994). Chaos as Metaphor for the Study of the Postmodern World: A Bahá'í Approach, *Annual Meetings of the Canadian Sociology and Anthropology Association,* Calgary, 10-13 June.

Wilburn, James R. (1983). Preface, in Carol L. Birch (ed.), *Unity in Diversity: An Index to the Publications of Conservative and Libertarian Institutions*. Metuchen, NJ: Scarecrow Press.

CHAPTER 14

Baha'i Meets Globalisation: A New Synergy?

Sen McGlinn

When Weber identified the synergy (*wahlverwandtschaft*) between Protestantism and the rationalisation of social control and production in 'modern' societies, both processes could be analysed in retrospect. This paper will attempt, more tentatively, to draw attention to the potential 'fit' between the dynamics of globalisation and the Baha'i Faith. In the 21st century, the Baha'i community is actually encountering the restructuring of global society, which was something that could only be anticipated in the 20th century. The character of the Baha'i Faith itself is still being shaped, in a three-way dynamic involving the community's scriptural resources, the traditions of practice it has built up over several generations, and the demands of a globalising society. No attempt will be made, therefore, to predict whether the Baha'i Faith will have a fruitful marriage with globalisation, or a short infatuation broken up by underlying incompatibilities. A comparison of the key dynamics of globalisation and corresponding Baha'i scriptures and practice will, however, identify aspects of the relationship that will be most interesting to monitor. We should begin with a definition of terms.

'Globalisation' and 'post-modern' in sociology refer to the process by which we move *from* the societies of the centralised nation-states of the 'modern' era *to* something which is structurally different. 'Globalisation' is the present active tense, and 'post-modern' is the future passive participle: 'that which will have been globalised,' as we imagine it. Globalisation is not just a matter of extending existing social structures to a global level: the extension requires and reinforces deep structural changes, which in turn demand changes in world-views.

The key dynamic of globalisation is the **functional differentiation** of society: that is, the shift from a unitary stratified society to an organic society in which politics, religion, science, and commerce are increasingly distinct spheres of life. Although the process of differentiation has roots in the earliest division of labour, there has been a sharp acceleration in Western Europe from the 14th to the 20th centuries. Distinct institutions of politics, economics, religion and science already existed, but their autonomy increased and, for the first time, we see theoretical claims that they *ought* to be autonomous. Some universities were freed from church control. Theories of national churches were advanced, to free the political sphere from papal control, and economic theories argued that trade prospers best where the state interferes least. Within the sphere of politics, the theory of the separation of the judicial, legislative and executive powers was worked out. The toleration of dissent developed into arguments for disestablishment, and churches were either constitutionally disestablished or withdrew from politics. These different institutions have also become distinct life-worlds: not only is the church distinct from the state and the academy, but the way we reason and relate to one another is different when we are sharing a Christian mass, arguing politics, doing science and setting up a trading company. It is accepted that we behave according to different logics in different spheres.

That brings us to the second dynamic of globalisation: **individualisation**. When society shifted from a unitary to a differentiated model, individual identity changed absolutely. In a unitary society, the individual has one identity: he might be a 'gentleman' in commerce, religion and politics for example. In a differentiated society each person learns to act in distinct ways in the different spheres, and maintains a distinct status in each. The poor cobbler may be a respected leader in the Methodist circle, the magistrate may be excluded from communion. That also means that individuals have more freedom in constructing their own identities, and are dealt with in each sphere as individuals and not as members of a family, group or class. Individualisation brings with it the possibility and concept of individual freedoms, and the claim of classes, ethnic minorities and women to share in them as individuals. I treat **feminism** as an aspect of individualisation, because society recognises the individual and not the family as its basic unit.

Spreading the individual identity across multiple life worlds causes a good deal of stress. How much stress depends on how rapidly world-views change to accommodate the new situation. Any substantial lag is experienced as moral chaos or a 'wrongness' in the world, and in the self. Individual responses to this stress can have dangerous social and political effects. The Baha'i Faith tells its followers that a radically different way of ordering the world (a New World Order) is not to be feared, and the Baha'i teachings anticipate the key dynamics of globalisation. These teachings could well alleviate some of the tension by supporting a world-view in which the differentiated and individualised society is not a threat, it is *the way things are meant to be.*

Another effect of functional differentiation has been that boundaries belonging to one sphere are not transferred to another. Trade is not confined by the boundaries of the state or the religious community, and religious communities cross political boundaries. **Global integration** is the process in which commerce, having become an autonomous sphere functioning according to its own logic, discovers that national and religious boundaries are irrelevant, and becomes a world economic system. Where trade leads, technologies of transport and communication follow, and this makes it possible for science and politics to be integrated globally. It is not yet clear whether religion too will become a global system.

The last dynamic of globalisation I will consider is **pluralism and relativism**, due to intercultural and inter-religious contacts and migration. When we speak of postmodernism in philosophy and the fine arts, we are referring mainly to this aspect of globalisation. Intercultural and inter-religious contacts and migration relativise truth claims and social norms. The family, we now know, is not a given: it is made by people in many different ways. The class system is not part of the divine order. Ideologies too are seen to be manufactured, their doctrines designed to support interests. Ideological states have given way to non-ideological states, and political theories which supposed that shared ideologies and values are the basis of social unity have given way to a model of society that is united, despite our differences, by our needs for one another.

The dynamics of **technological progress** and the convergence of material cultures are major contributors to globalisation, although I will not deal with these.

With one eye on Weber's work on the synergy between Protestantism and capitalist societies, I would now like to relate Baha'i doctrines and community structures to these dynamics of globalisation, looking for potential synergy between the Baha'i faith and postmodern society. In principle I am interested in whether Baha'i *scripture* and Baha'i *practice,* (the latter based mainly on Baha'i secondary literature), support functional differentiation, individualisation and feminism, global integration, pluralism and relativism in the Baha'i *religious community* and in the *world*. However lack of space will not allow sources to be presented for theory and for practice, for the world and the community, in relation to each of the six dynamics of globalisation.

Global Integration

As regards global integration, there seems to be no issue. The Baha'i terminology for this is 'world unity.' According to both its scriptures and its secondary literature, Baha'i teachings favour the extension of communications and of economic and political institutions to a global scale, based on the value that humanity is one people and the globe is one place. Evidence from the Baha'i literature in European languages and observations in the North American and Persian communities have shown that 'world-mindedness' or 'cosmopolitanism' is a strong characteristic of Baha'is.[1] Specific Baha'i teachings favour free trade and a universal currency, weights and measures, and Baha'i secondary literature has also endorsed these positions. Other Baha'i teachings oppose barriers to global integration, such as nationalism, prejudice and

1 See Keene (1967). Keene's 'characteristic statements' for world-mindedness are obviously drawn from the Baha'i teachings themselves, which invalidates his inter-religious comparisons (Keene: 145). Nevertheless his study does provide evidence of what has perhaps been too obvious to other observers to require empirical substantiation: the world-mindedness in the Baha'i scriptures is also an accepted and salient part of Baha'i self-awareness. Mehri Jensen (1986) has also used world-mindedness as a measure of Baha'i religiosity in Iran, but she does not report the specific rates she found. McMullen (2000) contains considerable anecdotal evidence for world-mindedness (see e.g. 170-72) but does not seem to have used any specific test for it. One of the most popular scriptural sources for the Baha'i vision of global integration is a letter written by Shoghi Effendi in 1936, and significantly entitled 'The Unfoldment of World Civilization'. (Shoghi Effendi, 1991: 161-206, especially 203-4).

exclusivism. The Baha'is have contributed to the 'thematisation of humanity,' for instance through the translation and global distribution of the Universal House of Justice's 1985 letter *The Promise of World Peace*, and through their participation in various international forums.

As for the internal dimension, it is evident that the Baha'i community itself is globally integrated, having spread and established its institutions in most parts of the world and most cultural areas, and having kept its communities in communication and communion with one another.

Pluralism

With regard to pluralism, the Baha'i teachings contain the relevant theory, under the headings of 'the oneness of mankind' (or sometimes, 'of humanity') and 'unity in diversity.' Baha'i practice has also been supportive of multi-cultural initiatives such as racial equality education. John Huddlestone. for example, says that 'one of the most effective ways of abolishing prejudice is to learn to appreciate the diversity of culture in the world and to see it as an enrichment of our total experience' (1989: 419). He then goes on to quote 'Abdu'l-Baha beginning 'Consider the flowers of the garden, though differing in kind ...'. This is typical of the presentations found in Baha'i literature, and is such a dominant theme in the Baha'i scriptures that further examples would be redundant.

When we look at pluralism in internal Baha'i practice, we have to distinguish between cultural pluralism, including racial pluralism, and other aspects of pluralism. As for *cultural pluralism*, Baha'i communities contain relatively high proportions of people who were born in another country or have lived long-term in another country, and almost all national Baha'i communities have a spread across the locally relevant variables, whether that be language, ethnic identity, class or religious background. Baha'i authors consistently advocate cultural pluralism. In our visual age, Baha'is have made an icon out of photographs and videos of groups of culturally diverse people. Such images are an important part of Baha'i socialisation and missionary work. Michael McMullen's description of the World Congress as 'global Baha'i dramaturgy' is a good example (2000: 3). Pilgrimage to the Baha'i holy places in Israel also reinforces the sense of global identity.

Some Baha'i authors have accepted cultural pluralism, while rejecting *religious pluralism*. Horace Holley, an extreme example, is against any form of social diversity. He says:

Baha'u'llah stood at that major turning-point of social evolution where the long historic trend toward diversity B in language, custom, civil and religious codes and economic practices B came to an end, and the movement was reversed in the direction of unity. The human motive in the former era was necessarily competitive. The human motive in the new era is necessarily co-operative (1976: 135-36).

This is a good illustration of the conservative instinct, since Holley wants to turn history back in its course, from society to a simple community, using religion to do so. As for religious diversity in particular, he says that

... the worldly conception of tolerance between conflicting creeds and sects is not unity - it is merely agreement to disagree. ... Without unity of faith and agreement on ... the laws and principles which come from God ... there can be no political nor economic unity.

David Hofman says that 'The strength of an organic society depends upon the unity of its millions of diversified individuals in a common ideology' (1960: 56). More recently, McMullen has said that 'Baha'is feel that this global solidarity will come about through adherence to a common ideology and recognition of a common global authority ... i.e., the Baha'i Administrative Order (2000: 4, see also 112). Huschmand Sabet writes 'It is a fatal fallacy to believe that a civilisation for mankind might be built up on a plurality of fundamental values' (1986: 76). Moojen Momen also considers a common ideology to be necessary to social unity.[2] His concept of the role of religion in society is explicitly drawn from the past when 'It was religion that was the cohesive force within the society.' apart from its nostalgic ring and present impossibility, this would leave religion with a shrinking role at best.

2 Moojan Momen [n.d.]: 'Baha'i Faith - Towards the Millennium' from http://www.gopbi.com/community/groups/pbcbahai. Another author with a Durkheimian concept of the function of religion (this time explicitly referring to Durkheim) is McMullen (2000: 12).

A global society that is held together by our need for one another and by the global nature of economics, politics and science has less and less need for religion or ideology as cohesive forces. Durkheim was able to perceive the cohesive function that religion had in *past* societies precisely because, in his own society, it no longer had that function. So a Durkheimian approach will hardly help us in thinking about the role of religion in the new world order.

Pluralism in terms of *sexual orientation* is not clearly addressed in the Baha'i writings, although the *Kitab-i Aqdas* refers to some behaviour - which might be male homosexuality or pederasty - as shameful. Baha'i authors reveal a variety of stances. John Huddlestone confidently describes homosexuality as abhorrent and also (inconsistently) as a medical problem, but there have also been networks and support groups for Baha'i homosexuals (1989: 424). There are some national Baha'i communities today in which diversity of sexual orientation is quietly tolerated.

Relativism

The relativity of religious truth-claims is endorsed in the Baha'i scriptures (Shoghi Effendi 1991: 58, 115) but not always in practice. Some Baha'i authors make absolute claims for the truth of the Baha'i revelation[3] but there is also a tendency in the apologetic literature to relativise, rather than reject, the truth claims of other religions. The acceptance of diversity of ideas within the Baha'i community is more difficult, especially as regards the public expression of ideas. My observation is that this varies between national Baha'i communities as a function both of the culture and of the policies of the National Spiritual Assembly. There is no adequate institutional protection for the right of individual expression which is recognised in theory. There appears to be a certain ambivalence about pluralism and freedom. Both are seen as good, but also as threats which must be kept in moderation, rather than strengths that should be maximised.

3 The Universal House of Justice does seem to have adopted that position: 'the Revelation of Baha'u'llah is the standard of truth against which all other views and conclusions are to be measured.' (Letter of 21 July 1968).

Individualism

Individualism, as a modern social philosophy, has its roots in the Enlightenment's rediscovery of epistemological individualism, which is endorsed in both the Baha'i scriptures and the secondary literature, where it is called 'the individual search after truth' or the rejection of 'blind imitation'.

In terms of *religious theory*, the Baha'i Faith continues a long trend in religious history by which the focus has shifted from the collective to the individual. As in Islam and Christianity (and late Judaism), salvation is not the well-being of the tribe but individual salvation. However the concept of an either-or judgement leading to one of two fates has given way to the belief that each individual grows towards an individual potential, the degrees of perfection being endless. It follows that salvation for me may not be salvation for you.

Baha'i religious duties are all individual obligations that cannot be fulfilled by proxy. The role of the prayer-leader has been abolished, except in the case of the obligatory prayer for the dead. Shaykh Ahmad's individualism in the Sufi path has been radicalised to something analogous to the 'shaykhood of all believers' (Cole 1997). All this points to a remarkably individualistic religious theory. At the same time, the Baha'i writings provide prescriptions not only for individual life but also for political life and the relations between states. Some Baha'i authors (McMullen 2000: 8) have regarded this as a shift from individual salvation to collective salvation, although it does not appear to me to involve any lesser emphasis on individual salvation.

In terms of *social theory*, this basis is reflected in a marked concern for individual rights over and against the state, and also over and against the religious collective. The latter aspect is reflected in an administrative system that is rational, democratic and participatory, and to some extent in a 'rule of law,' in that there is a formal appeal system. However since there are no formal legal procedures in practice, for instance to ensure that an individual who has suffered religious sanctions knows what he or she has been accused of, by whom, or on what evidence, the present appeal procedure is effectively an empty letter. The Baha'i scriptures do not provide details of the required procedures, but neither do they bar them: this is a matter to be worked out by and in practice.

The position of the internal dissenter – the heretic – is always an acid test for a religious theory of society. In the Baha'i case, those who have been declared to be 'covenant-breakers' are expelled and so excluded from every right within the religious community, but the Baha'is are also required to ensure they have full enjoyment of their civil rights.[4]

The Baha'i communities of the west began with a strongly Protestant – and to some extent millenarian – background, which involves an individualistic approach at least to religion (Stockman 1985: xix, 103; Will van den Hoonaard 1997: 26). However individualism in this sense is not the same thing as embracing individualism as a social philosophy.

Holley is one of the most collectivist of Baha'i authors (1976: 85). He says that the individual should accept 'guidance ... for his doctrinal beliefs, for not otherwise can he contribute his share to the general unity'. ... 'In comparison to this divine creation, the traditional claims of individual conscience, of personal judgement, of private freedom, seem nothing more than empty assertions advanced in opposition to the divine will.' Since he rejects the epistemological source of individualism, he naturally rejects individualism as a social philosophy as well. The Baha'i International Community refers in one statement to 'dogmas of consumerism and aggressive individualism'[5] which they feel dominate society. In another statement they say 'No aspect of contemporary civilization is more directly challenged by Baha'u'llah's conception of the future than is the prevailing cult of individualism ...'[6] Moojen Momen echoes this: 'Free-market capitalism,' he says, 'is principally a combination of laissez-faire economics and a strident individualism and consumerism. Having this as the ideology of a society is a paradox in that this ideology is itself destructive of society.'[7] If that were true, it would be remarkable that the societies afflicted

4 Letter from Shoghi Effendi to the Baha'is of Iran, cited in Schaefer et al. (2000): 257.

5 Statement 'Conservation and Sustainable Development in the Bahá'í Faith' (1995): http:/ /www.bic-un.bahai.org/ 95-0406.htm

6 Baha'i International Community, statement 'Who is Writing the Future' (2000): http:/ / www.bahai.org/ article-1-7-3-1.html.

7 *The Bahá'í World Today* [1996] http:/ / www.northill.demon.co.uk/ bahai/ intro9.htm.

with individualism have proved so successful. None of these authors support their views on individualism from the Baha'i scriptures.

Feminism

I am treating feminism here as an especially important variety of individualism, as a social philosophy that claims that people should participate in society and be treated by society as individuals, and not according to shared characteristics such as biological sex or gender identity. This principle is extensively treated in the Baha'i writings, and especially in reports of 'Abdu'l-Baha's talks in Western countries, under the heading of 'the equality of men and women.'

In practice the Baha'is have advocated equal rights for women in society, and have acted to raise the status of women, for instance through women's literacy programmes. Huddlestone (1989: 419-20) supports equal rights and the full public participation of women without reservation. Hofman stands out as somewhat of an exception: he says that women's place of honour is in the home, since the female represents Eros (1960: 68).

Although 'Abdu'l-Baha referred to 'the equality of men and women and their equal sharing in all rights,' Baha'i laws regarding inheritance and ritual duties distinguish between men and women as such (1978: 249). The theory on these points is complex, and some general references will have to suffice. As for the inheritance law, I have argued that the law provides a limited primacy for sons in inheriting from the father, and for the daughters in inheriting from their mother (McGlinn, 1995). This does not seem to be justifying unequal treatment for men and women as such. The ritual laws also exempt women from the duty of pilgrimage, although they may participate, and in practice do so equally with men. Menstruating women are exempt from fasting and obligatory prayer, but again they may participate, and menstruation and childbirth are not associated with ritual pollution. The same exemptions apply also to the sick, the elderly and those engaging in hard physical labour. Compliance with these religious laws is voluntary, and non-compliance does not affect a person's status within the community. There is therefore no direct contradiction with the principle that the *community* should treat members as individuals and not on the basis of their sex.

There has been a vigorous debate among Baha'is in recent decades as to whether the Baha'i scriptures exclude women from election to the Universal House of Justice. The textual issue is the same as that concerning the eligibility of women for the presidency in Iran. The Iranian constitution refers to the candidates for presidency as *rijal*, the same word that is used in the *Kitab-i Aqdas* to refer to the members of the House of Justice, and the issue is whether this means men only, or is an honorific address to persons of either sex. One might have expected that Baha'u'llah's own statements that women are counted as *rijal*[8] would be decisive, but the situation is not so straight-forward, for reasons that have been described in the unpublished paper 'The Service of Women on the Institutions of the Baha'i Faith' and more succinctly by Cole in 'Women and Baha'i Houses of Justice.'[9] I will omit the arguments here, and simply say that the 'theory' is not unambiguous: there are real textual grounds that have led some Baha'is, including the present Universal House of Justice, to think that women are scripturally excluded from that body. The practice however is clear, since it is decided by the Universal House of Justice. Women cannot serve on the Universal House of Justice, and votes for women are counted as invalid votes.

Differentiation

Differentiation in the social model and internal differentiation need to be addressed separately. As for *differentiation in society*, the Baha'i scriptures speak most clearly on the issues of church and state, and to a lesser extent on science and religion. In both cases the theory endorses an organic model in which different social organs co-exist and cooperate, each retaining its independent existence. The scriptural position on church and state is a major theme in the Baha'i writings, and has been described by Cole, Saiedi and myself: it need not be rehearsed here.[10] It is important to note that the Baha'i theory endorses the dif-

8 There are at least three such statements. One is translated in Research Department (1986), #7, 3.

9 Available at: http:// www.2.h-net.msu.edu/ ~bahai/ docs/ vol3/ wmnuhj.htm and http:// www.personal.umich.edu/ ~jrcole/ bhwmhous.htm

10 See Cole (1992) and (1998); Saiedi (2000: 360-70); S. McGlinn (1999). The last of these lists the major scriptural sources.

ferentiation of religion and politics on the basis of a high, not a low, valuation of politics. Politics is not rejected as dirty, it is the manifestation of the sovereignty of God, and therefore cannot be treated as subordinate to religion.

The theological arguments for this differentiation, based on the unknowable oneness of God and the differentiation of God's attributes, are in principle translatable to Jewish, Christian and Muslim theologies. Here the Baha'i Faith could contribute to the integration of religions in the post-modern order by showing why the functionally differentiated society is also the way the Kingdom of God is meant to be. For the individual believer, the implication of the organic model is that *religion is not everything*, which confirms what our life experience tells us, that we live in multiple worlds with their own ethics and logics. The metaphor of organic unity used in the Baha'i writings offers a way of making this abstract truth conceivable, by providing a representation of the differentiated global society as a body whose diverse organs have a common reference to a 'soul' which is not contained in any one organ. This should be sharply distinguished from monist uses of the organic metaphor in authoritarian religious and political theories (such as those of Hofman and McMullen, cited above), in which the coordinating agency is one of the organs.

Many Baha'i authors assume or argue a unitary concept of society and reveal a strong aversion to functional differentiation. Vafa Moayed describes the separation of church and state in Christianity and says 'The Baha'i concept is however radically different: the Baha'i Faith has a *monist* concept of human society' (1987: 57). Holley expresses a desire to establish a society centering on religion, in which religion dominates all aspects of life (1976: 63-64). David Hofman says that 'our dreadful Western civilisation has succeeded in dividing life (and therefore people) into separate compartments. Business, recreation, politics, religion, and social life are regarded as separate and distinct activities, to be assumed according to the time or day' (1960: 109). The point illustrated by Hofman would, I think, hold for the many other Baha'i authors who are critical of 'Western' civilisation: their actual target is functional differentiation, which they mistakenly believe to be a purely Western phenomenon. The same could be said of the anti-globalisation movement in general: the goal is not an end to international integration, but a return to a unitary social model.

Authors who claim that Baha'i teachings advocate theocracy, and that the Baha'i Administrative Order is an alternative system of government, are a particular case of the general aversion to functional differentiation. In the passage just mentioned, in which Hofman rejects the division of life in 'Western' society, he goes on to reject the New Testament verse 'Render to Caesar the things that are Caesar's, and to God the things that are God's' – a verse which Baha'u'llah cites as a proof text in *Epistle to the Son of the Wolf*.[11] This endorsement in turn was cited by 'Abdu'l-Baha and Shoghi Effendi in works that Hofman would certainly have known. Yet he, and Holley (1938: vii), reject this. The gap between scriptural theory and community practice could hardly be more glaring.

The rejection of the differentiation of society in these authors is combined with a strong advocacy of international political institutions and internationalisation. Huddleston, for instance, strongly advocates world free trade but presents an ideal of society without politics, and with much reduced structures, since morality is to take the place of institutions (1989: Chapter 29). In my view this should be interpreted as an anti-globalisation position, based on the rejection of functional differentiation. Some of the Baha'i authors who advocate theocratic government also advocate global political institutions or praise the United Nations, without any apparent awareness that global political systems must necessarily be secular.

Baha'is with a unitary world-view and a unitary self-image can resolve the religion and politics issue by refusing to participate in politics. David Hofman, for example, boasts that he has never participated in any election outside of the Baha'i community (1995: tape 7 side 2). But while politics can be avoided, science cannot. Baha'i authors' treatment of the relationship between science and religion reveals a unitary concept of truth, and a strong resistance to the plural roles that the individual is called on to play in different spheres. John Huddlestone says 'a scientist can become a Baha'i without having to split his mind into two separate and conflicting parts' (Huddlestone 1989: 415). Anjam Khursheed (1987) argues for a teleological theory of evolution, and seeks to show that the latest discoveries of physics are already prefigured in the Baha'i scriptures. His argument is directed

11 Pages 89-92. The Tablet to the Shah (Lawh-i Sultan) was available to Hofman and Holley in E.G. Browne's translation of 'Abdu'l-Bahá's *A Traveller's Narrative*: 113. The *New Testament* text is Mark 12: 17.

against the intellectual differentiation of science and religion, without addressing the relationship between their institutions. Similarly, the Universal House of Justice has expressed its disapproval of Baha'i academics who write 'as if they were non-Baha'is' and say that 'Scholarly endeavors are not an activity apart ... answering to standards and operating on authority outside it' ('it' being an 'organic process' of growth acting through the Baha'i institutions).[12]

The *internal differentiation* of the Baha'i community is one of its most remarkable features. The Baha'i term here is again 'organic unity,' a unity based on balance and harmony between elements and organs, rather than domination by one. In the *Kitab-i Aqdas* Baha'u'llah distinguished between the Houses of Worship and the Houses of Justice, separating liturgy and worship from administrative authority over the affairs of the religious community. I think this is an idea without antecedents, a stroke of genius or of inspiration. 'Abdu'l-Baha in turn distinguished between interpretative and doctrinal authority, vested in the Guardians, and legislative and administrative authority, vested in the Houses of Justice. This theoretical differentiation also exists in practice, although it is not always understood.

Conclusions

The Baha'i theory has a high degree of congruence with the dynamics of globalisation, in both its picture of the religious community and its picture of society. However, when we look at the practice we see a community that has a global identity and the means to consolidate it in individuals, but is unaware of how the various dynamics of globalisation fit together. The more conservative authors I have cited reveal a resistance to some aspects of globalisation. Their commitment to a unitary social model, as seen in the rejection of church-state differentiation, a negative evaluation of individualism, the belief that a society must be structured around a common ideology, the perpetuation of male dominance of religion, and in some cases outright rejection of religious and other kinds of pluralism, represents a serious problem for the Baha'i community.

If the Baha'is present their message in terms of an imagined future in which a unitary society is defined by a common ideology and ruled

12 Letters of 4 October 1994 and 10 December 1992.

by a theocracy, they will be marginalising their message. Individual believers will also be in a situation in which they have a religious investment in one view of how the world ought to be, while their daily experience tells them that this would be impossible and undesirable. As globalisation proceeds, the global economic, political and legal orders become steadily stronger, and it becomes ever more implausible to expect it to collapse, and ever more evident that what the Baha'is have been calling the 'old world order' is in fact the New World Order. The tension increases, and at a certain point an individual finds the implausibility of the world-rejecting position unbearable, and either leaves the community or embraces the social changes brought by globalisation as the fulfilment of Baha'i hopes.

The community faces a considerable intellectual challenge. The viability of a post-modern construction of the Baha'i Faith depends on having a coherent *religious* explanation of society, of religion and of their relationship. It is not sufficient simply to embrace post-modernity's own secular explanation of itself: Baha'u'llah must be re-envisioned as the prophet of post-modernity, as Cole (1998) has done. Exegetical traditions that have stood for generations have to be replaced with new readings. The 'imaginary' of an organic society has to be developed in rites, music and other arts, and in teaching the Faith, both internally and externally.

Some infrastructural changes are required if the Baha'i community is to flourish in a globalising society: censorship and other barriers to a civil society will have to be removed, the networks and interest groups that would constitute an internal civil society will have to be established, and the state of mind that sees diversity as 'internal opposition' to the true faith will have to be overcome. A community without a firm concept of the rights of individuals, and the criteria and infrastructure to guarantee these rights, is ill fitted for a post-modern society. While the Baha'i Faith is potentially a post-modern religion today, the unavoidable social inertia will probably ensure that the Baha'i community as a whole does not enter post-modern society for another two to three generations.

On the positive side, the Baha'i community has a strong sense of global identity. It represents a broad spectrum of the cultures of the world and has found effective means of teaching the message that 'humanity is one.' It has succeeded in building multi-racial communities even in hostile environments. If globalisation consisted simply of this, without involving any structural changes in society, the Baha'is would be in a good position. Moreover the Baha'is have a strong missionary drive and a strong work ethic, they value thrift and sobriety, literacy and higher education, altruism and community solidarity: these will continue to be success factors in the globalising world.

References

'Abdu'l-Baha (1978). *Selections from the Writings of Abdu'l-Baha.* Haifa: Baha'i World Centre.

Baha'i International Community (1995). Conservation and Sustainable Development in the Baha'i Faith.: http://www.bic-un.bahai.org/95-0406.htm.

Baha'i International Community (2000). Statement: Who is Writing the Future: http:// www.bahai.org/ article-1-7-3-1.html.

Browne, Edward G. (1891). *A traveller's narrative written to illustrate the Episode of the Báb. In the original Persian, and translated into English, with an introduction and explanatory notes by Edward G. Browne,* Cambridge.

Cole, J.R.I. (1992). Iranian Millennarianism and Democratic Thought in the 19th Century, *International Journal of Middle Eastern Studies* 24.

Cole, J.R.I. (1997). Individualism and the Mystical Path in Shaykh Ahmad al-Ahsa'i, *Occasional Papers in Shaykhi, Babi and Baha'i Studies,* no. 4.

Cole, J.R.I. (1998). *Modernity and the Millennium: The Genesis of the Baha'i Faith in the Nineteenth Century Middle East.* New York: Columbia University Press.

Cole, J.R.I. [n.d.] Women and Baha'i Houses of Justice, http:// www.personal.umich.edu/ ~jrcole/ bhwmhous.htm.

Hofman, David (1960). *The Renewal of Civilization,* (2nd revd. edn.). Oxford: George Ronald.

Hofman, David (1995). *David Hofman on Theocracy*: (Set of audio-tapes of lectures delivered in 1993): Live Unity Productions.

Holley, Horace (1938). Introduction, in Shoghi Effendi [Rabbani] (1991), *The World Order of Baha'u'llah.* Wilmette, Ill.: Baha'i Publishing Trust.

Holley, Horace (1976). *Religion for Mankind* (1st edn. 1956). Oxford: George Ronald.

Hoonaard, van den, Will (1997). The Baha'i Community of Canada, *Journal of Bahá'í Studies* 7: 3.

Huddlestone, John (1989). *The Search for a Just Society.* Oxford: George Ronald.

Jensen, Mehri (1986). Religion and Family Planning in Contemporary Iran, in Peter Smith (ed.) *In Iran, Studies in Babi and Baha'i History,* vol. 3. Los Angeles: Kalimat.

Keene, J.J. (1967). Religious Behavior and Neuroticism, Spontaneity, and Worldmindedness, *Sociometry,* 30.

Khursheed, Anjam (1987). *Science and Religion: towards the restoration of an ancient harmony.* London: One World.

McGlinn, Sen (1995). Some considerations relating to the inheritance laws of the Aqdas, *Baha'i Studies Review,* vol. 5.

McGlinn, Sen (1999). A theology of the state from the Baha'i writings, *Journal of Church and State,* vol. 41.

McMullen, Mike (2000). *The Baha'i: the religious construction of a global identity.* New Brunswick: Rutgers University Press.

Moayed, Vafa (1987). La separation des pouvoirs spirituel et temporel: une formule provisoire?, in the *Recueil des Conferences* of the European Francophone Association for Baha'i Studies, from the 1987 conference.

Momen, Moojan [n.d.] Baha'i Faith – Towards the Millennium: from http://www.gopbi.com/community/groups/pbcbahai.

Research Department, Baha'i World Centre (1986). *Women: Extracts from the Writings of Baha'u'llah, 'Abdu'l-Baha, Shoghi Effendi, and the Universal House of Justice,* comp. by the Research Department of the Universal House of Justice, Thornhill, Ont.: Baha'i Canada Publications.

Sabet, Huschmand (1986). *The Way out of the Dead End,* (tr. Patricia Crampton). Oxford: George Ronald.

Saiedi, Nader (2000). *Logos and Civilization,* Maryland, University Press of Maryland.

Schaeffer, Udo, Nicola Towfigh and Ulrich Gollmer (2000). *Making the Crooked Straight,* Oxford: George Ronald.

Shoghi Effendi [Rabbani] (1991). *The World Order of Baha'u'llah,* Wilmette, Ill.: Baha'i Publishing Trust.

Stockman, R. (1985). *The Baha'i Faith in America: Origins 1892-1900,* vol. 1. Wilmette, Ill.: Baha'i Publishing Trust.

The Baha'i World Today [n.d.] http:// www.northill.demon.co.uk/ bahai/ intro9.htm.

Lee, Anthony A. et al. *The Service of Women on the Institutions of the Baha'i Faith:* http:// www2.h-net.msu.edu/ ~bahai/ docs/ vol3/ wmnuhj.htm.

CHAPTER 15

Baha'ism: Some Uncertainties about its Role as a Globalizing Religion

Denis MacEoin

Towards a Definition (of sorts) of Globalization

I must assume that anyone reading this has a reasonably good idea of what Baha'ism stands for as a religion and as a social movement with as yet unrealized political ambitions. Globalization, on the other hand, is a widespread term with numerous interpretations. I hesitate to offer a definition of the latter to readers of this collection, many of whom are experts in that very topic. But I ought, at least, to clarify my personal views on the subject, and to specify some of the political and religious attitudes that seem to me to contradict it.

Globalization is a politico-economic process that has been gathering pace since the Second World War and the end of empires (America excepted). Conspiracy theorists apart, few would suggest that there is a centrally-organized 'globalization plan' or pre-conceived goals of any kind, even if globalization works towards such goals on a local or corporate scale. It proceeds through developments in technology, through free trade between nations, through the dissemination of science and information, through exercises in religious ecumenism, and through philosophical explorations of what encounters between nations, races, and religions may involve.

Its greatest expression to date must surely be the Internet, with its extraordinary ability to shrink distances and eliminate borders at the tap of a computer key. Ten years ago, searching for a rare book was a time-consuming activity that could take years. Now, however, one can search for a volume in seconds through websites that provide access to bookshops around the planet. From my study in the UK, I regularly order books from France, America, and Australia, and I can now buy recordings of Portuguese *fado* music from a Portuguese shop in Frankfurt, or *sencha* tea from several places in Japan.

Spaces close, not always with the best result. On the downside, globalization tends to homogenize cultures or to impose a variety of Western culture on non-western people or American culture on everybody else, including the French. Trade is eased, often with serious consequences for local producers or those employed in sweatshops by multinational companies. Cheap air fuel (kept that way by low taxation) means that it's cheaper to fly cherries in from Chile instead of transporting them by road from the farm just outside town directly to the supermarket.

In the religious sphere, globalization sets an ideal of harmony and cooperation, at the price of blurring important distinctions between belief systems. Inter-religious harmony is, in any case, a frail thing cultivated by people with irenic temperaments. The reality of religious behavior is still, in many ways, Catholic versus Protestant in Northern Ireland,[1] Hindu mobs in India, Islamic mobs in Kashmir, Jew versus Muslim in the Middle East, right-wing American fundamentalism spoiling for a fight with Islam, and Muslims on several continents *contra mundum*.

Globalization and Scientific Values

There is a link between globalization and science that is crucial and exciting. The virtues of science are neutrality, objectivity, and secularity. Just as there cannot be 'Jewish science', 'Muslim science', 'Hindu science', and so on, so there cannot be American globalization, British globalization, conservative globalization, or liberal globalization, and so on.

By its very nature, a globalized outlook threatens parochial interests and outlooks. Irish by birth, when I watch a French film or read a Persian poem or listen in awe to Cristina Branco sing *Aquele Tao*

1 Where a recent Queen's University survey shows that inter-community prejudice is worse than it was when the Troubles started over thirty years ago, even among three-year-old children.

Triste Dia or marvel at a piece of Arabic calligraphy – in all of these undertakings I transcend the 'Orangeism', the 'meat and two veg', the 'Kick the Pope' songs, and the constant bigotry of my Northern Irish origins. I am not alone.

The most important resistant culture and religion is that of Islam. Of course there are similar strains in Haredi Judaism, in militant Hinduism, in the German sects of North America, and in the Paisleyite variety of Protestantism. But Islam has stolen the stage, not only in its terrorist-militant forms, but even in most of its moderate incarnations. Although Islam is far from homogeneous, having two important divisions: Shi'i and Sunni, Sufi and non-Sufi; and more graduated variations between regional styles, it remains visibly less sectarian than any other religion of its size, with idealizing and universalizing pressures that reduce the impact of the divisions. Many Sufi brotherhoods have been and are highly shari'a-minded, many mystics have taken part in or led holy wars, the four Sunni law schools differ on minor points only, and Shi'is and Sunnis agree on more things than they fall out over.

Today, only a minority of Muslims are terrorists, but larger numbers will support the jihad-based struggle of the minority, while even larger numbers will condemn terrorism outright while agreeing with classical formulations regarding holy war, the priority of Islam, or the sacredness of martyrdom. It can never be accurate to say 'Muslims do this' or 'Muslims believe that'; but with some degree of caution it is easier to generalize about the Islamic world than most other religious congregations.

Muslim insistence on denying a fullness of human rights to women and religious minorities, the persistence of practices like female genital mutilation and honour killing, or the extraordinary continuance of a vicious anti-Semitism at most levels of society, in the popular press, on radio and television, even in school textbooks are all indications of a culture that has distanced and continues to distance itself from some of the most basic demands of a globalized society. Those Muslims most likely to embrace globalization and its consequences wholeheartedly will inevitably be partly or wholly secularized. It is secularization that provides the real test of openness to global values, not relatively insignificant distinctions of style between Cairo and Qum.

I think it is not untrue to say that any Muslim, if asked, would welcome the dissolution of the state of Israel and its replacement with a

Muslim Palestinian state. Some might seek the physical destruction of Israeli Jews, others might accept them as *dhimmis* under Islamic law, yet others might seek to exile them to any country that would have them. The thing is that the underlying desire to see Israel gone and Islam resurgent has a powerful influence on politics throughout the Muslim world, and this in turn makes Muslim involvement in global issues harder than it might be.

Baha'ism and Islam

Having said all this by way of preamble, let us return to the Baha'is.

What, the informed reader may wonder, has Islam to do with this? I had been tempted to make my title read: 'a post-Islamic response', but a moment's thought told me that we are definitely not living in a post-Islamic world, much as George Bush and his advisers might like to think so. The Baha'i faith, of course, is manifestly not a sect or school of Islam, and you will not find me arguing that. Baha'is do think of themselves as post-Islamic (and post-Christian, post-Buddhist, and so on), but that should not carry so much weight with the rest of us.

Although it has broken from Islam and offers a post-Islamic revelation, it is important to remember that Baha'ism does carry a heavy weight of Islamic influence, such that any intelligent examination of its position among other cultures must take account of this. Just as we can talk without contradiction of Judaeo-Christian this and that, so we can, I think, speak accurately about Islamo-Baha'i theology and theophanology, Islamo-Baha'i legalism, Islamo-Baha'i ritualism, Islamo-Baha'i morality, and so on.

A notable feature that Baha'ism shares with other New Religious Movements, and that distinguishes it fundamentally from major world religions, is the absence of any real polarity between Great and Little Traditions within the religion. It would be unrealistic to expect one so soon. But it would also be reckless to anticipate such a development as inevitable. In spite of their best efforts, the Baha'is have so far failed to develop either local cultures or a single universal one. What traces, if any, of a culture that do exist are manifestly too weak to provide a real identity for the religion, and as yet much too undeveloped to exercise a perceptible influence on local cultures, let alone on those of international stature. There is, for the present, no distinct Baha'i art, no Baha'i music, no Baha'i architecture,[2] no Baha'i literature (by which I mean, for example, poetry, *belles lettres*, and even fiction), no Baha'i cinema, no Baha'i cuisine, no Baha'i humour, and so on. It could take another century, and probably more, before such cultural expressions begin to emerge, if they do at all. More probably, by that time a global culture will have taken hold that will encourage Baha'i poets to write, composers to compose, or painters to paint in that context, rather than searching for a more limited form of religiously-defined expression.

But to anyone familiar with the movement, the absence of a distinct culture does not mean that Baha'ism has no flavour, that it is ersatz, that its books and rituals and doctrines are the blank products of unformed minds. What we actually find is a young religious tradition rich in Islamic cultural and religious referents, whose doctrinal, legal, and ritual core is colored throughout by 'Islamicity', if I may use such a clumsy term. Alongside this wealth of themes, symbols, rituals, mystical styles, and much else from Islamicate culture, there is an overwhelming sense of the abiding presence of Persian influence, from the literary style of the scriptures (even where written in Arabic),[3] to the design of book jackets, to the use of Persian chant in devotions, to the hanging of the *Ya Baha' al-Abha* calligraphic symbol on walls, to the availability of Persian food, to the physical and psychological presence of Iranian Baha'is in most Baha'i communities.

Because an assertion of independence from Islam has been of such importance to Baha'is almost from the inception of the movement (though, as is widely known), Abbas Effendi continued to attend the mosque until his death), there has been an understandable tendency

2 The existence of several *mashariq al-adhkar* and the various buildings that make up the Baha'i World Centre in Haifa have convinced some people that a recognizably Baha'i architecture does exist. I disagree. The Haifa buildings are either straight copies of the neo-classical design found in public buildings around the world, or developments of it, not least of forms found in totalitarian states. The better-designed *mashariq* have a very individual quality, but are very different among themselves, so that there is no coherent style.

3 It is worth noting the great differences in the Arabic styles of the Bab, Baha' Allah, and 'Abd al-Baha'. Only the third wrote in an authentic Arab style, as a result of Arabic lessons in early life and life in an Arabic environment after 1868.

for members to exaggerate the originality of everything from laws to common practices.

The 'External Influence' versus 'Divine Inspiration/Innate Knowledge' Debate

More recently, a debate has developed between liberal Baha'i scholars like Juan Cole on the one hand, and what I would term fundamentalists like Nader Saeidi and many others on the other. The former have propounded a scenario that puts the Bab, Baha' Allah and 'Abd al-Baha' deep within their cultural environment, and have identified a range of possible influences on their thinking, from Islamic mysticism to Western republicanism. The latter, arguing that all three figures were, in two distinct measures, divinely inspired from the moment they first took breath, deny any possibility of the slightest influence on their thought from any quarter whatever, other than God himself.

It's not my purpose here to enter into that debate, other than to say I find myself wholly on the side of the liberals, and that I find nothing in the Baha'i scriptures that cannot be ascribed to existing norms. This may seem like a minor internal debate, but the truth is that it has enormous significance for understanding the relationship between Baha'ism and the wider culture.

Because everything the Bab and his successors did or said is deemed to have come from their innate knowledge (*'ilm-i laduni*, an old Sufi term), it follows that all new ideas in Babism or Baha'ism must be treated as though wholly original, as though brought into the world *tabula rasa* from the mouth of the twin prophets. This creates an extraordinary ahistoricism, whereby all earlier examples of the phenomenon in question are simply ignored.

Thus, for example, the principle of the equality of men and women was enunciated by Baha' Allah, but not by the Bab. Despite that, orthodox Baha'is will attribute this same teaching to the Babi poetess Fatima Baraghani Qurrat al-'Ayn. My most strenuous researches have failed to reveal the slightest mention of this subject in Qurrat al-'Ayn's extant writings, and I doubt very much whether she gave the matter much thought. Certainly, I would not count her as an active promoter of women's rights, much less as the first woman in the world to adopt such a position.

It is quite understandable that earlier generations of Baha'is, lacking hard information about feminism in history, may have granted Qurrat al-'Ayn a primacy that was ill-justified. That they persist in doing so is less easy to comprehend. The historical position is clear. Open writing and debate about women's position in society, including detailed demands for equality between the sexes began in England and France from the fourteenth century and reached remarkable proportions by the late 16th.[4] By the time of Mary Wollstonecraft (1759-1797), the rights of women were firmly on the agenda for women in Europe and North America.

Baha'i insistence here and in many other areas on Baha' Allah's primacy is inconsistent with a worldview that recognizes the achievements of other cultures and religions. It resembles the old Soviet trick of claiming primacy for almost all modern inventions for Russia. Surely it should be enough that the Baha'is support the principle of male and female equality, without making a song and dance about a historically indefensible primacy.

Let me put all this in a somewhat different form. The Bab and Baha' Allah were never influenced through the whole range of their religion-making activities by the Buddhist, Hindu, Jewish, Sikh, Shintoist, Amerindian, African, Protestant, Confucian, Tibetan, Santerian, or any other significant religious tradition. Though that may sound like stating the obvious, the absence of any coloring from such sources is extremely relevant in the context of globalization. Quite simply, potential converts from those and many other traditions will see nothing familiar in Baha'ism on their first contact with it, but will instead be asked to take on board a host of ideas and acts of worship or personal routine saturated with Iranian, Arab, Sufi, Shi'i, Islamo-Christian and related norms. It's a one-way street, in other words.

By way of contrast, individuals from an Iranian, Shi'i, or Sunni Muslim background will have no difficulty in recognizing, say, the Baha'i *hajj*, or the practices of *ziyara*, *salat*, or *sawm* as cognates of

4 There is no space here for anything but the sketchiest of accounts. Readers looking for a complete picture of early pro-feminist writing should consult the 30-volume series *The Other Voice in Early Modern Europe*, edited by Margaret L. King and Albert Rabil Jr., Chicago, University of Chicago Press, 1996-). The central point is that a serious debate about the equality of women began in the 16th century, long before Babism or Baha'ism came on the scene.

Islamic ritual practices, even if the forms differ; they will feel at ease both with the style of Baha'i historical narrative, and with much of the content; they will recognize theological concepts such as *tawhid* (the divine unity), progressive revelation, and even the Manifestation of God (which has exact cognates in some Shi'i literature); they will find photographs of early Babis and Baha'is resonant with images of their own grandparents; they will find that the original scriptures are in languages they will understand or at least partly recognize; they will find some Baha'i imagery (such as the *ya baha' al-abha* symbol, the ringstone symbol, and the five-pointed star) essentially familiar; they will find the names of historical figures familiar and pronounceable; they will feel at ease with the style of chanting used in devotions; they will find 'Abd al-Baha's insistence that women wear headscarves unsurprising; they will have no problems with the ban on alcohol; they will have no difficulties with the extensive use of Quranic and *hadith* quotations in scripture; they will not be ill at ease with the use of *Allahu abha* as a greeting. I could go on, but I think the point has been made.

But how would a Scottish Presbyterian, say, or a Tibetan Buddhist or a Vodoun priestess or a Mormon elder react to all the above? Everything I have just mentioned will be unfamiliar, alienating, and often downright mysterious. There is no comfortable link between the Isle of Lewis and City of Shiraz, or between the Potola and the mansion of Bahji.

Oddly enough, the community that would find Baha'ism most familiar – Islam – displays the most negative reaction in fact, whereas a community without common referents (Hinduism) has proved a major source of converts.

Does Cultural Connectivity Matter?

Baha'is may say that none of this matters, because the main features of their religion revolve around matters like world government, world peace, and world brotherhood, or the administrative order, or international development. There's some truth in that, but I am not convinced that the Baha'i faith can travel so far from its roots as to become genuinely culture-free at heart. Matters like theology, the law, ritual, and sacred history are far more important in defining a religion than, say, involvement with the UN or advocating a world language or promoting racial harmony, activities which are common to many other religions and secular bodies.

At this point, I feel I am only scratching the surface of the problem. Practising Baha'is, at least those who aspire to some serious knowledge of their origins and beliefs, will say that they do not feel alienated by these elements of their faith. But many Western Baha'is find long Persian names, or historical accounts set in the alien world of 19th-century Iran, or even Shoghi Effendi's impossibly long periods difficult to read and digest. Converts from Christianity frequently find the Islamic-style legalism hard to link with earlier beliefs in the primacy of conscience.

Perhaps that does not matter, and perhaps it doesn't matter today how little new converts among tribespeople and other marginalized groups may understand these things.

But the children and grandchildren of these converts are, presumably, going to receive a more thoroughgoing Baha'i education, and we must assume that that will alienate them to some degree from their own traditions and belief systems. Indeed, such a process has to happen if Baha'ism is not to suffer the fate of so many earlier faiths and find itself overgrown by a congeries of beliefs and practices alien to its original nature. In fact, there appears to be a genuine disapproval of 'Little Tradition' features that 'corrupt' the 'pure' Baha'i teachings and prescribed practices.[5] Newly-converted tribes are put through 'deepening classes', the purpose of which is to acculturate them to Baha'i ways of thinking and doing.

And this is roughly where my worries centre. To speak of Baha'ism as a global religion and yet pursue a conversion and educational process which allows one culture (i.e. Baha'i/Islamic/Persianate culture) to dominate seems to me contradictory. Although official Baha'i teaching emphasizes a need for 'unity in diversity', one is often struck by an overriding stress on the unity side of the equation. This is because fear of sectarian division has led Baha'is to be cautious of words and behavior that might compromise the integrity of the *gemeinschaft*. Any attempt to introduce, say, Hindu prayers into Baha'i worship might be deemed contrary to strict orthodoxy.

5 On this, see Denis MacEoin (1994).

The Oneness of Religion

Baha'is preach their belief in the oneness of religion. But what does this really mean? In practice, it means something very similar to the Islamic belief (from which it is obviously derived) that there has only ever been one heavenly religion, and that it has been manifested historically by Judaism, Sabeanism, Christianity, and now Islam, or by prophets like Moses, Jesus, and Muhammad. The Islamic doctrine of the oneness of the heavenly religions had a side-effect of rendering Judaism and Christianity betrayed and corrupted faiths that had to be infantilized into 'protected peoples'. All others were out of the game entirely.

The Baha'i faith widens this a little, by artificially incorporating Buddhism and Hinduism as divine religions, while stripping both of them of everything that makes them 'Buddhism' or 'Hinduism'. There is no scriptural indication that other faiths (Sikhism, Jainism, Shintoism, Maori religion, the new Japanese religions, African religions, Mormonism, Candoblé, Vodoun and so forth, together with the innumerable sectarian variations in them and in the larger faiths) have any value whatever. Standard Baha'i texts on progressive revelation or world faiths simply ignore them.[6] They are certainly not considered by Baha'is to be divinely revealed, nor are their founders (where one exists) considered Manifestations of God.

This in itself means that, as far as a large proportion of mankind is concerned, the only possible interaction with Baha'ism is either to convert or to remain resistant. Neither seems appropriate in a globalization context.

Baha'i Dogmatism

But this is not all. Like Islam, Baha'ism is a dogmatic religion. Very clear lines are drawn between truth and falsehood ('This, verily, is the truth, and all else naught but error', Baha' Allah).[7] This means, for example, that Christian belief in the Trinity, in the status of Christ as God incarnate, in the resurrection of Jesus, in the divine origin of the

6 One exception is Amerindian religion, which is credited with a chain of oral prophecies believed to foretell the advent of Baha'ism.

7 Baha' Allah (1956) *Lawh al-malika*, in *Gleanings from the Writings of Baha'u'llah*, trans. Shoghi Effendi: 255.

Church and the liturgy, in the status of Mary as Mother of God, in the intermediary role of the priesthood, in the salvific power of confession and the forgiveness of sins, in the intercession of the saints, in the resurrection of the dead, in the infallibility of the Pope, in the efficacy of the sacraments, and so much else that is absolutely fundamental to all Catholics (other lists could be made for other churches) are all regarded as errors or worse by Baha'is.

Similarly, the absence of a Buddhist belief in God is not only considered false, but is subject to extreme revisionism, as in the Baha'i book by Jamshid Fozdar, *The God of Buddha*.[8]

It is hard to see how this essentially intolerant attitude can hope to further the aims of globalization, in which no one culture or set of beliefs should be allowed to dominate. Baha'is have for a long time claimed that their faith is a strong force in bringing together disparate religious traditions. But we have only to look at the content of Baha'i-managed World Religion Day events to see them as ham-fisted attempts to declare all previous religions as precursors of Baha'ism, all conforming to basic ideals of one God, a succession of prophets, one true faith from Adam to Baha' Allah, and so on.

This divisive approach is accentuated by the intensity of the Baha'i international missionary effort, an endeavour that has for many decades now dominated Baha'i activities in all continents. Baha'is do not set out to bring religions closer in an ecumenical manner, but rather seek to convert Hindus to Baha'is, Buddhists to Baha'is, and even Northern Irish Protestants to Baha'is. Positively understood, globalization is not about proselytizing, but about mutual respect, tolerance, and an abandonment of earlier beliefs about one religion's superiority over another.

In its favour, it is worth remembering that Baha'ism has broken from Islam in a number of important areas. It has abolished *jihad*, it no longer punishes apostasy,[9] and it contains strict rules for the tolerant treatment of religious minorities of all kinds, whether 'People of the Book' or not. But the urge to convert and to establish Baha'i states and an eventual 'Baha'i World State' rather undermine what might have been an important ecumenical role for the faith.

8 Fozdar, Jamshid K. (1973).

9 It does, of course, punish dissidence ('covenant-breaking') by total excommunication.

Globalization and Secularization

Let's leave the purely religious aspect for the moment, and take a look at some other aspects of Baha'ism that may create problems for a serious Baha'i role within a broader globalization process. It is, I think, axiomatic that healthy globalization must involve the spread of democratic forms of government, a monitored attachment to human rights, and – more controversially – a gradual secularization of societies across the globe.

Though much criticized in some quarters today, secularization has for some time now been seen as a prerequisite of democracy, liberalization and socio-economic progress. I would not be the first to suggest that nothing would further the peace progress in my native Ireland more than a massive injection of secular values on both sides. Certainly, the development of democracy and human rights legislation has been markedly more positive in mainly secularized countries, such as those in Europe, than in the Islamic world or other religiously determined societies.

Even though the simple secularization thesis has been abandoned in the face of a wave of determined religious revivalism, there seems to be no evidence that religions can work easily with modernization, other than in mechanical, technological ways. Ideological aspects of modernity, such as women's rights or the rights of the individual to freedom of conscience and expression (including the right to change one's religion and to dissent), tend to meet with resistance in the religious realm, particularly from Islam, where apostasy is, strictly speaking, punishable by death, and simple questioning as often as not equated with apostasy.

I have said before that, like Islam, Baha'ism is, by its very nature, a dogmatic religion. I'm not saying that that is, in itself, a bad thing to be. Many people seek precisely the sort of security and certainty that such a religion can bring. But their certainty in dogmas may be bought at a high price for their fellow citizens.

Dogmatism is particularly visible in the system of Baha'i law, the *shari'a,* based on Islamic norms but in this case sent down from heaven by Baha' Allah. Baha'i behaviour in most things can be determined from the *Kitab al-aqdas* and related texts, and in future fresh laws and rulings are expected to be delivered (under divine inspiration) by the Universal House of Justice.

Although the Baha'i *shari'a* is, as yet, far from as detailed as its Islamic model, or, for that matter, its eccentric precursor, the Babi *shari'a*, it does contain injunctions that ensure the Baha'is will be unable to modify their stance on certain issues, much as modern Muslims have resisted social change through a reluctance to alter or even reinterpret their own legal code.

Two matters may bring Baha'is into increasing dissonance with liberal social opinion in the West, particularly in Europe. One is approval of capital punishment, including its use in cases of arson (where the perpetrator may be burned to death), the other, famously, is prohibition of active homosexuality. Europeans (and a considerable number of Americans) have come to regard capital punishment with abhorrence, and opposition to it has come to be identified with a sense of compassion and justice that is socially more adult than the baser motives of revenge that surround executions.

Acceptance of homosexuals as worthy fellow citizens has come to symbolize respect for our fellows and the vital importance of tolerance in all parts of the social sphere.

To become identified with intolerance while preaching the abolition of prejudice may do the Baha'is harm in precisely those social contexts that may be most supportive of the positive aspects of globalization. A religion that tells men how long they may grow their hair, or that even provides detailed directions on how to eat (as laid down in Baha' Allah's *Lawh al-tibb*) is likely to fall out of favor with a majority of independent-minded people in the West, and with growing numbers of people in developing countries who are only now learning how to break away from their own stultifying traditions and petty injunctions.

Religion and Secular Norms

This almost certainly means that, whatever role religion may play in the globalization process, it is always likely to be out of step with secular achievements. Here are some examples: the refusal of the Iranian government to recognize Baha'is, Hindus, Buddhists and others as citizens, or to accord Jews, Christians, and Zoroastrians full legal rights; the illegality of preaching or converting to non-Muslim faiths within Islamic countries; the blatant intolerance displayed towards all non-Muslim faiths by Saudi Arabia; the persistence of caste divisions in India; the opposition until recently of both the Russian and Greek Orthodox churches to the legal recognition of Catholicism, Judaism, and other faiths; the insistence by the Afghan Taliban that Hindu citizens wear badges indicating their faith; the long-standing interference in politics by the American Christian right; the imposition of shari'a law on animists in southern Sudan; the concealed involvement of the Unification Church in the restore Nixon campaign; the role of the Dutch Reformed Church in promoting and justifying apartheid; the belated acceptance of black converts by the Mormon church; the support given to the Ceaucescu régime by the Romanian Orthodox Church, and obstacles created for young members to join the pro-democracy movement; the banning of various religious movements by the state of Brunei, which actively promotes Islam; the close involvement in right-wing politics, high finance, and academia of the Catholic order *Opus Dei*, especially in Spain; the insistence of several religious groups in the United Kingdom on the right to provide their children with separate education to that of the majority, an attitude long established in Northern Ireland, which is nobody's model for a healthy democracy capable of taking part in the globalization process; and so on.

All of the above, tedious as it may be, is only part of a broad picture that shows most religions to have a reactionary and intolerant side which often dominates, and to be quite incapable of providing a secure basis for democratic processes and the rule of law in keeping with the International Declaration of Human Rights. It is because of this that secularists like myself are forced to conclude that the only healthy way forward is through a thoroughgoing secularization that keeps the hands of priests and *ulama* off areas like freedom of thought and the right to dissent.

Baha'ism, by way of contrast, sees no true globalization, no true international unity, other than by means of religious forces. And, most importantly, it sees those religious forces as inhering exclusively within itself.

The Promised Day is Come

To understand this (and what is to come) correctly, one has to read Shoghi Effendi's 1941 treatise, *The Promised Day is Come* and related texts, from which I can only quote very selectively here.

The main thrusts of this central text are, first, that the Bab and Baha' Allah have come to usher in the Day promised in all the holy books; secondly, that both prophets suffered terribly at the hands of clergy and rulers alike; thirdly, that all religions, but Islam and Christianity in particular, have gone into rapid and permanent decline as retribution for their rejection of these two figures, so prominently prefigured in their scriptures; and, lastly, that the future of humanity is glorious and will culminate in a global world political system provided by the Baha'i faith and the emergence of one world religion (which obviously is not going to be Islam, Christianity, or Hinduism).

In other words, all the events of the past one hundred and fifty years or so have been set in motion by the appearance in the world of the Baha'i revelation. Even secular events like wars and revolutions ultimately owe their appearance to the earlier emergence of Baha'ism and its rejection by the forces of ignorance, bigotry, and arrogance.

The 'Decline' in Religious Influence

Shoghi Effendi expresses the decline in religious influence throughout the text, as in the following declaration:

> The decline in the fortunes of the crowned wielders of temporal power has been paralleled by a no less startling deterioration in the influence exercised by the world's spiritual leaders. The colossal events that have heralded the dissolution of so many kingdoms and empires have almost synchronized with the crumbling of the seemingly inviolable strongholds of religious orthodoxy. That same process which, swiftly and tragically, sealed the doom of kings and emperors, and extinguished their dynasties, has operated in the case of the ecclesiastical leaders of both Christianity and Islam, damaging their prestige, and, in some cases, overthrowing their highest institutions. (Shoghi Effendi, 1941: 71)

With regard to Islam, he says:

> The dissolution of the institution of the Caliphate, the complete secularization of the state which had enshrined the most august institution of Islam, and the virtual collapse of the Shi'ih hierarchy in Persia, were the visible and immediate consequences of the treatment meted out to the Cause of God by the clergy of the two largest communions of the Muslim world. (*ibid.*: 86)

This message is hammered home in numerous other passages too long to quote here. Christianity is treated in much the same way:

> Indeed, ever since the Divine summons was issued, and the invitation extended, and the warning sounded, and the condemnation pronounced, this process, that may be said to have been initiated with the collapse of the temporal sovereignty of the Roman Pontiff, soon after the Tablet to the Pope had been revealed, has been operating with increasing momentum, menacing the very basis on which the entire order is resting. Aided by the forces which the Communist movement has unloosed, reinforced by the political consequences of the last war, accelerated by the excessive, the blind, the intolerant, and militant nationalism which is now convulsing the nations, and stimulated by the rising tide of materialism, irreligion, and paganism, this process is not only tending to subvert ecclesiastical institutions, but appears to be leading to the rapid dechristianization of the masses in many Christian countries. (*ibid.*: 99)

Whether Shoghi Effendi will one day be proved right, and we will see the utter decline of all religions save Baha'ism, it is not for me to argue. What is more interesting here is his almost inadvertent support for secularization (as in the 'rapid dechristianization of the masses in many Christian countries' mentioned above). In some of his letters from around the 1930s and 40s, he speaks with great approval of the secularizing policies of Reza Shah in Iran. The more the Pahlavi regime tried to reduce the influence of Islam, the more Shoghi gave it his backing. He writes more than once of the benefits this situation gave to the previously persecuted Baha'i community. And many Baha'is, with their Western education (acquired abroad or in Baha'i schools), their ability to act as entrepreneurs outside the narrow confines of the Bazaar, their international contacts, their attraction to subjects like science, engineering, medicine, or architecture, acted as important conduits for the secularizing process.

Perversely, both Shoghi Effendi and subsequent conservative Baha'i writers in Persian and English have shown themselves to be stridently anti-secular, to the point where their fulminations could comfortably be exchanged with those of their fundamentalist Christian cousins. What they see as a decline in public morality, a breakdown in law and order, and the spread of individualism and excessive personal freedom chimes perfectly with the main concerns of right-wing Christian and Muslim writers.

Many of these Baha'i thinkers are particularly exercised by the thought that modern men and women are given the freedom to make their own decisions on issues like morality. The Baha'i preference is for a society governed by divine law and instruction, for the only true freedom lies in absolute and unquestioning obedience to the Law of God and its elevation above the human intellect and conscience.

This can be carried to ridiculous lengths, as in the ruling that couples seeking to marry should first obtain the consent of all living parents, even if the couple be in their forties or fifties and parents themselves. That is a barely-concealed method of guaranteeing arranged marriages for almost everyone.

This distaste for the freedoms, rights, and responsibilities that make up secular society sometimes results in blatant contradictions. For example, Udo Schaefer, a major advocate of 'the Law above all' approach to social relations writes that' 'most people' are at present inclined to the idea of a concrete, apodictic religious law with its absolute, non-questionable, obligatory nature as much as the devil loves holy water'. Later, he actually quotes with approval part of an interview with a French sociologist who speaks of the way in which young people in Europe have abandoned organized religion.[10]

Considering that Shoghi Effendi and other Baha'i writers have thought that the abandonment of the established churches was a sign of God's hand at work in society, punishing the detractors of the Baha'i faith, and clearing the way for its coming triumph over the religions of the past – it seems odd that Schaefer should regret the spread of secular values so much.

Shoghi Effendi got his prophecies badly wrong when he predicted the ongoing decline of faiths, almost all of which are currently experiencing waves of regrowth. He got it wrong, of course, by trying to impose a grand scheme on everything and everybody. His 'Divine Plan', a plot made up of the future advent of a new world order, the need for God to punish those responsible for the sufferings of the Bab, Baha' Allah, and their followers, and an overriding desire to believe and demonstrate that history is not something made by human beings, but rather thrust upon them by a divine puppet-master proved itself constantly prone to rebuttal by the simple march of human events.

10 Udo Schaefer (2000: 321).

The Baha'i Dilemma

So, the Baha'is have a dilemma. They don't want the process of secularization rolled back, since this would mean either the regeneration of old faiths that ought to be on their way out or the forward march of new religions whose temporal success would surely negate a Divine Plan that has no role for them. Since it is far from likely for the foreseeable future that Baha'ism alone will both challenge secularism and supplant it globally, it looks as though the Baha'is will have to accept a secular society for a long time to come. In any case, only a tolerant secular society, the sort of society that grants human beings their liberty to think and speak and write as they wish, can provide the context for any forward movement of the Baha'i faith. But since the Baha'is don't really like secular society and make a point of adopting a conservative position on many issues that will only serve to alienate the best minds and most tolerant participants in such a society, they aren't likely to get very far.

What does this imply for Baha'ism and globalization? If my argument is correct, that a global society needs to be a secular society, then it suggests that the Baha'is won't know which way they are going. If they choose secularization because it means toleration for their own beliefs and activities (something they certainly do not find in Muslim societies), their anti-secular attitudes will probably result in their marginalization or some sort of unholy alliance with the Christian right. If, on the other hand, they prefer to promote firm religious belief, we have already shown the problems this may create between them and the adherents of other churches and faiths.

Summary

To sum up: it seems to me axiomatic that Baha'ism can be characterized as:

- Intolerant of other religions, yet tolerant of their adherents (but not their priesthoods).
- Triumphalist with regard to the defeats of other faiths.
- Intolerant of the best aspects of secular society, such as freedom of thought and speech, freedom to dissent, freedom to reject religion, and so on, which are important factors in creating a tolerant global society.

- Ambivalent towards secularization, which offers them advantages and helps fulfill prophecies, but emphasizes freedoms for which they do not care too much.
- Intolerant towards internal dissent, to the extent that non-conformists may lose their voting rights or be excommunicated.

The foregoing may seem to most people reading this paper a contradiction of what they believe the Baha'i faith to hold dear. How could Baha'ism be intolerant of other religions, for example? I think I have provided enough evidence above to show that this is really the case, notwithstanding World Religion Day and the willingness of Baha'is to take part in inter-faith activities. It may be true that Baha'is will never actively persecute the members of other faiths. But Shoghi Effendi, whose views are never challenged in Haifa or elsewhere, seemed to think it a matter worth rejoicing over that Christians, Muslims, and others were subjected to humiliation and worse during his lifetime.[11] The Universal House of Justice, despite clear evidence to the contrary, has continued to pursue a vision of a world falling into irremediable decay, and the continuing infliction of divine vengeance on all non-believers. To my knowledge, no modern Baha'i authorities have tackled the topics of the meaning of the Holocaust, AIDS, global warming, etc. in the context of God's supposed plan for mankind.

I do not doubt that the Baha'is will contribute to what they see as half-way measures towards world unity, while working in their own fashion towards the establishment of a Baha'i World Commonwealth somewhere in the future. They will continue to participate in conferences on world unity and peace, they will continue to show a concern for human rights (and to publish booklets on human duties, which they

11 He is never anti-Semitic; but it has to be borne in mind that the idea of divine punishment being visited on the people of specific religions begs the question whether the Holocaust may not be read in this light. It would be interesting for some Baha'i thinkers to discuss this and the modern Jewish debate about the Holocaust (see under the term *hester panim*). What was God's will in the Holocaust remains a central theological topic completely neglected by the Baha'is. If, like the present writer, one considers the Shoah to be the most important event of modern history, possibly of all history, it is axiomatic that a religion that regards the modern era as the beginning of a new religious dispensation should do some hard thinking about the theological meaning of six million Jewish deaths.

see as essential corollaries to rights), and they will continue to enter into some sort of dialogue with the followers of other faiths, even if this is only window-dressing, since they don't actually believe those other faiths to be anything but distortions of some pristine faith. They will – with total justification – protest to the UN and other bodies about the persecution of Baha'is in Iran, and yet enjoy a thrill of satisfaction every time Islam meets with a setback there or elsewhere.

My conclusion is that, if the Baha'is are going to get anywhere in their contribution to globalization, they will have to reinvent themselves, and I'm not sure they will be willing or able to do that. A less Islamicist religion, one that was better able to adapt itself to circumstances, rather than believing circumstances should adapt themselves to its universal prescriptions, might accomplish much. Obsolete laws would be placed where they belong, silly historicist theories would be cast aside, absolute scriptural rulings would be interpreted in a more liberal fashion, and ethics would bend to accept things that human beings, in their foolishness and dignity, have found to be of benefit. But Baha'ism has inherited from Islam a rigid core and a thoroughgoing authoritarianism that sit uneasily beside its seeming openness, and it is this that may, as the very nature of the global enterprise develops, make it a dinosaur.

References

Baha'u'llah (1956). *Gleanings from the Writings of Baha'u'llah*, trans. Shoghi Effendi, Birmingham: Templar Printing Works.

Shoghi Effendi (1941). *The Promised Day is Come*, Wilmette, Ill.: Baha'i Publishing Trust.

Fozdar, Jamshid K. (1973). *The God of Buddha*, New York: Asia Publishing House.

King, Margaret L. and Albert Rabil Jr. (eds.) (1996-). *The Other Voice in Early Modern Europe*, Chicago: University of Chicago Press.

MacEoin, Denis (1994). *Ritual in Babism and Baha'ism*, London: IB Tauris.

Schaefer, Udo, Nicola Towfigh and Ulrich Gollmer (2000). *Making the Crooked Straight*, Oxford: George Ronald.

Contributors

Juan R. I. Cole is Professor of Middle Eastern and South Asian History at the University of Michigan. He is author of *Modernity and the Millennium: The Genesis of the Baha'i Faith in the Nineteenth-Century Middle East*, New York: Columbia University Press, 1998 and numerous other works.
Email: jrcole@umich.edu

Lynn Echevarria is the Coordinator and Instructor for the Women's Studies Program at Yukon College, Whitehorse. She holds a Ph.D. in Sociology from Essex University, with a dissertation entitled, *Working Through the Vision: Religion and Identity in the Life Histories of Bahá'í Women in Canada*.
Email: lechevarria9@klondiker.com

Annika Hvithamar holds a Ph.D. in Sociology of Religion from the University of Copenhagen. She is working on a post-doc research project at the Department of History of Religions at the University of Copenhagen.
Email: ahvit@hum.ku.dk

Stephen Lambden holds a Ph.D. from the University of Newcastle upon Tyne (UK) where he taught a course in Baha'i Studies. Now he is a Research Scholar at Ohio University in Athens, Ohio. His many publications include contributions to *Encyclopedia Iranica* and the Kalimat Press Studies in *The Babi and Baha'i Religions series.*
Email: lambden@ohio.edu

Todd Lawson is Associate Professor of Islamic Thought in the Department of Near and Middle Eastern Civilizations at the University of Toronto. Among his published studies is 'Qur'an Commentary as Sacred Performance', in Johann Christoph Bürgel and Isabel Schayani,

(eds.), *Iran im 19. Jarhundert und die Entstehung der Baha'i-Religion*, Hildesheim: Georg Olms Verlag, 1998: 145-58.
Email: todd.lawson@utoronto.ca

Zaid Lundberg is a Ph.D. student in History of Religions at the University of Lund, Sweden. He is currently working on his dissertation entitled *The Guardian and the Globe: Shoghi Effendi's Early Discourse on Globalization and the Baha'i Faith.*
Email: zaid.lundberg@pub.malmo.se

Denis MacEoin holds a Ph.D. from King's College, Cambridge. He taught English at the University of Fez in Morocco, and Arabic and Islamic Studies at the University of Newcastle (1981-1986). When his post was terminated by its Saudi sponsors, he embarked on a career as a writer of fiction. His numerous academic publications include *The Sources for Early Babi Doctrine and History: A Survey*, Leiden: E.J.Brill, 1992.
Email: maceoin@btinternet.com

Sen McGlinn is a student of Islamic Studies and Persian at Leiden University and is preparing a dissertation on Baha'i political theology. His publications include: 'A theology of the state from the Baha'i writings', *Journal of Church and State*, vol. 41, 1999.
Email: sonja@bahai-library.org

Moojan Momen is a Fellow of the Royal Asiatic Society. His numerous publications include: *The Phenomenon of Religion: A Thematic Approach*, Oxford: Oneworld, 1999.
Email: momen@northhill.demon.co.uk

Wendi Momen holds a Ph.D. in International Relations from the London School of Economics. She is Justice of the Peace and Chair of the One World Trust. Her publications include: *A Basic Bahá'í Dictionary*, Oxford: George Ronald, 1989.
Email: wendi@northhill.demon.co.uk

David Piff holds a Ph.D. in Sociology of Religion from University of Copenhagen. He is Senior Archivist at the U.S. National Archives and

Records Administration, Pacific Region (San Francisco). He is author of *Baha'i Lore*, Oxford: George Ronald, 2000.
Email: david.piff@nara.gov

Robert Stockman holds a Th.D. in History of American Religion from Harvard University and is an instructor of religious studies at DePaul University in Illinois. His numerous publications include: *The Bahá'í Faith in America,* vol. I and II, Wilmette, Ill.: Baha'i Publishing Trust 1985 and 1995.
Email: rstockman@usbnc.org

Fereydun Vahman holds a Ph.D. in Iranian Philology from the University of Copenhagen where he was Associate Professor. His numerous publications include: 'The Bahá'í Religion and the Orientalists' in *Proceedings of the fifth annual seminar on Persian Literature and Culture,* Darmstadt: Academy of Landegg, 1994: 137-175. He is Fellow at Yale University.
Email: vahman@hum.ku.dk

Will C. van den Hoonaard is Professor of Sociology at the University of New Brunswick, Fredericton, Canada. He has authored a number of books, including: *The Origins of the Bahá'í Community of Canada, 1898-1948,* Waterloo, Ontario: Wilfrid Laurier University Press, 1996.
Email: will@unb.ca

Margit Warburg is a sociologist of religion and Professor at the Department of History of Religions at the University of Copenhagen. Her numerous publications include: *Baha'i,* Salt Lake City: Signature Books, 2003.
Email: warburg@hum.ku.dk

Morten Warmind is Associate Professor of Sociology of Religion at the University of Copenhagen. He has published articles in Danish on minority religions and Ahmadiyya.
Email: warmind@hum.ku.dk